"As a leading global expert on colorism, Dr. Hall eloquently, poignantly invites the reader to investigate the melanin misconceptions that shape our lived realities. *Interdisciplinary Perspectives on Colorism: Beyond Black and White* features a seminal perspective on the historical, colonial and contemporary legacies of colorism, while turning an eye to what the future holds."

—**Amrit Dhillon, Podcast Host: Shadeism**

"*Interdisciplinary Perspectives on Colorism: Beyond Black and White*, is riveting and illuminating! . . . I highly recommend this book. It is a must read, if we truly are to understand and gain insights into Colorism one of society's most complex issues amongst people of color. It pertains to the causes or impacts per assimilation, bleaching, attractiveness, brown racism, income disparities, identity politics and the resultant physical (e.g., stillbirths) and mental health challenges.

Professor Hall, who is one of the leading colorism scholars, argues persuasively and convincingly for the need of a paradigm shift from old, outdated models of colorism to more evidence-based models of colorism and melanin, that enlighten, educate, and potentially could impact and shape social policy that ultimately inform, improve, and save lives in our Black communities."

—**Dr. Richard G. Majors, Consulting Counselling Psychologist, former Clinical Fellow, Harvard Medical School, and bestselling coauthor of the classic** *Cool Pose: The Dilemmas of Black Manhood in America*

"In this provocative and challenging tour de force, Professor Ronald E. Hall unveils the sordid underpinnings of the societal hierarchy that privileges lighter skin over darker skin. This book exposes the historical, cultural, and economic forces that have led to colorism supplanting racism as the main engine of stratification as well as the adoption of extreme measures like skin bleaching, which can cause dire health outcomes. Anyone interested in racial, gender, and social equity should read this book."

—**Joni Hersch, Cornelius Vanderbilt Professor of Law and Economics, Vanderbilt University**

"In this stirring and profound work Dr. Hall exposes readers to the taboos of colorism heretofore dismissed from public discourse. In detail are dramatic accounts of a skin color hierarchy rooted in history and culture that privileges light-skinned persons and denigrates their dark-skinned counterparts. This book is a must read for those seeking a glimpse into the future social environment of mankind."

—**Kevin Brown, Richard S. Melvin Professor, University of Indiana Maurer School of Law**

INTERDISCIPLINARY PERSPECTIVES ON COLORISM

This timely and unique book explores the concept of colorism, which is discrimination based on the color of a person's skin, in a world where arguably light skin is privileged over dark, and one's wealth, health, and opportunities are impacted by skin color, sometimes irrespective of one's racial background.

In the context of our multi-cultural and increasingly global society, and the historical backdrop of slavery, the text takes a unique approach by moving from personal anecdotes to adopting a scientific perspective grounded in empirical evidence. Hall explores how skin color is a more effective framework for examining prejudice and discrimination, as racial identities become increasingly mixed due to inter-racial unions and immigration. He argues that racism as discrimination by race is contrived, polarizing, and non-quantifiable, and that it is often skin color that is used to "identify" race, often inaccurately. With skin color being a visual and physical characteristic, with race-based prejudices attached to it, the author shows how skin color can be a loaded identifier of value and identity. In a world where the objective measure of skin color crosses racial boundaries and where race will become increasingly indiscernible over time, the ultimate aim of this book is to prepare for the social future of mankind that has already begun to take shape.

Split into three parts, examining historical, contemporary, and potential future perspectives on colorism, this is a fascinating reading for students and academics in psychology, social work, education, criminal justice, and other social sciences. The text will also be useful for providing validation for including colorism into the public domain.

Dr. Ronald E. Hall is Professor in the School of Social Work, at Michigan State University, USA. Dr. Hall's research comprises more than 150 (co)-authored publications, interviews, and presentations pertaining to colorism, including 15 books. He testified as an expert witness for America's first case of colorism litigation between African Americans: *Morrow v. IRS*.

INTERDISCIPLINARY PERSPECTIVES ON COLORISM

Beyond Black and White

Ronald E. Hall

NEW YORK AND LONDON

Cover image: © Getty Images

First published 2023
by Routledge
605 Third Avenue, New York, NY 10158

and by Routledge
4 Park Square, Milton Park, Abingdon, Oxon, OX14 4RN

Routledge is an imprint of the Taylor & Francis Group, an informa business

© 2023 Ronald E. Hall

The right of Ronald E. Hall to be identified as author of this work has been asserted in accordance with sections 77 and 78 of the Copyright, Designs and Patents Act 1988.

All rights reserved. No part of this book may be reprinted or reproduced or utilized in any form or by any electronic, mechanical, or other means, now known or hereafter invented, including photocopying and recording, or in any information storage or retrieval system, without permission in writing from the publishers.

Trademark notice: Product or corporate names may be trademarks or registered trademarks, and are used only for identification and explanation without intent to infringe.

Library of Congress Cataloging-in-Publication Data
A catalog record for this book has been requested

ISBN: 978-1-032-29950-1 (hbk)
ISBN: 978-1-032-29938-9 (pbk)
ISBN: 978-1-003-30288-9 (ebk)

DOI: 10.4324/9781003302889

Typeset in Bembo
by Apex CoVantage, LLC

CONTENTS

Preface ix

Historical 1

  1 Introduction 3

  2 The Colonial Origins of Colorism 17

  3 Field Negro and the House Negro 28

  4 Fancy Girls and Run 'Round Men 39

  5 The Mulatto Hypothesis 50

Contemporary 63

  6 Colorism by Education 65

  7 Colorism by Occupation 75

  8 Colorism by Income 86

  9 Health Risks in Stillbirth Colorism 95

10	The Bleaching Syndrome	107
11	Brown Racism as Pre-colorism	118

Future   131

12	Colorism as Racism in the 21st Century	133
13	Conclusion	145

Index   *154*

PREFACE

It is my contention that slavery and colonial subjugation are bygone historical hostilities that for the most part have been dismissed from the annals of polite social discourse. However, people of color and of African descent in particular continue to manifest the impact of so-called racial transgressions. They are enabled by the most esteemed of social scientists, who as intellectual icons are trained with hardly any reference at all to the implications of skin color as it pertains to quality of life for people of color. The senior operatives of academic journals, academic books, and other scholarly commentaries are then subsequently dominated by a Eurocentric worldview. Therefore, all matters of non-Eurocentric life space significance become reduced to trivia for reasons of social or racial incongruence. Furthermore, those who teach at some of our most prestigious universities, which serve a substantially diverse population, labor in the wake of an intellectual void. They have not the faintest idea of just how the implications of skin color as pertains to colorism impact the social environment of non-European people of color across extensive spans of time and today on a global scale.

In any society not fascist or authoritarian, I have ascertained from the literature that idealized, power structure groups necessarily dictate or hold sway over their less endowed counterparts. Said groups provide evidence of our numerous human flaws in directing the destructive behavior of others. Manifestation of this human tendency is recapitulated in colorism. The dynamics of colorism enabling intra-race discrimination are compulsory to the comprehension of Western culture in both the modern era and historical years past. It is this intra-race discrimination that has contributed to the appeal and legitimacy of white supremacy.

As an ideology, white supremacy is covertly associated with colorism because it too is Western culture, and it too is thus an extension of Western civilization. Subsequently, white supremacy then necessitates an unspoken, collective notion of "us" against "them" by dissecting mankind into races and ignoring our rank as a common earthly species. Furthermore, it is plausible via colorism that what associated Western civilization with racism is the idea that being of or in proximity to European ancestry is superior to all other human identities. Extended from that belief by people of color is thus self-subjugation in their worship of a presumed divine alien ideal. Their corrupted sectarianism overrides the possibility that we of the more skeptical, darker-skinned masses might conclude otherwise.

Struggles with colorism as centrifugal to people of color help define and determine our existential reality. Our role in that determination includes the deconstruction of sanctified melanin misconceptions, the illumination of racial inequalities, and, if necessary, moves to completely dismiss the acknowledgment of "race" from the annals of Western intellectual discourse. Given to the challenges of colorism, our labors have not been consequential. They are not without precedent but in fact exist as an eternal continuum wedded to the seductions of a Western assumed "scientific" eugenic temptation. People of color and their conscientious allies must become cognizant of their unique role in the deconstruction of the race concept; that of articulating for the raceless whole of humanity, and ultimately of a civil passage to our destined nirvana. Enabled by a need to be woke academy, intellectual operatives divorced from the holy shrines of racial speculations will contribute. Their toils nourish an effort to purge the race concept and advance the body of academia to the zenith of knowledge where it must prevail.

As one who values knowledge and the academic process, I have agonized constantly over the manner in which the life space realities brought by colorism in a racist context have been trivialized by the intelligencia status quo. On more than one occasion, I have encountered operatives of that status quo. They carry on as human service academics in social work and other social sciences or they carry on as human service practice professionals in social work and other social sciences. Their credentials qualify them as supposedly trained in exact competence to address some of the keenest aspects of human dysfunction as if their methodologies are comprehensive of the entire human universe. Despite their successful navigation through some of the most rigorous and prestigious of scholastic institutions, they emerge having been seduced by a contrived distortion of existential facts. Subsequently in their efforts they harbor ignorance given to the social and cultural gaps that have been perpetuated by the trivialization of colorism. In fact, most social science faculties with Eurocentric worldview have gone through their entire educational experience absent reference to colorism content. Their lacking is dramatically extended to social work professionals and others in human service practice fields clueless to non-white ailings. While such ideals as diversity and social justice dominate social work, rhetoric manifestations are cursed via delinquency in actions. Therefore, it will come as no surprise that students, faculties, and social work practitioners alike have not known of or understood the significant role of colorism in the formulation of conceptual, social, and behavioral models. If enlightened by colorism it would provide a cogent explanation of truths beyond domains of the Eurocentric worldview. Unfortunately, as per the aforementioned and other reasons, the topic of colorism has remained an unspeakable taboo in practically every sector of the "legitimate" academy and practice domain. From my own personal perspective as a humble member of the same academy, I see this as a harbinger of ignorance. It serves the perpetuation of incompetence which stagnates the progress of civil evolution that humanity cannot for a moment tolerate.

The social consequences of a transgression—overt or covert—can be neither understood nor assessed for logic without an all-encompassing dispassionate frame of reference. This is true at the local domestic level as well as at the global international level. The chapters in this book are dedicated to exposing the heretofore taboo and secret canons of colorism that humanity be rescued from the Eurocentric worldview. It will illustrate with conscientious clarity the social environment of victim people of color who contribute to their own demise in the aftermath of having idealized alien Eurocentric norms. It will characterize the unspoken notion of hierarchy manifested by a multitude of human conditions including a history of colorism, contemporary implications of colorism, and anticipation of a future permeated by the trappings of color. While the content herein may offend and/or confound the traditional academic "ivory tower" operative, it must be conveyed without hesitation nevertheless. It will take readers beyond the exaggeration of racial significance, exposing a manifestation of discrimination brought by colorism among those who would be otherwise considered victims. It will address the forbidden implications of skin color that promises to simplify and expose social criteria otherwise undetectable in a racial context. Doing so is not an attempt to minimize or denounce the academy's earned esteem and its distinguished icons of social work and other disciplines. It is instead an honest effort to objectively serve as a mirror in which academic institutions and their intellectual workforce may view a reflection of themselves and their manner of thought. This should not imply my assumption that what is described about the colorism phenomenon set forth in the following pages is complete and accurate without flaw. Rather, it is a well-intended attempt to promote fruitful dialogue that will spawn a productive season of scientific growth. Cultivating such an outcome is to plant the seeds of growth for this book's ability to expose all forms and manner of self-denigration in a more accurate and applicable context of colorism. While I realize there are disadvantages in this undertaking, the most obvious of which are stereotyping, treatment methodology, and social misrepresentation, I do not feel I have unlimited options. I am both very aware and concerned about this and in no way wish to contribute to it, although I do not deny that what I have written can be misused by those who would choose to do so.

Some of my colleagues in the academy will argue that to write about the unspeakable taboo of colorism among people of color will do more harm than good. Despite the fact, it is my humble opinion forged from the transgressions of academia that confronting such a provocative issue is literally a healthy and socially appropriate way to advance civilization and the advent of peaceful human interaction. While this may appear an insignificant strategy, as a start is where the ultimate bliss of solutions begin.

In the finality of my following speculations, I believe the problem for any writer or academic operative who attempts to characterize an issue as complex as colorism will always be their potential exposure to factual errors. Overcoming the obstacles of so-called racial boundaries proves increasingly formidable when conveyed in the context of colorism. When that interpretation reaches publication, we run the risk of doing a disservice to all including ourselves. In the significance of self-worth, I have determined that dignity and respect for the human condition not as a race but a species worldwide take precedent. The elimination of race for purposes of humane evolution will be the hoped for offspring of such an effort. Therefore, the need to advocate for the significance of colorism in lieu of racism for me is inspired by maintaining openness and a willingness to confront new ideas. New ideas can only bring solace to the eventuality and hence future and a new era. Furthermore, those of us considering whatever criteria stained by the rumors of intellectual and cultural inferiority indulge an extremely dangerous luxury. By virtue of our having been victimized there is a tendency to portray the Eurocentric worldview simultaneously as the absence of virtue. However, the denigration of dark skin espoused in colorism has not divorced us from the sting of similar accusations. We seek refuge under the victim cloak as if setting us morally apart from the racism of our oppressors. We seem to feel that because we are most often the victims of colorism, we have earned the right to cast an exclusive moral stone. We take no responsibility for our role in colorism and have deluded ourselves into ignoring the implications of colorism because racism seems more critical.

Akin to unadulterated speculations, humanity of whatever gender, race, or skin color cannot deny the dignity and divine worth of another without somehow diminishing some measure of their own. For in the image of one's victim is a replication of one's assumed perfect self. Study of the implications of colorism and racism in that believed perfection will provide a glimpse of what we have become. Believing that, it is my sincerest hope that those who read this book move past stereotypes or loyalty to falsehoods desired as fact. They must focus, instead, on the quality of life for all peoples globally as closely linked members of a common genetic family.

Ronald E. Hall, Ph.D.

Historical

1
INTRODUCTION

Colorism is a term that pertains to a human social function subject to explanation by ecology. Succinctly put, ecology relative to a branch of science proceeds to investigate the relationship, if any, between organisms and, in this case, their social environments (Kailash, 1997). From the existence of ecology often used in the field of social work is the scientific and empirically verifiable ecological perspective (EP) of colorism. The EP is utilized by science as a social construct that allows for integrating colorism and other manifestations of human behavior into an organized concept such as the W. E. B. DuBois (Black, 2007) notion of double consciousness or Hall's (2016) notion of the Bleaching Syndrome. The EP is thus indicative of a metaphor that enables the configuration of people and their social environments into a common frame of reference where one is defined in context of its relationship to the other.

Considering the realities of colorism via the EP allows for the exposition of social discrimination transgressions brought by the stresses of a racist social environment. In a racist society, there is significant reluctance to attribute discrimination to anything other than race for fear of challenging validity of the traditional race discourse. The academy overall has contributed significant investments to race validity. In actuality, the culpability of race per the EP overlooks the biopsychosocial environmental experience encountered by people of color as pertains to their skin color designated as race. The more encompassing EP considers that the "bio" takes into consideration the implications of genetic endowment for human behavior. Unlike race, skin color is an objective, scientifically verifiable biological human trait. As a social reality it allows for the social function or social dysfunction of human organisms that contribute to human quality of life. Academic research to date has not fully or adequately investigated the social pathologies associated with the consequences of certain genetic endowments. What's more as endowment the genetic heritage of skin color does not dictate social ills or health risks among

DOI: 10.4324/9781003302889-2

people of color independently. That is the aftermath of an unnecessary societal skin color stigma.

The "psycho" of biopsychosocial relative to the EP takes into consideration the implications of psychological endowment of the individual. Here the EP considers the adaptive strategies extended from environmental demands that in consideration of colorism is pathological (Beverly, 1989). In the context of colorism where people of color are forced to endure various forms of discrimination in a racist environment on a daily basis may manifest in disease such as high blood pressure or hypertension. For women during pregnancy may lead to stillbirths as a consequence of toxic substances ingested by women of color who seek escape from the stigmas associated with their dark skin.

In consideration of the EP "social" content becomes a part of the environment." The social aspect of the environment involves an ability to carry out roles in relation to other members of the group, community, and/or society at large. These roles, no less per the EP, also contribute to what comprises the environment (Green & Ephross, 1991). The racist implications of race implied by skin color can be illustrated given the stereotype of African-Americans as human inferior. That presumed inferiority permeates the social environment often unspoken where African-Americans' IQ as one example is advocated by "scientists" as evidence of black inferiority. This encourages stress extended from the environment which facilitates disease and other problems encountered by people of color due to their constant struggles with stress to compensate for their dark skin.

No less theoretically relevant to the biopsychosocial apparatus of people of color per the EP is also the concept of adaptation. Adaptation is too often confused with adjustment to the environment but in fact is distinguishable. Adjustment pertains to a passive effort to accommodate an abusive environmental situation (Mackey & O'Brien, 1999). Since 1619 in landing of African slaves at Jamestown, Virginia even under the yoke of slavery, African-Americans, i.e., people of color have never sought adjustment to a racist environment. The prevailing racism is all but irrelevant in the context of adjustment. On the other hand, adaptation for African-Americans and other people of color contains a therapeutic dimension and may be proactive. Therefore, relative to adaptation, human organisms include an attempt to engage "goodness-of-fit," considering "goodness-of-fit" is reference to person and the environment for the fulfillment of needs, aspirations, and other quality-of-life human conditions (Thissen, 2013). Exemplified by a historical African-American chronology Negro Suffrage, Civil Rights, and the recent Black Lives Matter movement are "goodness-of-fit" efforts. African-Americans may carry the memory of such experiences with them throughout the life span and well into later years. This is true whether their experience was direct in personal involvement or indirect via identification with other African-Americans who took part personally. In the event that fit be ill suited or the environment changes, as per adaptation, people of color as human organisms will actively attempt change in themselves, the environment, or both. Various attempts to change the latter have been exacerbated by displays of racism. People of color per skin color subsequently encounter environmental stresses imposed upon their psyche. Ultimately, unlike adjustments per the EP, adaptation accommodates the preferred needs and objectives of the human organism relative to its biopsychosocial environment. Unfortunately, that adaptation imposed on by colorism can also be destructive and detrimental (Schwartz, 1999).

In consideration of the EP, the pro-activity of adaptation should by no means imply that passivity of the organism is totally irrelevant. In the context of Martin Luther King Jr.'s non-violent movement was an account of passivity that amounted to a goal-directed end. Given the EP, people of color as human organisms may actively choose to be passive in certain extreme situations such as response to racism and/or colorism. When this takes place in an adaptation context, the critical dynamic involved is psycho system control. That control is manifested in making the decision to be passive or nonviolent. What's more, passivity in the context of adaptation may include the manipulation of a race- or color-dominated environment. This can be accomplished as in peaceful protest aimed at obtaining a moral advantage, etc. (Erwin & Kipness, 1997). Therefore, adaptation may take place whether the movement is by active confrontation or passive avoidance for a specified objective. Unfortunately, by colorism or racism per the EP while goals may be attained or set, in adaptation they exact a penalty that requires an informed familiarity with racism to fully comprehend.

Racism

Racism, according to Banton (in Kitano, 1985), refers to the efforts of a dominant race group to exclude a dominated race group from sharing in the material and symbolic rewards of status and power. It differs from the numerous other forms of domination in that qualification is contingent upon observable and assumed biosystem traits in this case skin color (Wilson, 1992). Said traits imply the inherent superiority of dominant race groups that are then rationalized as a natural order of the human social universe (Minor & McGauley, 1988).

From the EP, Banton's traditional view of racism is hereby referred to as primary. The most zealous proponents of primary racism profess that persons of European descent being light-skinned are superior to those of African or non-European descent being dark-skinned as a matter of fact (Welsing, 1970). They postulate that Europeans have been biologically endowed with capacities necessary to bring about civilization. Efforts to civilize were initially a thinly veiled form of primary racism devoted to rationalizing the right of Europeans to embark upon a worldwide mission aimed at European domination (Daly, Jennings, Beckett, & Leashore, 1995). By way of domination, Europeans left no terrain of the human environment untouched by their existence. After centuries of said domination, the racist mission to "civilize" non-Europeans has necessitated a universal, almost mystic belief in the power of race to elevate or taint (Hyde, 1995).

As per the EP, primary racism permeates the human biopsychosocial environment. By virtue of disparity in power, dominant primary group Europeans proceeded to exploit less powerful intermediate and tertiary race groups deemed such by their proximity to European (Gordon, 1998). The prevailing racism is pathological retarding human growth, human health, and human system functioning. As pathos of the environment, primary racism eventually disrupts the normal growth and development potential of the various human entities. Dominant groups then exercise political and economic power on the basis of skin color interpreted as race and other observable bio system criteria for access to and control of wealth (Sahay & Piran, 1997; Chestang, 1995). Such pernicious management of power is toxic to human existence overall manifesting as various social problems. Similar to the biological impact of disease, it impairs and by circumlocution eventually revisits the dominant groups from which it emerged.

Contrary to traditional views, primary racism is then a major stressor that afflicts the entire human population (Schuchman, 1997). It extends to perpetrators as well as victims via formidable distortions of moral criteria. While dominant race groups are not unaffected, the heaviest burdens are arguably borne by the victim vulnerable, colonized, and racially disenfranchised. It orchestrates the environment in which the system development and functioning of all human organisms must thrive. Over the life span, enormous consequences are visited upon vulnerable populations in their adaptive response to primary racism (Daniel & Daniel, 1998). Spurred on by self-preservation and a corrupted sense of humanity, dominated groups eventually tolerate and contribute to the prevalence of racism in the human social environment. Subsequent to their adaptation, dominated race groups then become a factor in the pain and suffering of their own demise. The consequences thus reciprocate in the systems of both dominant and dominated groups. Hence, extended from dominant race groups is the traditional primary racism and from dominated race groups the heretofore-unacknowledged intermediate and tertiary manifestations.

As per the EP, intermediate racism refers to the efforts of a dominated race group individual to exclude another dominated race group individual from sharing in the material and symbolic rewards of status and power (Sidel, 2000). By virtue of having been conquered, colonized, or otherwise subjugated by Europeans' primary racism, intermediate racism is perpetrated by those group individuals who occupy an intermediate status on the primary racial hierarchy. They are thus below the status of European descent and due to colorism regarded as being above that of African descent. Their skin color and other bio system features may be intermediate as well making them lighter than those of African descent and darker than those of European descent (Hall, 1994).

Intermediate group racism differs from primary group racism in that qualification is contingent upon submission to European domination and valuing European norms at the expense of self and other dominated groups. This qualifies as a version of no less destructive adaptation. Said adaptation in becoming norm validates the assumed superiority of dominant race groups that are then accepted as a natural order of the biopsychosocial universe.

Intermediate group racism prevails because primary group racism has become ubiquitous to the human social environment. Among intermediate race groups it is historical via colorism, having manifested long before their ancestors reached the Americas or Europeans visited their homeland. The once colonized forefathers of intermediate race Nicaraguans considered race to have an influence upon the psychosocial system of common folk. Mestizos—the racially mixed—refer to the darker-skinned Costenos—persons of African descent—in derogatory terms (Lancaster, 1991). For Cuban-Americans, the idealization of the European bio system has existed historically despite the attempts of Castro's Revolution to eliminate it. Status in Cuba is continually based on gradations of skin color and affects all aspects of Cuban life covertly as well as overtly (Canizares, 1990). Furthermore, Asian intermediate race groups from India, Pakistan, Bangladesh, and Sri Lanka once settled in the United States constantly seek ways to prove themselves "white" (Mazumdar, 1989). In the process, vehement forms of intermediate group racism are perpetrated against dark-skinned persons including those of African descent.

The most zealous proponents of intermediate group racism thus idealize European bio systems and accept their superiority as a matter of fact. They are convinced that Europeans have been endowed with the genetic capacity necessary to civilize the human environment. That acceptance is a thinly veiled form of intermediate group racism devoted to rationalizing the status of intermediate groups as being superior to those of tertiary group descent. By way of assumed superiority, intermediate group racism in the social environment such as that of Asians is manifested in their alteration of native bio systems.

As per the EP, tertiary group racism refers to the efforts of a dominated race group member to exclude another dominated race group member from sharing in the material and symbolic rewards of status and power (Spencer, 1998). In perpetuation skin color is employed as an all too often measure of function. Extended from the white supremacy ideology light skin per primary group racism precipitates intra-group conflicts by notation of superiority. In this instance colorism may be dramatically carried out against same race individuals whose melanin content significantly differs from their counterparts. This dynamic among those who were light-skinned during the antebellum were referred to by African-Americans as "House Negroes" and the dark-skinned as "Field Negroes." In a speech delivered on November 10, 1963, in Detroit, Michigan Malcolm X commented on the "House Negro."

> The House Negroes—they lived in the house with master, they dressed pretty good, they ate good 'cause they ate his food—what he left. They lived in the attic or the basement, but still they lived near the master; and they loved their master more than the master loved himself. They would give their life to save the master's house quicker than the master would. The House Negro, if the master said, "We got a good house here," the House Negro would say, "Yeah, we got a good house here." Whenever the master said "we," he said "we." That's how you can tell a House Negro.
>
> *(Brietman, 1965, p. 10)*

Many "House Negroes" were in fact the psychologically dominated, light-skinned offspring of the master class by slave concubines. More often their subjection to domination encouraged them to embrace the master's primary racism as their own where the end result was tertiary group racism via colorism. By manifestation of the master's politics, "House Negroes" found fault with the assumed crudeness of and "inferiority" of "Field Negroes" who could not appreciate or contribute to the more advanced aspects of white culture (Jenkins & Tryman, 2002). That is not to suggest that existence outside the master's residence facilitated African-Americans' access to a better quality of life in the absolute. However, it is to suggest that a disproportionate number of the black antebellum affluent by tertiary group racism were "House Negroes" who had accommodated the domination of black people by the master class (Lambert, 2005). They clearly understood the implications of their racial and political proximity to that class for quality of life and aristocratic status within the color conscience antebellum hierarchy (Banks, 2000). By virtue of African-Americans having been conquered, colonized, or enslaved, tertiary group racism was perpetrated by light-skinned members of most stigmatized groups who occupy a tertiary status on the primary racial hierarchy. They may be of African descent by racial heritage but may or may not exhibit African bio system characteristics. Their features may then vary and function in the perpetration of tertiary group racism in the social environment of tertiary groups.

Tertiary group racism differs from primary and intermediate group racism in that qualification is contingent upon submission to alien norms at the expense of self and members of the native bio system group. Said norms validate the assumed inferiority of tertiary groups that are then accepted as a natural order of their biopsychosocial universe. Less attention is given to the superiority of dominant and intermediate groups. However, the assumed inferiority of tertiary groups impacts their psychosocial systems and today is a matter of judicial record. Tertiary group racism is no doubt colorism in the modern world that emerges from documented ancient history long before European conquest or otherwise European domination had occurred.

Colorism

Primary, secondary, and tertiary group racism is gradually giving way to colorism. Any remaining reference to racism is a consequence of Western scholarship committed to the validation of a race/racism concept. In fact, as biracial births increase, comes the waning validity of a race decrease attributable to the emergence and visibility of colorism. The existence of colorism has been known by people of color for most of human history. The terms may vary across culture and historical era, but colorism exists no less. Colorism has prevailed in Asia, Africa, and various other locations globally. Considering people of color at large, the longevity of colorism post-colonization and the Atlantic slave trade, as a topic of public discussion has remained an ethnic taboo (Moore, 2008). In both definition and documented terminology until recently colorism has thus remained a taboo in matters of public discourse. Its eventual documentation is credited to the modern-day literary icon African-American Alice Walker. Walker first made documented mention of colorism as pertains to people of color in the context of African-Americans. Her reference was published in 1983 on the pages of *Essence* magazine popular among African-American women. At first thought Walker referred to colorism as being an issue relative to African-Americans exclusively. However, following careful study and measured speculation, she revised her perspective of the issue to incorporate the participation and inclusion of all people of color consisting of Native-, Asian-, and Latinx- as well as African-Americans.

In specific detail, Walker defines colorism as an issue commensurate with racism (Nakray, 2018). Similar to racism, colorism is an immoral act that operates on the basis of melanin content in human skin. Said content is responsible for the degree of hue in human skin commonly referred to as skin color. Subsequently, people of color who contain the maximum in melanin content will be observed as having dark skin. Conversely, those having a minimum of melanin will by observation have light skin. As a biological trait, the level of melanin has social consequences that pertain to colorism considered basis for a potent social transgression that dominates the life space environment of dark-skinned people of color. This life space transgression is the reality of discrimination that exists in the shadows of the more traditionally preferred reference to racism (Goldenberg, 2014). This preferred racial reference has discouraged attention to an otherwise dominating impact of colorism that has imposed on people of color globally. Little known by the Eurocentric academy is the existence of colorism long before the impact of European influences. Among the most dramatic of primary examples as a template for all people of color is the history of colorism in ancient India.

Without any doubt ancient India is one of the oldest civilizations in the world. Initially colorism in what is known as India today did not exist as a social pathology or cultural taboo (Mohan, 2016). In fact, ancient India was originally a conglomeration of different races and distinct cultures with many similarities, which gradually formed the nation today referred to as India. Therefore, by skin color, the citizens of India were dramatically varied in their amount of melanin, but they were also varied in facial features based on the Indian geographical area where they resided. Thus, Indians from the northern most regions were/are more fair-skinned having a yellowish skin tone and facial features more akin to their southeast Asian counterparts. What's more, south Indians from the Dravidian's family tree are for the most part darker in skin color. That is to say, the physical environment has greatly shaped the physical features of Indians today including their skin color. In addition, having dark skin was initially not a stigma or unspoken social taboo (Picton, 2013). Thus, an acceptance of diversity in physical attributes relative to feminine beauty until recently did not accrue on the basis of skin color. The fact that skin color is a significant attribute in modern India necessitates an explanation of how it came to be.

Ancient India as now was perhaps the most socially complex society in the world. The broad orderings and sub-orderings in India seem very multifarious and confusing to outsiders as a lot of classifications are often overlapping: region, religion, caste, sub-caste, Jati, Gotra, Kula, Varna, language, etc. Any effort to simplify the aforementioned categories beyond a point can lead to distortions of social reality. The earliest classification, as found in Rig Veda, was not through birth but the hierarchy that was determined by one's occupation. At some point in Indian history, this arrangement eventually became birth based and very rigid. Thousands of castes and sub-castes came into existence from the Varna categorization. Ultimately, the classification system became oppressive. The much-cited Purush Sukta in Rig Veda explains how the four orders in society originated from the self-sacrifice of Purusha, the primeval being, who destroyed himself so that appropriate social order could emerge (Dube, 2013).

Among the four caste-relevant orders of Indian society are Brahmin: born from the head; Kshatriya born from the arms; Vaishya born from the thighs; and Shudras born from the feet (Dube, 2013). It is compulsory to acknowledge the fact that this was a symbolic categorization. As a metaphorical categorization system, all four caste classes existing in Indian society symbolically emerged from the same body and have different but equally important functions in the overall of Indian society not irrelevant to colorism today.

No less pertinent to the issue of colorism in ancient India is the Hindu texts. For a period of time, the Vedic Hindu texts were in unwritten form. Existing as unwritten allowed for a diversity of interpretation, which eventually became an extensive misinterpretation. The aforementioned occupational system was (mis)interpreted in that noble occupations were given higher status and polluting and unclean occupations given lower status. Marriages and mixing of the different Varnas were rare and for the most part not allowed, though certain instances show intellectuals from lower strata being accepted as saints and given higher status and acceptance in society at large. Many saints and highly respected Rishis were children of parents other than those from upper castes. The great writer of Mahabharata, Maharshi Veda Vyas, for instance was the son of a rishi and Satyavati, who was the daughter of a fisherman (Dusharaj) belonging to a lower caste (Mittal, 2006).

The significant heterogeneity of ancient India was obviously reflected in skin color as well as occupation. At the onset, there were reasons to think that there was a difference in the light skin color of Aryans (immigrant "noble" population) and their enemies who were the darker-skinned tribal populations that had yet to be ranked in status by color. The two groups were constantly at war over territory and other measures of wealth. Their appearance was noted by various excerpts from the Rig Veda, which distinguished Indians on the basis of skin color that had as yet implied anything pertaining to status or social stigma. However, the previous historical differentiations in color provided a vehicle for colorism that prevails in modern India today. It is well-known but not a popular topic of Indian discourse. The arrival of light-skinned British colonials to the Indian continent was critical to the evolution of colorism there. With the experience of British invasion, the prospects of colorism in India were exacerbated and no less apparent among all people of color globally today.

The evolution of colorism in India is not unique among people of color. There may exist various nuances as to how it came about but its existence is no less a fact. In ancient Japan, the Middle East, Latinx America, and various locations abroad, colorism has exacted social consequences upon the people. Women valued for their physical attributes suffer additional consequences compared to men. Of note is the ancient Japanese notion that light skin compensates for seven blemishes in a woman (Wagatsuma, 1968). In fact, while seldom acknowledged colorism relative to people of color is also apparent among Eurocentric populations who are charged with assessing people of color. In all Western locations inhabited by persons of European descent, colorism may be applied to people of color as a measure of character, intellect, attractiveness, and unfortunately in courts of law guilt or innocence (Viglione, Hannon, & Defina, 2011). Thus, skin color prevails as an omnipotent physiological trait that historically and contemporaneously potentially permeate all categories of human existence and quality of life. Despite the fact, its actuality has been all but denied as per academic bias and overlooked by the various institutions of social science pedagogy committed to the discourses on race.

Academic Bias

The academic investment in race is a product of power. In the well-established fact that race is a contrived concept, it nevertheless exists as the preferred system of human demarcation and category notation. In law, politics, etc., when it is necessary to organize human populations, they are consistently differentiated on the basis of race. Said differentiation is more often by skin color designation. Such terms as Negroid, Caucasoid, and Mongoloid have been discontinued in use and now considered offensive. As pertains to colorism during the antebellum such terms as mulatto, quadroon, and octoroon have been similarly discontinued as they too have been found to be offensive. Unfortunately, the concept of race although false has been maintained in the details of official documents (Billinger, 2007). The ability of the race concept to survive is owed to participating operatives of the scientific academy.

As racial tolerance has gained global acceptance via diversity and human equality, race while still prevalent is becoming increasingly unpopular for reasons not irrelevant to a colorism reality. The white supremacy ideology has been reduced to profanity and the rhetoric of only the most extreme, racist factions (Mascolo, 2017). Those nations that took part in colonization and the demonization of their colonial subjects have moved to various measures of reconciliation reflected most dramatically in their rhetoric. At the pinnacle of such reconciliation is the aftermath of South African apartheid where white Afrikaners have facilitated the adoption of laws and policies absent white supremacy in public discourse. In the aftermath of its racist past South Africa now boasts of black judges, doctors, lawyers, and successful business operatives. The ultimate of change is perhaps symbolic in the election of a black citizen to the office of South African President.

Various scholars have suggested that bias does in fact exist in the scientific literature, particularly as pertains to colorism, though it is not unique to this area of social science study. In an article published by Stanley Sue in 1999, he clearly and eloquently articulates the manner in which academic bias in the publication of literature is fostered and maintained. Vehemently, he asserts that popular and accepted norms for defining the rigor of a study are flawed and lend themselves to bias under the guise of the pursuit of rigorous scientific investigation. Furthermore, he suggests that not all scholars are held to the same standard with regard to the generalizability of their work. Dr. Sue's investigation is endorsed by the published reports of multiple authors, who through careful and rigorous review, substantiate his claims regarding the inclusiveness and generalizability of their research findings (Nagayama, Hall & Maramba, 2001). It is a possibility that because of the historical preponderance of Euro-American researchers, Eurocentrism became a bias that set the "gold standard" for how academics approached their subject matter (Stinson, 1979). Recent studies of bias in scientific fields such as medicine suggest that an ethnocentric bias exists in journals such that authors of varied nationalities only cite and attend to the work of their fellow countrymen (Stephenson, 1997).

Eurocentric and ethnocentric bias are assumptions that have been methodically challenged by a handful of academics who, in the early 1970s, established the aggressive push toward inclusiveness regarding issues of racial and ethnic diversity that might encompass colorism. Though noteworthy strides have been achieved in the last 30 years or so, significant issues published in the leading journals have generally remained a recapitulation of the Eurocentric race perspective. Such a perspective considering race remains loyal to a Western intellectual ideal where colorism and other skin color issues have been subjugated. As such, it might be argued that the academy remains a bastion of Eurocentric thought and Eurocentric bias despite the globalization of knowledge and the influx of racially and ethnically diverse scientists into the intellectual endeavor (Mathis, 2002). Verily, the trivialization of issues such as colorism is then likely a manifestation of certain scholars who have a limited knowledge or a limited range of diversity issues. In essence, scholarship as per social science is then an outgrowth of a Western Eurocentric approach to understanding the human psyche and the resulting prospects of human behavior. What's more given that research scholarship was advanced by the works of European scientists over centuries it is not surprising that academia, even with its advanced modern-day focus on issues of diversity, is lagging in redressing Eurocentric bias as pertains to the global and historical acknowledgment of colorism in published works.

In preparation for the future, colorism via skin color must replace racism via race as the most objective and applicable measure of the human social experience. In detail the human experience is most given to adaptation and the EP. The continuation of race will not only prove increasingly irrelevant but also promote sustained polarity that can only disserve scientific investigation. Where biracial births increasingly allow for indistinct racial features, academy personnel will be confronted by research challenges unprecedented. In the aftermath absent choice, they will seek an applicable construct. Heretofore skin color and colorism are their only viable alternatives (Smart, 2019).

Social scientific investigation as a profession is not immune to the criticisms leveled against other intellectual fields. Recent developments in the area of cultural diversity and ethnic minority content have supported the assumption of Eurocentric bias in recent years by suggesting that no one person exists outside a cultural milieu. Even the most well-intentioned among scholars falls victim to socialized prejudices (McIntosh, 1989). These prejudices, while often stealth and masked, are frequently manifested in the continued teaching and research of non-inclusive theories and the limited inclusion of ethnic minority focused research in the top-tier journals (Ritchie, 1994). As an example, in noting the work of Carl Jung (1969), whose theories are widely used in higher education, makes the point. Jung is identified as having maintained quite a controversial and negative (many would say racist) view of African-Americans (Tinsley-Jones, 2001). Yet, despite the fact Jungian theory remains a staple of the academic realm. The same is true considering many of the celebrated theories universally applied and taught in all of social science (Pedersen, 1987).

Suggestions of a Eurocentric bias per colorism in social science is often met with resistance in the form of repudiation. An example of such repudiation is Merton's (1973) work in which he supposedly articulates four norms that protect peer-reviewed journals from bias: universalism, communalism, disinterestedness, and organized skepticism. Universalism contends that issues published in journals are independent of personal criteria and subjective desired outcomes. Communalism pertains to the public availability of such issues. Disinterestedness assures that objective scientific investigators disassociate their personal bias and prejudices from their conclusions. Lastly, organized skepticism requires any conclusions drawn via the scientific method be subjected to standard universal procedures of scrutiny, replication, testing of rival conclusions, and peer review. Inherent in these arguments is the idea that scientists can separate themselves from the world views and cultures within which they intellectually develop and exist. Furthermore, these arguments suggest that even when scientists fail to acknowledge and minimize their own prejudices, colleagues (via peer review) serve as a buffer against bias.

More recent arguments in support of Merton's theories pertaining to bias include Koehler (1993), who reports that most social scientists endorse Merton's ideas and believe themselves to practice them in peer review. Such fervent arguments were developed to dispel the notion that Eurocentric bias does little to alter the real experiences of researchers interested in publishing in the area of cultural diversity such as the prospects of colorism focused on people of color. This renders the EP all but totally irrelevant or if relevant insignificant. Unfortunately, for all intents and purposes bias then remains a formidable obstacle to the incorporation of a colorism reality subjugated by the auspices of race. This is so despite the fact that race will be all but totally irrelevant by end of the 21st century as it is currently increasingly becoming so. Resolution and preparation for the future will necessitate a sea change and require a comprehensive re-education of the academy and society at large. Therefore, in an effort to reduce race bias in preparation for the future and coming millennium will require a thorough discourse on colorism beginning with its colonial origins

References

Banks, T. L. (2000). Colorism: A darker shade of pale. *UCLA Law Review, 47*(6), 1705–1746.
Beverly, C. (1989). Treatment issues for black, alcoholic clients. *Social Casework, 70*(6), 370–374.
Billinger, M. (2007). Another look at ethnicity as a biological concept: Moving anthropology beyond the race concept. *Critique of Anthropology, 27*(1), 5–35.
Black, M. (2007). Fanon and DuBoisian double consciousness. *Human Architecture: Journal of the Sociology of Self-Knowledge, 5*, 393–404.
Brietman, G. (1965). *Malcolm X speaks*. New York: Grove Press.
Canizares, R. (1990). Cuban racism and the myth of the racial paradise. *Ethnic Studies Report, 8*(2), 27–32.
Chestang, L. (1995). Is it time to rethink affirmative action? No! *Journal of Environmental Psychology Education, 32*(1), 12–18.
Daly, A., Jennings, J., Beckett, J., & Leashore, B. (1995). Effective coping strategies of African Americans. *Social Work, 40*(2), 40-48.
Daniel, J., & Daniel, J. (1998). Preschool children's selection of race-related personal names. *Journal of Black Studies, 28*(4), 471–490.
Dube, S. C. (2013). *Indian society* (p. 50). New Delhi: National Book Trust.
Erwin, E., & Kipness, N. (1997). Fostering democratic values in inclusive early childhood settings. *Early Childhood Education Journal, 25*(1), 57–60.
Goldenberg, B. (2014). White teachers in urban classrooms: Embracing non-white students'. *Urban Education, 49*(1), 111–144.
Gordon, D. (1998). Humor in African American discourse: Speaking of oppression. *Journal of Black Studies, 29*(2), 254–276.
Green, R., & Ephross, P. (1991). *Human behavior theory and social work practice*. New York: DeGruyter.
Hall, R. (1994). The 'bleaching syndrome': Implications of light skin for Hispanic American assimilation. *Hispanic Journal of Behavioral Sciences, 16*(3), 307–314.
Hall, R. (2016). The bleaching syndrome: Manifestations of a post-colonial pathology among African women. *African Journal of Social Work, 6*(2), 49–57.
Hyde, C. (1995). The meanings of whiteness. *Qualitative Sociology, 18*(1), 87–95.
Jenkins, R., & Tryman, M. (2002). *The Malcolm X encyclopedia*. Westport, CT: Greenwood Press.
Jung, C. (1969). *The archetypes and the collective unconscious* (R. F. C. Hull, Trans., 2nd ed.). Princeton: Princeton University Press.
Kailash, (1997). Human ecological stress and demographic decline: A case of Negritos of Andamans. *Indian Journal of Social Work, 58*(3), 382–402.
Kitano, H. (1985). *Race relations*. Englewood Cliffs, NJ: Prentice Hall.
Koehler, J. J. (1993). The influence of prior beliefs on scientific judgments of evidence quality. *Organizational Behavior and Human Decision Processes, 56*(1), 28–55.
Lambert, D. (2005). *White creole culture, politics and identity during the age of abolition*. Cambridge: Cambridge University Press.
Lancaster, R. (1991, October). Skin color, race and racism in Nicaragua. *Ethnology, 30*(4), 339–353.
McIntosh, P. (1989, July–August). White privilege: Unpacking the invisible knapsack. *Peace and Freedom Magazine*, pp. 10–12, Women's International League for Peace and Freedom, Philadelphia, PA.
Mackey, R., & O'Brien, B. (1999). Adaptation in lasting marriages. *Families in Society, 80*(6), 587–596.

Mascolo, M. (2017). The transformation of a White supremacist: A dialectical-developmental analysis. *Qualitative Psychology, 4*(3), 223–242.

Mathis, D. (2002). *Yet a stranger*. New York: Warner Books.

Mazumdar, S. (1989). Racist response to racism: The Aryan myth and South Asians in the US. *South Asia Bulletin, 9*(1), 47–55.

Merton, R. (1973). *The sociology of science: Theoretical and empirical investigations*. Chicago: University of Chicago Press.

Minor, N., & McGauley, L. (1988). A different approach: Dialogue in education. *Journal of Teaching in Social Work, 2*(1), 127-140.

Mittal, J. P. (2006). *History of ancient India: From 4250 to 637 AD* (p. 447). New Delhi: Atlantic Publishers.

Mohan, J. (2016). The glory of ancient India stems from her Aryan blood: French anthropologists 'construct' the racial history of India for the world. *Modern Asian Studies, 50*(5), 1576–1618.

Moore, J. (2008). The paper bag principle: Class, colorism, and rumor and the case of black Washington, DC. *The Journal of Southern History, 74*(1), 222–223.

Nagayama Hall, G. C. & Maramba, G. G. (2001). In search of cultural: Diversity recent literature in cross-cultural and ethnic minority psychology. *Cultural Diversity & Ethnic Minority Psychology February, 7*(1), 12–26.

Nakray, K. (2018). The global beauty industry, colorism, racism and the national body. *Journal of Gender Studies, 27*(7), 861–863.

Pedersen, P. (1987). Ten frequent assumptions of cultural bias in counseling. *Journal of Multicultural Counseling & Development, 15*(1), 16–24.

Picton, O. (2013). The complexities of complexion: A cultural geography of skin color and beauty products. *Geography, 98*, 85–92.

Ritchie, M. H. (1994). Cultural and gender biases in definitions of mental and emotional health and illness.

Sahay, S., & Piran, N. (1997). Skin-color preferences and body satisfaction among South Asian-Canadian and European-Canadian female university students. *Journal of Social Psychology, 137*(2), 161–171.

Schuchman, K. (1997). *Social structure and immigrant identification: Impact of race, economic participation*. New York: Adelphi University, DSW.

Schwartz, A. (1999). Americanization and cultural preservation in Seattle's settlement house: A Jewish adaptation to the Anglo-American model of settlement work. *Journal of Sociology and Social Welfare, 26*(3), 25–47.

Sidel, R. (2000). The enemy within: The demonization of poor women. *Journal of Sociology and Social Welfare, 27*(1), 73–84.

Smart, H. (2019). Operationalizing a conceptual model of colorism in local policing. *Social Justice Research, 32*(1), 72–115.

Spencer, M. (1998). Reducing racism in schools: Moving beyond rhetoric. *Social Work in Education, 20*(1), 25–36.

Stephenson, J. P. (1997, November). Medical journals turn gaze inward to examine process of peer review. *JAMA, 278*(17), 1389–1391.

Stinson, A. (1979). Community development in an era of perspective search. *Social Development Issues, 3*(3), 6–21.

Thissen, D. (2013). The meaning of goodness-of-fit tests: Commentary on "goodness-of-fit assessment of item response theory models". *Measurement: Interdisciplinary Research and Perspectives, 11*(3), 123–126.

Tinsley-Jones, H. A. (2001). Racism in our midst: Listening to psychologists of color. *Professional Psychology-Research and Practice, 32*(6), 573–580.

Viglione, J., Hannon, L., & Defina, R. (2011). The impact of prison time for Black female offenders. *Social Science Journal, 48*(1), 250–258.

Wagatsuma, H. (1968). The social perception of skin color in Japan. In J. Franklin (Ed.), *Color and race* (pp. 129–165). Boston: Daedalus.

Welsing, F. (1970). *The Cress theory of color confrontation and white supremacy*. Washington, DC: CR Publishers.

Wilson, M. (1992). What difference could a revolution make? Group work in the new Nicaragua. *Social Work with Groups, 15*(2–3), 301–314.

2
THE COLONIAL ORIGINS OF COLORISM

Although Native-Americans as people of color had similarly brutal experiences with slavery, the arrival of Africans at Jamestown to the American shores in 1619 was markedly different. It was much more brutal and given to more extensive longevity. Natives were considered the original inhabitants of the Americas, Africans were kidnapped and brought to the New World via slave ships. A short time later their blood would be mingled with that of the Native population. Such mixing of blood made for a distinct skin color in offspring. The journey of both peoples was cruel and inhumane, but many managed to survive. Those who did, could not have imagined what lay ahead for the future. Kidnap and enslavement were the circumstances for the lot of African slaves, but this was not the first experience Africans had had with slavery (Stampp, 1956; Herskovits, 1968). It was an all-too common practice in many parts of the African continent for the males of defeated tribes to be enslaved and sold like chattel by victors.

The European version of African enslavement differed from any practiced by Africans. In the European version, slaves were not only regarded as inferior, but they also had lost their status as whole human beings (Meier & Rudwick, 1966). In fact, Native-American peoples had not been so demeaned as the US Constitution regarded Africans legally as 3/5 human (Franklin, 1969). Nowhere in recorded human history was this acute form of denigration known to exist.

Similar to that of Native-Americans and Africans, the skin color of Latinx people of color contrasted with that of European colonists. Such a contrast was equally obvious owing to the extremely high concentration of melanin in the skin of Afro-Latinx in particular and those who had mingled blood with Native peoples. Dark skin evoked a sexual dilemma in the psyche of colonists which enabled the perpetuation of colorism via offspring. Perpetuation was perhaps most intensified by the sight of a slave woman. At night in the cabins of slave women, colonial males lived out their sexual fantasies; by day they extolled the virtues of fidelity in an attempt to

DOI: 10.4324/9781003302889-3

absolve themselves of any impending guilt and to control the urges of colonial white women (Disch & Schwartz, 1970). Ordinarily the contradiction in such behavior would have evoked guilt. But this is perhaps a marvel of the colonial slave master mentality, in that for all his sexual exploitation of slave women, guilt never became an ethical issue (Kovel, 1984). This ability to circumvent any impending guilt was critical to sustaining colonial institutions responsible for perpetuating colorism.

While sexual contact between colonial males and their female slaves encouraged miscegenation, the supremacy attitude toward slaves that allowed the behavior to flourish eventually led to Civil War in the States (Kinder, 1986). Thus, while colonial males violated their own color-coded ethics without legal or social consequences, any slave and/or male of color sexually engaged with a colonial female was immediately accused of rape (Wood, 1968). The urges colonial males could not control in themselves were invested in a slave they could dominate. By the time overt slavery as an institution had been dismantled, Western civilization had become fertile ground for villainizing people of color by whatever forms necessary. The impending fear similar to Africans but as pertains to Latinx people of color aroused fantasies of "hot" blooded putas and knife welding "bandits." As a result, the Latinx male in the minds of colonial aggressors in many South American locations were frequently thought of in the role of beast, seeking vengeance for his "women" having been violated (Hernton, 1965). It is this fantasy of African and Latinx fear that incited much of the historical colorism aimed at people of color around the world and continues as justification for negative images today existent in the form of stereotypes.

Prior to the age of computer technology, print media was the primary vehicle for communicating colonial images of people of color in the form of stereotypes. What observers could not learn about people of color by word of mouth was left to what they could read, or the literate could read to them. Although print was an established form of business, it was a largely unregulated industry (Tebbel, 1963). This allowed the unscrupulous to incite for the purpose of increasing profits (Silberman, 1964). It also served as a colonial means to convey negative images which facilitated the existence of colorism by dehumanizing people of color. In rationalizing their stereotype print media used buzz words for Latinx victims like "wetback," "greaser," and "illegal" immigrant to evoke passion and anger among the mainstream community.

The ability of print to stereotype people of color has had quite an impact on how they are perceived (St. John, 1967). That impact increased with the use of photographic technology. The camera offered the ability to freeze a detailed likeness of a person of color suspected as a culprit in crime, who could then be recognized on sight. Motivated by profit, photography applied lighting, pose, attire, etc., to create whatever stereotype deemed necessary. It is debatable why the media stereotypes people of color. But what cannot be disputed is the fact that too often colorism is served by their contrasting complexions.

Slavery in South America is less dramatized in US literature perhaps given to implications of the US antebellum. But slavery is relevant to the early experience of all people of color in both the North and South Americas. The contrast of their dark skin was a daily reminder to the colonial power structure of the need for domination in order to reaffirm its presumed superiority. Thus, a brand of discrimination in colorism was to follow much later that compromised non-white efforts to assimilate. Throughout history, it insured that people of color would never be accorded equal status with their colonial counterparts. The forces that had once kept slaves in bondage were effectively used to exploit their descendants. Policies such as "Jim Crow" became standard procedure in every form of interaction between the dominant group colonials and their dominated group subjects (Hertel & Hughes, 1988). This meant that people of color such as Native-Americans, whose ancestors had roamed free and uninhibited across wide open American spaces and erected civilizations superior to any in Europe now found it extremely difficult to even feed themselves. Thus, given their circumstances, the quality of life for people of color and their families suffered. Said suffering resulted in their lessened ability to thrive as productive humanity which was espoused by some as a rationale for colorism. According to the vestiges of colorism, people of color were obviously not fit for civilization because they lacked the innate capacities of culture inherent in the capacities of colonial operatives (Lawler, 1978).

Colonization

The act of colonization is defined as the peopling of foreign territory—usually third world—previously settled by a native population with emigrants from the mother country (Kitano, 1997). Since the existence of the Roman Empire, the aforementioned colonial powers have dealt with their third world subjects, i.e., people of color in one of three ways: eradication, exclusion, or assimilation (Kitano, 1997). Ironically it is the assimilation experience of people of color and other victim group populations that has inspired their tendency to colorism.

Colorism enabled by slavery is a function of the colonial experience. One of the most comprehensive accounts of the colonial experience was written by a black psychiatrist named Franz Fanon (Macey, 2012). Life for Frantz Fanon began as a resident of the French colony of Martinique on July 20, 1925. He was not considered poor and in fact his family most likely qualified as a member of the black bourgeoisie. The elder Casimir Fanon was employed as a customs inspector. His mother, Eléanore Médélice, was proprietor of a hardware store located in downtown Fort-de-France, which was the capital of Martinique. Most of Fanon's social peers tended to assimilation and idealization of white French culture. Fanon grew to adulthood in such an environment eventually idealizing French culture and history as his own. That idealization of French culture would change upon entering high school when he was exposed to the philosophy of negritude. The works on negritude was espoused by a Martinique scholar named Aimé Césaire, who was an active critic of Western European colonization. Conflicted by his middle-class assimilation and Martinique's colonial status in 1943 Fanon left the country. At the age of 18, he joined with the Free French army during the culmination of WWII that his homeland be rescued from its colonial oppressors (Macey, 2012).

Fanon's colonial experience served his perspective well. He eventually finished training as a psychiatrist and authored among the most widely read accounts of the colonial mentality to date. It is a classic titled "Black Skin White Masks." Fanon's belief was that the colonial mentality pertains to the internalized attitude of inferiority experienced by the subjects of colonization. Such a mentality pertains to the belief by the colonized that the cultural traditions of the colonizer are superior to that of the colonized. This idea is frequently used by postcolonial intellectuals in discourse as pertains to the transgenerational impact of colonialism upon previous colonies in the aftermath of decolonization. It is more often applied as an operational construct for organizing colonial domination in historical colonial experiences. In the social and behavioral sciences Fanon's notion of the colonial mentality that facilitates colorism has been used to explain collective depression, anxiety, and other ailments widespread in the aftermath of colonization (Fanon, 1967).

The genesis of modern-day colorism is owed to elements of the Atlantic slave trade as well as European colonization. Slavery for the most part was attributed to the capture of Africans abducted from their homelands and dispersed abroad by a means unprecedented in human cruelty. Colonization, on the other hand, was not limited to Africans but pertained to a much broader sector of humanity. European nations, including Britain, Spain, Portugal, and the Dutch Netherlands, were active participants in the trade of human chattel. Thus, modern-day colorism is no less an extension of the colonial era that has imposed on human social systems worldwide.

European colonization at various locations in Africa, Asia, South America, and the Caribbean has long since ended. Unfortunately, the subjugation suffered by people of color has not been resolved. Most of the previously colonized nations are now proud, independent sovereignties but the psychological effects of their colonization remain. The colonial idealization of light skin is evidence ever visited upon the non-white psyche. It is apparent among people of color who, having suffered under colonial transgression, act out various forms of colorism against other equally subjugated or victimized populations. The most dramatic display of this suffering is demonstrated by the colorism implications of dark skin in the colonial aftermath.

The colorism implications of dark skin in the colonial aftermath are germane to the so-called racial hierarchy among people of color. Kitano implied that colorism in the aftermath of colonization is an extension of cultural stratification and is based on a system that consists of a dominant light-skinned Western and dominated dark-skinned non-Western populous (Weber, 1946). It is then the contention of Weber that societies are divided between those who rule and those who are ruled, and that dominant groups tend to draw lines around themselves in order to control the quality and consistency of interaction (Mazumdar, 1989). They exhibit a tendency toward closed systems and the ordering of people into hierarchies based on proximity to dominant group ideals. People of color, because of their skin color, were generally placed at the bottom of the colonial hierarchy (Buwalda-Macatangay,

1998). As emancipated slaves or immigrants arriving from non-white countries most could not speak the language very well; they were less familiar with Western culture; and sometimes lacked the necessary resources to succeed. Furthermore, many had not the education and competitive skills required for rapid mobility and unlike those of European descent, their dark skin was alien to the Western mainstream norm.

From the colonial origins of colorism in the modern era is the manifestation of discrimination by and among people of color. To fully comprehend the advent of colorism requires an examination of European colonization and the equally dominant Western influence. Both factors played a role in the creation of a skin color hierarchy that people of color may initially have found objectionable. Thus, according to Powell, it should not come as a shock that an unexpected number of African-American soldiers during the Spanish-American war deserted the armed forces while serving in the Philippines and that many joined the Filipino struggle for independence (Gilchrist, 1985). Despite such noble efforts in the aftermath is a hierarchy ever so subtle but nonetheless existent among colonized people of color both at home and abroad. In every country having been colonized and/or dominated by colorism a hierarchy exists under colonial circumstances. Among the noted are Cuba, Brazil, Panama, Jamaica, Japan, Puerto Rico, etc. In fact, Cuba is regarded by some such as Cuban intellectuals as the most colorism society in the Hispanic Caribbean. The physical, social, and cultural mores that the European Spaniards exported to Cuba were thus shaped and modified so as to effectively sustain aboriginal populations under a colorism system of colonization. The beneficiary of course was the colonial motherland. The success of this system in another colonial product such as the Philippines was largely dependent upon the experience of the first generation of locals to be colonized (Pratt, 1950). Although their lives and those of later Filipinos were directly impacted, the mixed race in particular in association with dark-skinned and light-skinned Filipinos would continue manifestations of colonization.

The ability of colonial victim populations to act out colorism depends principally on somatic visibility and assumed Western superiority. However, the mere belief in superiority is not enough to sustain the phenomenon. Mechanisms must be constructed to stigmatize and reinforce differentiation. Included are (a) the use of stereotypes, which leads to avoidance; (b) the use of legal barriers and norms, which leads to a competitive disadvantage; and (c) isolation of the previously colonized group (Kitano, 1997). How a colonized group is treated by the dominant population is a function of its perceived threat, its unpopularity, and the enforcement power of the colonizing entity. Frequently, the eruption of violence rationalizes extreme actions that may ultimately include extermination. In the aforementioned prevails exiles, refugees, and various acts of cultural genocide. The more excessive actions tend to occur when colorism by prejudice, discrimination, and segregation have exacted their toll to the extent of becoming norms.

Among a large majority of people of color who act out colorism is hard evidence of colorism whereby they internalize colonial ideals for physical beauty.

In referring to such ideals, Hoetink uses the concept of "somatic norm image" (Hoetink, 1967). By definition "somatic norm image" is "the complex of physical somatic characteristics accepted as ideal" (Hoetink, 1967). Therefore, every psychologically healthy group considers itself aesthetically superior to all others by comparison. However, as pertains to colonization, a Western somatic norm implies the belief that superiority is physiologically based in an alien racial category determined by skin color. Any deviations from the ideal category are presumed inferior enabling various social and political objectives to be acted out. As a result, the psychological implications of colonization among subjects are then as follows: (a) somatic ideals are continually rooted in colonial ideals, although it is seldom articulated in polite circles; (b) by virtue of colonization such ideals are inculcated by victims as the norm and a prerequisite to their tendency to colorism; (c) the tendency of victims to colorism in the aftermath of colonization has necessitated manifestation of a skin color hierarchy; and (d) in the outcome prevails a less-tolerant population characterized by their idealization of European physiology as ideal somatic norm.

Considering the skin color ideal, people of color are lacking in their ability to conform to the ideal skin color and are thus classified as "minorities." A few among members of the academy have applied the concept of "minority" under the rubric of race. If a designated so-called racial group is distinct, i.e., viewed as unique and as being bound by cultural ties, "minority" is a valid term. It is only when colorism and other distinctions are associated with denigration that the concept of "minority" takes on special significance as pertains to hierarchy (Kubota & Yoshida, 1998). The fact is that Italians have experiences comparable to "minorities" especially during their arrival to Elis Island. But, they were less victimized by colorism due to their light skin. Unlike people of color, they were not perceived as permanently alien not only by the dominant segments of society but also by members of the minority population as well (Kubota & Yoshida, 1998).

Due to their social experience, people of color post-colonization exhibit a color-based hierarchy commensurate with colorism. In the context of colorism light skin contrasted by dark skin is strictly applied to social and political group interaction. Subsequently, while mainstream groups are differentiated by socially selected cultural and ethnic traits, people of color are selected by socially selected physical traits not irrelevant to skin color (Hyde, 1995). Designation by physical group traits would have little or no meaning for people of color if there were no implied stigma. Unfortunately, per colonization origins people of color are perceived as alien due to perceptions and definitions held by members of the traditional, mainstream norm. Whereas some such as Italians characterized by light skin did not fit the Western ideal initially and totally, they were not differentiated as permanently alien having satisfied the skin color norm. They thus do not regard themselves as stigmatized nor are they so regarded by the nation in toto (Hyde, 1995).

Relative to people of color dark skin is germane to their somatic make up hence how they are perceived. Dark skin in a post-colonial era presupposes interpretation as a peculiar phenomenon that has been demonized extended across historical era and geographical location. In the modern era, no other somatic trait so essentially defines people of color as an out-group in Western societies than dark skin. On the other hand, for reasons of mental health and overall sanity a self-defined concept of skin color as per identity is critical to the emotional and psychological well-being of a people. That well-being is illustrated in the works of Cooley. As per the classic literature, Cooley constructed a concept referred to as the "Looking Glass Self" (Cooley, 1902). "The Looking Glass Self" is a descriptive metaphor which portrays identity as a reflection of the self in public perception. From that perception the core of identity via colorism is fashioned. A similar analysis for identity was proposed by Mead. Mead contends that identity is in fact a product of social interaction with others that gives unlimited potency to colorism (Mead, 1934). Therefore, the identity is completed and acted out once the host has moved from the "I" to the "me" perception of self. In addition to the works of Mead and Cooley, Nobles extended the concept of "I" and "me" to group memberships that might have implications for so-called race (Nobles, 1973; Cross, 1987). As suggested by Nobles is the fact that group membership assigns a "weness" to the identity development process. What's more, Erickson (1968) at first professed that identity is not static. He contends that by physiological characteristics considering skin color it may evolve from a complex of decision-making experiences. However, commensurate with tradition, Erikson eventually concluded that final identity is fixed "at the end of adolescence" (Erickson, 1968). Colorism as a product of the colonial experience dramatized during adolescence is apparent via analysis of people of color who idealize light skin. By virtue of such idealization, they display an attempt to realize a "weness" in which they are merged with the colonial population even at the risk of their personal well-being.

In the aftermath of identity formation impacted by colorism once people of color migrate to Western countries, they denigrate the self per idealization of light skin. As a result, they act to develop their identities motivated by a pathological self-concept manifested not only in the idealization of light skin but other non-white physiological characteristics such as the bleaching and straitening of hair, and alteration of eye folds. Confronted by an intense self-hatred they may experience feelings of inferiority which accommodates a paternalistic attitude toward the Western mainstream that contributes to the perpetuation of colorism. They imitate colonial group behaviors assumed necessary as a means of escape from identification with the despised non-white population. Thus, people of color, having relative darker skin, act out self-hate in a variety of ways ascribed to colorism. When opportunities are consistently made available by light skin, those who have darker skin as Fanon would contend experience despair, regardless of race, ethnicity, nationality, or immigration status.

The Aftermath of Colonization

In the historical aftermath of slavery and colonization, people of color are no less colonized as pertains to their psyche and quality of life. Those who manage entry into the upper classes are not unfamiliar with hierarchy as pertains to skin color. Enabled by the benefits of education and less threatening circumstances, people of color today are more likely spared the violence and overt hostility of previous generations. However, their unique features and in particular dark skin remained alien to the Western colonial gene pool and for reasons of colorism marks them permanently ineligible for all but marginal acceptance into the mainstream of traditional society (Hall, 1994). Their inability to gain acceptance is a critical aftermath of colonization that poses psychological consequences assumed due to dark skin.

The psychological consequence of colorism facilitates colonial structures because it implies the ability of colonial descended groups to impose their ideals absent consideration for the latter's reaction (Hall, 1994). Without regard to the particular methods used, colonial descended groups may then construct a social universe extended from the ideals of the colonial self. What's more, aside from the more obvious aggressive colonial tactics, psychological colonization may also thrive and derive influential behavior as pertains to personal status. Therefore, in modern-day Western societies, dominant group Europeans and their non-European subjects are thrust into a position to impose their ideals upon people of color who seek escape in an effort to value their skin color as norm (Hall, 1994). On a subliminal level, descendent colonials and those victimized by colorism may act out psychological colonization without ever making conscious or overt decisions to do so.

The willingness of people of color to adhere to colonial ideals is rooted in their having been socialized to pursue the "American Dream." In pursuit of the "American Dream," research suggests dominant groups then acquire power directly by emphasizing competence and action. People of color victimized by colorism acquire power by virtue of identification and/or submission to the colonial ideals, which manifests in their willingness to denigrate other people of color (Hoetink, 1967). In view of the status, differential between colonials and the colonized is thus tantamount to societally based institutional servitude.

Among spoils of the colonial aftermath is the influence and memorialized tradition of Eurocentrism. Eurocentrism pertains to the pursuit of "knowledge" couched in a colonial context. Said context has enabled an impact on the thinking of scholars worldwide (Stinson, 1979). This otherwise obvious assumption is not the least subject to legitimate dispute. The Western academy and other colonial influenced intellectual institutions exist as little more than a recapitulation of a colonial world order. That world order has been dominated by a Western geo-political power structure since the rein of Europe's colonial imperialism. Additionally, as the product of a geo-political entity, "knowledge" pertaining to what is and is not an intellectual priority extends for the most part from Europe (Hagen, 1982). Subsequently, until 1945 social science was centralized in the colonial efforts of such operatives as France, Great Britain, Germany, Italy, and the United States. What's more, despite the emergence of people of color in the intellectual generation of knowledge, the academy remains largely given to the ideas and ideals of a limited colonial perspective (Joyner, 1978). The results produce a portrayal of colonial transgressions free of oppression and an intellectual mentality hostile to the reality of hostile facts. It then follows as a matter of simple logic that colorism has been trivialized while race has been rendered both valid and a priority. In order to correct such intellectual failures, the generation of "knowledge" must bend to facilitate study of taboos such as colorism. The inability to do so will bring accusations of elitism from the very groups factual scientific knowledge proposes to serve (Tambor, 1979). The result of this elitism is that "knowledge" will be reduced to something that serves colonization in both shape and substance.

Eurocentrists who denounce the existence of colorism have facilitated the canonization of race without engaging conclusive debate or empirical analysis of colorism. In a loosely organized cultural and intellectual conspiracy, they resort to methods opposed to scientific rigor. Their hegemony is neither scientific nor ethical, but in fact a pseudo-scientific colonial collaboration designed to standardize the existential reality of human life by Eurocentric dimensions. In the aftermath, the significance of colorism is all but dismissed from the colonial experience and that which is existentially real. Such a compromise of science and intellectual integrity discourages the intellectual rigor which could provide new solutions to old world problems. Having evolved to a post-colonial era vastly more diverse than years past will require change commensurate with diversity.

Colorism Versus Racism

With respect to colonization, there are a number of reasons why scholars should consider colorism as an alternative to racism. First, the significance of colorism is well known and, if skillfully addressed, will likely enable study of colonized people of color worldwide (Hurdle, 2002). Second, discussions of racism as per discrimination for most involved conjures up images of legal conflicts with the potential to charge emotions; when it is associated with stereotype it encourages knee-jerk condemnation of an entire people, their social structure, lifestyle and other aspects of their being (Bridges & Steen, 1998). Ultimately it is intensely polarizing. The traditional subjugated race groups will impair the ability of same to thrive in a Eurocentric post-colonial environment unless more rational less polarized factions prevail. Third, colorism must be viewed in proportion to its consequence in the lives of people of color. To do otherwise will accommodate Eurocentrism rendering "knowledge" as pertains to colorism a less accurate portrayal of people and the "facts" conveyed about their lives.

Aside from racial constructs, the most efficient means of addressing colorism via colonization is to become more amenable to a universal global perspective. Discourse pertaining to the less relevance or irrelevance of race will enable that effort (Hall, 1992). Social scientists so enabled will then be in a better position to study and accurately portray colorism by and among victim group populations. Equally important is the impact of colorism upon the world at large. An advantage of such a perspective includes the ability of scholars to create tolerant environments by the building of bridges beyond race or what is politically exploitable. The focus on such bridges to people of color should be their language, history, cultures, colonial influences, etc., rather than the stereotypes and assumptions associated with their so-called race or color. What's more, during an era of more frequent contacts between the world's various so-called race populations, scholars are confronted by issues and perspectives on colorism which did not require consideration in years past (Harvey, 1995). They are thus challenged in future study to develop more comprehensive concepts less confined to Eurocentric or race traditions. That consideration is compelled to remain consistent and viable without interruption to sustain the emerging diverse world order.

Lastly, aside from slavery and colonization as origin of colorism transgression is not extraneous to the ecological reality as pertains to people of color (Hall, 2001). Their role in the perpetuation of colorism must be addressed including the decoding of Eurocentric concepts, illumination of hegemonic inequalities, and other moves to intellectual discourse. Through the prescripts of struggle, people of color have not been immune to participation, but in fact is arguably a matter of their willing participation. The academy at large must then become cognizant of their unique role, that of advocating for a more accurate representation of "facts" (Barnes, 2001). Doing so in the interest of illustrating the actuality of colorism is no more rigorous than in the antebellum, post-slavery, post-colonization of black culture that evolved the "Field Negro" and the "House Negro."

References

Barnes, S. (2001). Stressors and strengths: A theoretical and practical examination of nuclear, single-parent, and augmented African American families. Families in Society: The Journal of Contemporary Social Services, 82(5), 449-460.

Bridges, G., & Steen, S. (1998). Racial disparities in official assessments of offenders: Attributional stereotypes as mediating mechanisms. *American Sociological Review*, 63(4), 554–570.

Buwalda-Macatangay, M. (1998). Filipinas in Europe get ready for year 2000. *Philippines International Review*, 1(2).

Cooley, C. (1902). *Human nature and the social order*. New York: Schreiber.

Cross, W. (1987). A two-factor theory of Black identity: implications for the study of identity development in minority children. In J.S. Phinney & M.J. Rotheram (eds) Children's Ethnic Socialization. Pluralism and Development Newbury Park, CA: Sage Publications

Disch, R., & Schwartz, B. (1970). *White racism* (2nd ed.). New York: Dell.

Erickson, E. (1968). *Identity youth and crisis*. New York: Norton.

Fanon, F. (1967). *Black skin, white masks*. New York: Grove Press.

Franklin, J. (1969). *From slavery to freedom* (3rd ed.). New York: Vintage.

Gilchrist, M. (1985). *The Philippines annexation debate: As contained in four selected speeches*. MSU: 109285THS. Retrieved from https://journals.sagepub.com/doi/10.1177/00113921030516006

Hagen, J. (1982). Whatever happened to 43 Elizabeth I, c.2? *Social Service Review*, 56(1), 108–119.

Hall, R. E. (1992). Bias among African Americans regarding skin color: Implications for social work practice. *Research on Social Work Practice*, 2(4), 479–486.

Hall, R. E. (1994). The Bleaching Syndrome: Light skin, psychic conflict and the domination model of western assimilation. *The Indian Journal of Social Work, Tata Institute of Social Sciences, Deonar Bombay, India*, 405–418.

Hall, R. E. (2001). *Filipina eurogamy: Skin color as vehicle of psychological colonization*. Manila, Philippines: Giraffe Books.

Harvey, R. (1995). The issue of skin color in psychotherapy with African Americans. *Families in Society, 76*(1), 3–10.

Hernton, C. (1965). *Sex and racism in America*. New York: Grove.

Herskovits, M. (1968). *The American Negro*. Bloomington: Indiana University Press.

Hertel, B., & Hughes, M. (1988). The significance of color remains. *Social Forces, 68*, 1105–1120.

Hoetink, H. (1967). *The two variants in Caribbean race relations: A contribution to the sociology of segmented societies* (E. M. Hookykaas, Trans.). New York. Hispanic American Historical Review, 48(3), 465-467

Hurdle, D. (2002). Native Hawaiian traditional healing: Culturally based interventions for social work practice. *Social Work, 47*(2), 183–192.

Hyde, C. (1995). The meanings of whiteness. *Qualitative Sociology, 18*(1), 87–95.

Joyner, C. (1978). The historical status of American Indians under international law. *Indian Historian, 11*(4), 30–36, 63.

Kinder, D. (1986). The continuing American dilemma: White resistance to racial change 40 years after Myrdal. *Journal of Social Issues, 42*, 161–171.

Kitano, H. (1997). *Race relations*. Englewood Cliffs, NJ: Prentice-Hall.

Kovel, J. (1984). *White racism: A psychohistory*. New York: Columbia University Press.

Kubota, K., & Yoshida, F. (1998). Intergroup discrimination and attitudinal similarity in majority and minority groups. *Japanese Journal of Psychology, 11*(2), 116–124.

Lawler, J. M. (1978). *I.Q. heritability and racism*. New York: International Publishers.

Nobles, W. (1973). Psychological research and the black self-concept: a critical review. Journal of Social Issues.

Macey, D. (2012). *Frantz Fanon: A biography*. Brooklyn, NY: Verso Publishers.

Mazumdar, S. (1989). Racist response to racism: The Aryan myth and South Asians in the US. *South Asia Bulletin, 9*(1), 47–55.

Mead, G. (1934). *Mind, self and society*. Chicago, IL: University of Chicago Press.

Meier, A., & Rudwick, E. (1966). *From plantation to ghetto*. New York: Hill and Wang.

Pratt, J. (1950). *America's colonial experiment*. New York: Prentice-Hall.

Silberman, C. (1964). *Crisis in black and white*. New York: Random House.

Stampp, K. M. (1956). *The peculiar institution*. New York: Vintage Books.

Stinson, A. (1979). Community development in an era of paradigm search. *Social Development Issues, 3*(3), 6–21.

St. John, R. (1967). *Encyclopedia of radio and television broadcasting*. Milwaukee, WI: Cathedral Square Publishing.

Tambor, M. (1979). The social worker as worker: A union perspective. *Administration in Social Work, 3*(3), 289–300.

Tebbel, J. (1963). *The compact history of the American newspaper*. New York: Hawthorne Books.

Weber, M. (1946). From Max Weber: essays in Sociology. New York: Oxford University Press

Wood, F. (1968). *Black scare*. Los Angeles: University of California Press.

3
FIELD NEGRO AND THE HOUSE NEGRO

The antebellum period in American history was a time of great turmoil and social change. It was generally regarded by historians as preceding the Civil War and proceeding the War of 1812. Some historians also contend that the antebellum period includes the years from the ratification of the US Constitution which occurred in 1789 to the start of the American Civil War. It was a dramatic display in the rise of slave abolition and the eventual polarization of the nation. The primary opposing factions were the abolitionists and those who supported the institution of slavery. At the same time the American economy was experiencing a shift taking place in the North where manufacturing was emerging in the midst of an Industrial Revolution. Economics in the South evidenced the same events. There a rise in cotton sales elevated the status of plantations to the focal point of a thriving economy. Joined by the annexation of new territory and efforts at land expansion in the western area of the country inspired the popularity and reinforcement of American individualism and the widely held notion of Manifest Destiny. The message in such inspiration was that white Americans and white American institutions were morally superior. Subsequently, due to such superiority white Americans had a moral obligation to export their superiority wherever and whenever possible (Historynet, 2021). Their ability to do so required the mental indoctrination of Africans to dissolve their humanity for purposes of human bondage.

The dissolution of man's humanity was a global conspiracy inspired by slave traders and their European allies. A most descriptive explanation of this crime against humanity can be had in the context of Behaviorism, Psychoanalysis, and cultural paradigms. Taken as a composite the aforementioned is an effective framework for reducing the wills of a *Homo sapien* to that of a docile brute. Behaviorism incorporates role-playing. Role-playing can be reduced per a superficial performance that may have little impact on the individual role-player. Further study may suggest that role-playing does in fact significantly impact inner feelings. By a requirement

DOI: 10.4324/9781003302889-4

to conform and act out directives may enable self-deprecation or evidence of self-hatred. The issue is not limited to the role player alone but may extend to observers. In the eyes of observers those considered "deviants" are bound to meet the obligations of their role. As per sociologist Erving Goffman, victims may respond via "hostile bravado" or "defensive cowering," etc. Others disagree with Goffman but do accept the significance of role-playing where identity is concerned. In reality behavior is critical to the manufacture of self.

Psychoanalysis by Sigmund Freud has brought disagreement from some by whose expertise is specific to the psychological dynamics of slavery. Some among the scholars of slavery have inculcated the concept of "significant other." This significant other concept was a variation of Freud's Oedipal complex. According to the Oedipus, complex was reference to the authoritarian relationship between the white master and the black slave. In Psychoanalysis, the "sambo" invention was a product of a loveless, brutal relationship where black culture, black family life, or white institutions such as the church and state provided no rescue. No doubt, slaves relative to the master do not accurately move to the child's evolution from "object-choice" and internalize the master's Freudian superego. However, in consideration of power differentials between master and slave was simulation of a father-child relationship that allowed the master to exercise total control of his bonded subject.

The final aspect of slavery pertains to the cultural implications. Here the emphasis is less about the individual psyche and more about the social character of the slave personality. In this instance Bernard Meltzer suggests that "[t]he mind is social in both origin and function. It arises in the social process of communication. Through association with the members of his groups, the individual comes to internalize the definitions transmitted to him." In particular this arrangement is most apparent in face-to-face interactions between slaves and slave masters. Subsequently, slaves had less opportunity for individualism that more civil societies encourage. Thus, in combination Behaviorism, Psychoanalysis, and cultural criteria allow for a comprehensive explanation of indoctrination as pertains to the slave mentality (Harris, 1992).

Considering indoctrination for purposes of human bondage slaves were not aloof to the social movements taking place. Despite operating under the limitations of bondage, slaves and black free conducted passive forms of resistance including damaging equipment, working slowly, or keeping their culture and religious beliefs viable. Given to a passive strategy, such resistance was more often conducted in secrecy. While passivity was practiced, there were occasions of open rebellion where slaves despite insurmountable odds willingly risked their lives to escape bondage for the human right to freedom. During this antebellum period, a number of plots and rebellions took place. Historically noted included Gabriel's Rebellion in 1800 in Richmond, Virginia; the uprising in Louisiana in 1811; and the events of Denmark Vesey's conspiracy. Said conspiracy was exposed in 1822 in Charleston, South Carolina. Perhaps the bloodiest and most noted of slave rebellions to occur in US history took place in August 1831. It was led by a black male slave named Nat Turner, who organized other slaves to rebel in Southampton County, Virginia.

During the uprising approximately 60 whites were killed. Following the conclusion of this event, the state killed 56 innocent slaves whom it contended were guilty of taking part. Beyond authority of the state were the actions of white citizen militias and violent mobs that were organized in the aftermath. Their murders resulted in a reported 100 to 200 innocent slaves being killed. Given to white paranoia brought the adoption of slave codes and slave laws that limited the movement of slaves and their ability to peacefully gather in groups. Despite such tight restrictions the continuation of slave plots and slave rebellions in slave-holding states were a fact well before and during the Civil War. This black slave rebellion was not limited to the participation of blacks enslaved under the constraints of bondage but included whites.

In October 1859, a radical white American known as an abolitionist named John Brown led a contingent of followers to conduct a weapons raid. They were to capture a US arsenal at Harpers Ferry, Virginia, that is today known as West Virginia. Their objective was to eventually arm participants including slaves for a general slave uprising. Unfortunately, the raid failed, and John Brown accompanied by his followers were put to death. Northerners sympathetic to his cause made of John Brown a martyr. His celebration as a martyr stoked Southern fears that Northern white Americans intended to wage a war with the South that would necessitate the wholesale killing of their lot. John Brown's raid and the resistance carried out by black slaves were dramatic events culminating in the American Civil War (Historynet, 2021). It was also significant in the cultural emergence of a disgruntled, fearless class of dark-skinned slaves inspired by their work conditions and experienced brutality who came to be known as Field Negroes.

Field Negroes

Field Negroes by skin color were more often dark. The colorism imposed upon dark-skinned Field Negroes more than likely was not by intension. The fact that Field Negroes tended to be dark-skinned with some occasional exception was more often a function of their assignment to hard labor in the most intense heat commensurate with their unadulterated biological heritage. Field Negroes who worked hard under the most brutal of conditions were located at the bottom of the hierarchical structure of the slave system. Their quality of life was a daily struggle to overcome the unprecedented challenges imposed upon them by the slave system. In addition to being lowly ranked they were also considered less intelligent, which resulted in severe beatings when they failed at carrying out a work task correctly or did not produce as much crop as slave owners expected of them. Unbeknownst to the slave master such behaviors were more of a slave's method of conducting passive resistance. Being male or female, old or young was often insignificant. Women and children on occasion were apt to be assigned the worst field tasks by the master's authority (HierarchyStructure, 2018).

Dark-skinned Field Negroes were treated much worse than their counterparts. They were also considered as animals no more than a horse or a pig. They were forced to take on the most demanding and exhausting of physical labor. As a consequence of such work, Field Negroes were known to despise their less African counterparts most of whom happened to be light-skinned. Their work and their skin color made for a distinct boundary between blacks in general and Field Negroes who worked under intense sun and heat as they plowed the soil, and picked and planted the crops. While it is easily assumed that most Field Negroes were dark-skinned males in fact a significant number of Field Negro women were involved in strenuous work in some cases amounting to 80% of those assigned. Under the most brutal of conditions, Field Negro women then picked cotton, sugar cane, rice, and tobacco. They worked long schedules that today would be illegal averaging 14 hours per day, and perhaps longer during harvest times as needed. The work week included all seven days as Sunday was a half day. The normal expectations of a patriarch slave society where less was expected of women did not pertain to Field Negro slave women. More often than not they were required to perform work under the same strains of violence and brutality as Field Negro men. This meant that they carried extremely heavy loads and used large iron tools. Their physical well-being was not of the master's concern. What's more despite such labor challenges when pregnant Field Negro slave women were expected to do no less work until such time as they gave birth.

On a few occasions, elderly slaves, children, and pregnant women were assigned less physical work such as weeding and cleaning related chores. They were all under the constant watchful eyes of an overseer who made certain that Field Negroes were carrying out their assigned chores according to plan. They were forced to maintain a constant work pace and productivity. Anyone caught slowing their pace could be whipped or otherwise punished by the overseer assigned to managing their lot.

The bare necessities provided to Field Negroes were just enough to sustain their existence in enough health to work. Clothes were an obvious example as they were allowed no more than the thinnest of sheets to cover themselves. In the winter Field Negro slaves were only given a single allotment of clothing as they were in the summer. They slept in cramped shacks with dirty, damp mud floors. When winter arrived the roofs of such shacks often leaked letting in snow and cold air. For food Field Negroes after a day of hard work were provided a mere fraction of the proper nourishment needed. What they ate was little more than cornmeal, salt herring and pork. This they consumed in not three but two meals a day. In the morning it was breakfast and at night about 12 hours later it was dinner. No doubt for reasons of profit slave owners provided the bare minimum of what was required for human existence. Condiments such as tea, coffee, sugar, and salt were not provided.

When Field Negroes were intending to marry, there were objections to their doing so by law. What's more, any master who commenced to abuse their slaves could not be held accountable for their actions by the same authority of law. Therefore, slave couples could be separated by their masters if he made a decision to sell either one of them. If marriage of a sort was attempted, the marrying couple could expect no formal ceremony to be conducted. All that was necessary, though illegal, was obtaining permission from the master to live together. Under the most challenging of these circumstances Field Negroes attempted to form some semblance of a family not irrelevant to social configurations today.

Whether or not they were married Field Negro men and women could be sold by their masters to other masters. At auction they were bought under two slave auction arrangements: "highest bidder" and "grab and go auctions." During sale, slaves were directed to a pen where one by one they were raised upon platforms where they were examined by potential masters. Similar to any other chattel, masters searched for strong, healthy slaves. Slaves had to submit to being poked, prodded, and forced to open their mouths for inspection. The administrator of the auction set the price for a starting bid. Those interested announced a higher and higher bid. Ultimately, the person who provided the highest bid would then be presumed to have purchased a slave.

The "grab and go" slave auction arrangement was a terrifying experience for the slaves being offered for sale. They were often confused about the process of their being sold. Masters who took part in these auctions agreed to pay a fee to the slave owner. Those who had come to purchase were given a ticket for each slave they bought. To maintain control, punishment of slaves such as whips and chains were ever present. They were used to either keep slaves busy at work or to prevent them from attempts to escape. As previously stated, there were no laws or protection for slaves. They could all be punished or abused at the slave owner's discretion. An owner who might catch a slave stealing or even a suspicion of theft might punish the slave by cutting off a limb, ear, or hand without being held accountable. Such severe forms of abuse were dramatized in the popular Roots series where LaVar Burton as the slave Kunta Kinte had his foot cut off after an attempt to escape. If the suspected crime were more serious, the master might torture the Field Negro or even put him to death. Such punishments were usually reserved for infractions such as murder or rebellion. Ultimately slave owners spared no form of brutality such as hanging, flogging, and quartering to exact control and domination over their human property. Not only did such brutality serve to control the individual slave but set an example for other Field Negroes who might consider acting out what they observed in the actions of others (Chen, 2012).

The brutality experienced by Field Negroes was a strategy carried out by slave owners to enforce sub-human working conditions and make willing animals of mankind. Field Negroes under such conditions worked the fields from sunrise to sunset and at harvest time they might do an 18-hour workday. In a personal account Frederick Douglass described such conditions when he too was forced to work under the yoke of bondage orchestrated by a slave master. He provided a detailed narrative in his autobiography titled "The Life of Frederick Douglass" that was published in 1881:

> We were worked in all weathers. It was never too hot or too cold; it could never rain, blow, hail, or snow, too hard for us to work in the field. Work,

work, work, was scarcely more the order of the day than of the night. The longest days were too short for him, and the shortest nights too long for him. I was somewhat unmanageable when I first went there, but a few months of this discipline tamed me. Mr. Covey succeeded in breaking me. I was broken in body, soul, and spirit. My natural elasticity was crushed, my intellect languished, the disposition to read departed, the cheerful spark that lingered about my eye died; the dark night of slavery closed in upon me; and behold a man transformed into a brute!

(Douglas, 2020)

It was under such working conditions as those experienced by Frederick Douglas that fashioned the predisposition of Field Negroes and distinguished them from their light-skinned slave counterpart in House Negroes. House Negro was a fitting notation considering that House Negroes whose name derives from their occupational charges resided in the master's house. This should not suggest to any extent that the circumstances of living in the master's house was any less brutal. House Negro occupants were no less slaves than Field Negroes and considered no less inferior to whites. However, their residential location in the master's house made for an effective boundary. It precipitated colorism via hierarchy that became a cultural construct devised by the slave master and internalized by the slave subject. In the aftermath was a differentiation between Field Negroes and House Negroes that facilitated colorism long after expiration of the antebellum.

House Negroes

Resident and work assignment in close proximity to the master are what gave the House Negro their differentiation and separation. The process of converting a slave into a House Negro was not contingent upon residence alone but included their intentional socialization. The term used was called "seasoning" which produced a slave given to discipline and prone to obedience. In fact, under the circumstances many House Negroes were the master's sons and daughters by their captive often Field Negro slave women. Any assumption that life for House Negroes was more humane is merely an error in judgment. The treatment of House Negroes was in fact coercive and extremely brutal. Coercive and brutal methods were devised to convert them into beings which lacked any cultural memory that would accommodate the slave's belief in black inferiority and white supremacy in three years' time (Phillips, 1914, p. 546). Historians contend that approximately 20% of Africans kidnapped to American shores perished in the aftermath of a seasoning process (Friends of Society, 1842, p. 19).

Attributed to the seasoning process slaves were divided into three categories that consisted of New Africans or saltwater Negroes; Old Africans; and Creoles. By definition New Africans or saltwater Negroes were considered those who had just arrived from their African homeland. With their cultural memory still active they spoke indigenous languages, maintained African names, and displayed a strong cultural connection with their ancestors. Due to culture such slaves were considered by slave owners to be the most dangerous as were Field Negroes and the most likely to rebel. Their Old African counterparts consisted of those Africans born in Africa but who had spent a considerable amount of time living and working on the master's plantation. They were more often middle-aged or as their name implied elderly Africans. The third group referred to as Creoles included Africans who were born and raised in the Americas. Their life cultural experiences were not given to Africa but the Americas and limitation of the master's plantation. In the process of seasoning Creoles and Old Africans were the most preferable choice to convert into House Negroes.

The House Negro was uniquely prepared for his or her slave duties. Their daily chores included maintaining the domestic life and home of the plantation master. Therefore, they were responsible for cooking; cleaning; running errands; caring for domestic animals; sewing and repairing clothes worn by the master's family; performing common household tasks; and when needed tending to the master's children. While House Negroes seldom commenced to hard labor, they worked extended hours completing their chores. Their lives were dedicated to the social needs of the master and his immediate family. Most obvious of such dedication in particular pertained to the master's children. House Negro women especially most often assumed the role of wet nurse and surrogate mother to white newborns. House Negro men might assume the role of their playmate and personal servant to adolescents as well as their drivers. Drivers in such circumstances served as an extension of the overseer who worked for the master. If they had been seasoned well House Negroes monitored the work of other slaves, disciplined them using violence and took part in the capture of runaways.

As a part of psychological conditioning and confiscation of their humanity House Negroes were often given hand-me-down clothes from the master's closet. Being separated from the assigned slave residence, House Negroes might reside in nearby rooms in the master's house. When meals were consumed having served as cooks House Negroes ate the master's leftovers which despite being leftovers were a better quality of food than the typical cornmeal, pork, or salt herring that Field Negro slaves ate. Most importantly while it was illegal for slaves being taught to read and write not a few House Negroes learned from the wives and children of the plantation's master.

House Versus Field Negroes

Given to the work differentiations between House Negroes and Field Negroes a hierarchy had begun to form that was exacerbated by colorism. Initially these differentiations were not a conscious intended strategy by the master class but eventually seemed to serve a purpose. In fact, on more than a few occasions House Negroes often being the master's offspring were characterized by light skin. On the other hand, the large majority of slaves were Field Negroes and being of unadulterated descent were characterized by dark skin. In close proximity to the master class was not irrelevant to the social and psychological predisposition of House Negroes. Therefore, sharp social class distinctions among slaves had begun to take shape initially irrelevant but now for a purpose. Conspicuous by light skin House Negroes came to represent the more privileged and refined class among those relegated to bondage. Eventually by close proximity to the master and residing in his home, with relative ease House Negroes internalized and hence idealized the master's way of life (Ingraham, 1860, pp. 34–36). White workers such as overseers used this distinction to their advantage to control both slave factions. For example, when House Negroes acted in some manner that was disapproved, they would be threatened with directives to work the fields. Subsequently, slave masters, overseers, and any others responsible for the management of slaves intentionally stoked division among slaves. This would insure, slave control and that they would remain socially isolated, both physically and psychologically, despite having blood ties. House Negroes who were caught fraternizing with Field Negroes in extreme situations might be subject to flogging or some other form of punishment (Williams, 1838, p. 48). In actuality the historical stereotype of the content House Negro and the defiant Field Negro portrayed in film were both a mythic and simplistic interpretation. The experiences of House Negroes and their Field Negro counterparts in reality were much more complicated than reported. However, by colorism their lives were symbolized as dramatically distinct. One such distinction pertains to the treatment of House Negro slave women compared to Field Negro slave women.

Less referenced by white historians are accounts of the harsh and demeaning experiences House Negro slave women were forced to endure on a daily basis. As a result of their appeal to white masters, House Negro slave women were routinely raped by the plantation owner. This sexual deviance thrust such women into the dynamics of familial social conflicts. Particularly if the master were married, his interactions with his slave woman victim exposed her to any number of moral transgressions. The master's wife might resent the presence of a House Negro slave woman frequently more attractive than she. That attractiveness is marked by the fact that mixed-race, light-skinned House Negro women were called "Fancy Girls" for their exotic looks which appealed to white masters. The master's daily rape of such women was a constant reminder to his wife of marital infidelity. The wife responded by not confronting her husband but by assaulting House Negro women in slapping their faces, boxing their ears, and flogging for reasons not of her doing. Rather than face the reality of her husband's infidelity, the master's wife confronted his victim.

Further evidence of the demeaning of House Negro slaves is provided in their required deference to members of the master's family regardless of age differences. Elder House Negro men were expected to address the teenage and adolescent children of the master as sir and ma'am respectfully. When elder House Negro women often serving as wet nurses for white infants interacted with children, they were expected to refer to them as adults (Jacobs, 1861). What's more as pertains to Field Negroes, House Negroes were required to inform on their counterpart to the master or overseer in the event of a planned rebellion. However, House Negroes less given to the master's domination might perform the role of spy and assist in the efforts of a planned rebellion. Living in the master's proximity these House Negroes had access to valuable information including the master's daily habits, hopes, fears, strengths, and weaknesses. Such information if known by Field Negroes would be critical in staging a successful rebellion. Thus while work assignment and colorism imposed significantly upon the two factions, the omnipotence of the slave system considering its coercive, violent, and humiliating methods of socialization would come to impact black Americans well into the 20th century and beyond (Encyclopedia.com, 2019).

The Slave Psychology

As a basic question of slave psychology is the question as to the existence of Field Negroes and House Negroes in how they came to be. Both slave factions were no less members of a despised and oppressed group who in various ways came to identify to some extent with their oppressor. The dynamics of such identification cannot occur unless slaves are subjected to some form of violence. Such violence must come via threats or actual physical attack. For slavery to have been successful required House Negroes and Field Negroes both to be forced to endure psychological and emotional pain that would eventually compromise their human spirit. This will be necessary if they are to tolerate an otherwise unnatural and brutal state of human existence (Turner, 2014).

For the most part those referred to as House or Field Negroes previously regarded themselves with pride and self-respect. Africans have existed in the flow of pride and respect from the dawn of humanity. In fact, according to scientific investigation they are the dawn of humanity located nowhere other than the African continent. Had they not emerged no European master, no Asian-, Latinx- or Native-American people of color would come to exist. Alternatively, if Europeans, Asian-, Latinx-, and Native-American people failed to emerge Africans would be no less a reality of humanity. Furthermore, House Negroes and Field Negroes would likely not have come to be at least as a cross-racial phenomenon. That is because there is a natural human affinity for a life-fulfilling existence among Africans as among all people. That's because there are no substantial biological differences between human-beings as pertains to the enthusiasm for life, and the tendency for pride and self-worth. Few other aspects of the human spirit and viable existence are more significant than the innate desire for freedom. The existence of House Negroes and Field Negroes is evidence of such human traits as the requirement of freedom having been broken. Consequently, since freedom is the natural and preferred state of human existence requires the convergence of humanity to brute or animal. Only in this manner might human beings be receptive of an unnatural state of human existence such that they themselves be forced to cooperate in their own demise and denigration.

Field Negroes and House Negroes whose ancestors reached America by way of the European Slave Trade descended from people who resisted their enslavement in any way that they could (Turner, 2014). The abduction and imprisonment of Africans in the slave dungeons along Africa's coastal waters were feats commensurate with an international crime. Similar to the division stoked upon Field Negroes and House Negroes slave traders working for a slave master clientele would pay Africans to go into the interior of the continent to capture young Africans. Most of them were captured when they were between the ages of 14 and 22 years. They did not go willingly but known to have fought to maintain their freedom. Western historians have said little about those Africans who jumped ship committing suicide rather than submit to a life of bondage. In fact, on a number of occasions the success of those who fought back resulted in death for the slave traders. The unfortunate Africans who failed to escape or defeat their captors experienced a brutal Atlantic crossing. On ships they lay naked, dehumanized, and forced to recline in proximity of their own feces (Burroughs, 2018). Not until the middle of the 17th century would British law as per the slave trade require that African slave captives be clothed. By such time the unadulterated dark-skinned captives who would be Field Negroes had begun the psychological processing of a brute. Given to their adulterated lineage light-skinned House Negroes were sparred.

While slavery was a common human phenomenon by psychology the European version was unprecedented. It succeeded in reducing Africans to the classification of chattel or animal property. While Africans assisted in the capture of Africans never had captives been reduced to the property of another. That is because the Field Negro and the House Negro did not exist serving no practical purpose. By virtue of this notion of property Africans were also reduced to something less than a human being in Europe's legal structure. That legal status has been transported to America in Field Negro and House Negro social psychological orientation. The differentials in skin color were further served by the black community at large regardless of free or slave status. Evidence of this commonality in the assessment of blacks by skin color advanced the prospects of colorism in the attractiveness associated with the light skin of mixed-race blacks. In the white master class community, it manifested pertaining to light-skinned black women referred to as "Fancy Girls" for their exotic beauty. In the black community at large it manifested pertaining to light-skinned black men for their exotic handsome appeal to black women manifested in the existence of run 'round men. While Fancy Girls were the desire of white men, run 'round men were the desire of black women. However, both instances characterized the reality of colorism that reinforced the traditions of slavery no less than the antebellum traditions that differentiated Field and House Negroes.

References

Burroughs, R. (2018). Recaptured Africans: Surviving slave ships, detention, and dislocation in the final years of the slave trade. *The Journal of Interdisciplinary History, 48*(3), 420.

Chen, M. (2012). *The life of a field slave*. Retrieved October 18, 2021, from https://fieldslaves.wordpress.com/2012/09/19/hello-world/

Douglas, F. (2020). *Narrative of the life of Frederick Douglas*. London: Collins Classics.

Encyclopedia.com. (2019). *House slaves: An overview*. Retrieved October 18, 2021, from www.encyclopedia.com/humanities/applied-and-social-sciences-magazines/house-slaves-overview

Friends Society of New England Yearly Meeting. (1842). *An appeal to the professors of Christianity in the southern states and elsewhere, on the subject of slavery*. Providence, RI: Knowles and Vose.

Harris, J. (Ed.). (1992). *Society and culture in the slave south*. New York: Routledge.

HierarchyStructure. (2018). *Racial hierarchy in slavery*. Retrieved October 18, 2021, from www.hierarchystructure.com/racial-hierarchy-in-slavery/

Historynet. (2021). *Antebellum period: Facts, information, and articles about the antebellum period*. Retrieved October 18, 2021, from www.historynet.com/antebellum-period

Ingraham, J. H. (1860). *The Sunny South, or, the southerner at home: Embracing five years' experience of a Northern governess in the land of the sugar and the cotton*. Philadelphia: G.G. Evans.

Jacobs, H. (1861). *Incidents in the life of a slave girl*. Boston: Published for the Author.

Phillips, U. B. (1914, April). A Jamaica slave plantation. *The American Historical Review, 19*(3), 543–558.

Turner, D. (2014). Review of African American slavery and disability: Bodies, property, and power in the antebellum south, 1800–1860. *Disability & Society, 29*(9), 1505–1506.

Williams, J. (1838). *Narrative of James Williams, an American slave: Who was for several years a driver on a cotton plantation in Alabama*. Boston, MA: Anti-Slavery Society.

4
FANCY GIRLS AND RUN 'ROUND MEN

The origins of Fancy Girls and Run 'Round men are attributed to inter-racial couplings. Although such arrangements were forbidden by law, black and white Americans had been intimately involved before, during, and since the antebellum. While inter-racial arrangements with Native-, Asian-, and Latinx-Americans had also been designated a societal infraction, it was that between blacks and whites that brought the most intense objections. Subsequently just prior to turn of the 21st century such an issue reached the US Supreme Court in Loving v Virginia (Grossman, 2016).

The emergence of inter-racial marital patterns beset by skin color per colorism represent a critical turning point in Western marital jurisprudence. A decision on inter-racial marriage in the United States was litigated in the case of a white male named Richard Loving and a black female named Mildred Jeter. Attributed to the illegality of marriage between different races the couple left their Southern town of Central Point, Virginia, and traveled to Washington, D.C. Upon arrival, they were officially married on June 2, 1958. Once they returned home, the newlywed couple took up residence in the house of the bride's parents while the groom built themselves a home of their own.

In July 1958, the Lovings were arrested by police in the couple's bedroom during early morning hours for having violated Central Point's prohibition against inter-racial marital unions. Sometime later, they were remanded to stand trial. Shortly thereafter in January 1959, the Lovings pleaded guilty to violating Sections 20–58 of the Virginia state code. Said code specifically forbid a white person and a black person from obtaining a marriage license from another state. For those who violated the law were consequences, which included incarceration in the state penitentiary for 1–5 years. The law did not define white or black objectively. By assumption, "white person" was in reference to those having "no other admixture of blood other than white or Native-American. If Native-American, one-sixteenth

DOI: 10.4324/9781003302889-5

was the limit. "Black person" by the "one-drop" theory referred to those "in whom there is ascertainable any Negro blood." This marital tradition entered into law was intended to preserve white racial integrity (Duignan, 2016).

Once found guilty of a crime, the judge in the Loving v. Virginia case sentenced the plaintiffs to a year in jail. However, the judge then suspended sentence on the condition that both plaintiffs agreed to vacate the state immediately never to return as man and wife for a specified period of 25 calendar years.

Following adjudication, the Lovings relocated back to Washington, D.C., where they filed suit in a Virginia state court dated November 1963. It was their contention that Sections 20–58 and 20–59 were a breach of the Fourteenth Amendment. Eventually the Virginia state court rejected the Loving's proposal for redress. After local court, the Virginia Supreme Court of Appeals agreed to review the case. It upheld the constitutionality of 20–58 and 20–59 but vacated sentences given that the condition under which they were suspended was considered "unreasonable." Rationale for this decision rested upon Naim v. Naim in 1965 (Duignan, 2016). In that case, the Appeals court determined that, regardless of the statutes' application of racial classifications relative to the criminal offenses concerned, equal protection under the law was not violated because the penalties were applied equally to "white" and "colored" citizens. At conclusion of the Appeals court decision the Lovings subsequently refiled their case to the US Supreme Court. The Supreme Court then heard oral arguments pertaining to Loving v. Virginia on April 10, 1967.

The US Supreme Court led by Chief Justice Earl Warren in a unanimous decision reversed the Loving's convictions. It initially dismissed the Naim court's interpretation of the equal protection clause in the suggestion that "we reject the notion that the mere 'equal application' of a statute containing racial classifications is enough to remove the classifications from the Fourteenth Amendment's proscription of all invidious racial discriminations" (Duignan, 2016). In the aftermath was a rejection of Virginia's belief that the constitutionality of the statutes, considering their compliance with the equal protection clause rested on whether they served a cogent purpose. Conversely, the Warren Court proclaimed citing Korematsu v. United States adjudicated in 1944 (Duignan, 2016), "the Equal Protection Clause demands that racial classifications, especially suspect in criminal statutes, be subjected to the 'most rigid scrutiny'"—in contrast to the less-demanding "rational-basis" standard—"and, if they are ever to be upheld, they must be shown to be necessary to the accomplishment of some permissible state objective, independent of the racial discrimination which it was the object of the Fourteenth Amendment to eliminate" (Duignan, 2016). Further contention by the Court was that "there is patently no legitimate overriding purpose independent of invidious racial discrimination which justifies this classification" (Duignan, 2016).

Due to its litigation the Warren Court further served as a means of memorializing that the right to marriage by choice is "'one of the 'basic civil rights of man,' fundamental to our very existence and survival" (Duignan, 2016). For this contention, the court articulated reference to its decision in Skinner v. Oklahoma adjudicated in 1942 (Duignan, 2016). According to Skinner v. Oklahoma, denying marital freedom "on so unsupportable a basis as the racial classifications embodied in these statutes" (Duignan, 2016) is tantamount "to deprive all the State's citizens of liberty without due process of law" (Duignan, 2016). Subsequently the US Supreme Court overturned Loving v. Virginia, which established inter-racial marriage as legal in 15 other states (Duignan, 2016). This decision did not begin inter-racial couplings between black and white Americans but simply made them legal. Inter-racial unions began during the antebellum and is the historical origin of Fancy Girls and Run 'Round men.

Fancy Girls

In racial heritage Fancy Girls and Run 'Round men would be considered biracial. The existence of biracial Americans should have confounded so-called scientists. Dramatically for Northern readers scanning the January 30, 1864, issue of Harper's Weekly for news from the South, a large engraving on page (Mitchell, 2016) brought the war home in an unexpected way. Drawn from a photograph, it featured eight recently freed slaves from Union-occupied New Orleans. At the back of the portrait stood three adults. In the foreground were five children ranging in age from 7 to 11 years. Instead of the coarse garments worn by most enslaved people in the South, they were well dressed, the men and boys in suits and the girls in dresses and petticoats. But it was not their attire that confounded readers. Rather, the pale skin and smooth hair of four of the children overturned a different set of Northern expectations about the appearance of people enslaved in the South: that a person's black heritage would always, somehow, be visible and that only "negroes" could be slaves.

It was no accident that the young "white" slaves resembled the children of the magazine's white middle-class readership, which is to say Northern children who were far removed from the threat of enslavement, or so their parents liked to think. The sponsors of the group from New Orleans anticipated precisely the kind of effect such children might have on Northern middle-class readers. As "the offspring of white fathers through two or three generations," the Harper's Weekly editors explained, "they are as white, as intelligent, as docile, as most of our own children."

Not surprisingly, the lightest-skinned children caused the most stir among Northern editors and audiences. The two lightest-skinned girls seemed to have the greatest appeal, judging from the large number of cartes de visite that survived of them. Harper's Weekly wrote: "to all appearance, she is perfectly white. Her complexion, hair, and features show not the slightest trace of negro blood." With their fair skin and elegant dress, the two girls evoked for most viewers the "Fancy Girls" sold in the New Orleans slave market. The fate that awaited these girls as concubines to white men was clear to most viewers at the time. Their tender youth compelled Northerners to renew their commitment to the war and rescue girls like these (Mitchell, 2016).

Biracial Fancy Girls were considered exotically beautiful by both black and white races. The fact of physical attractiveness attributed to light-skinned biracial black girls and women like those on the slave auction block went challenged by none. They were a mainstay of the Southern antebellum called "Fancy Girls" for their feminine ideals. As "Fancy Girls" biracial slave women frequented the Quadroon Balls in New Orleans and other Southern cities. As per urban vernacular "Fancy Girls" were eventually dubbed "yella" in reference to dark skin that had been lightened via white genes. By today's standards "yella" Fancy Girls having benefitted from the mulatto hypothesis lived a life by slave standards of relative financial luxury. Such luxury approximates the black version of a denigrated princess. As princesses they are celebrated for their light skin, straight hair, and often exotic-colored eyes. In every way their features approximated that of the white ideal institutionalized as an icon of feminine beauty.

The feminine ideal of Fancy Girls meant that they were prone to a type of exploitation that those slave women with dark skin would less often encounter. In some sections, a sub-surface type of polygamy grew that approached an institutional norm. In addition to slaves free biracial Fancy Girls became the mistresses of white men by whom they were supported and by whom they reared families of biracial children. In some cases, these biracial Fancy Girls were deserted, with or without income for their support, when the man married a white woman; in other cases, the extra-legal relationship was continued and the family was supported in addition to the lawful household and the legitimate children. This type of dual family arrangement was particularly open and highly developed in New Orleans, Mobile, and certain other points of the Lower South (Rabinowitz, 1978). The free biracial girls, whose families were frequently persons of some wealth and culture, aspired to such unions and, so long as there was hope of contracting one, they scorned to marry with non-white black or biracial men. Some of the pillars of American history are guilty of such moral lapses, including the third president of the United States, the highly respected Thomas Jefferson.

While this moral lapse could be expected of lesser men, it is widely held by serious scholars, such as Barbara Chase-Riboud and William Cobett, that Thomas Jefferson engaged for many years in sexual intercourse with a 14-year-old biracial minor: a Fancy Girl slave named Sally Hemings (Stember, 1976). It is perhaps the most famous and controversial case of a Western "gentleman" keeping a "black" mistress. In this instance, Jefferson was an author of the "Declaration of Independence" and a historical legend.

According to Russell, Wilson, and Hall (1992), in 1772, Thomas Jefferson married a widow named Martha (Wayles) Skelton, the daughter of John Wayles, a prosperous local plantation owner. Martha's father, a widower, kept a beautiful biracial slave named Betty Hemings. Shortly after Thomas and Martha's marriage, the slave gave birth to a daughter, Sally, who, in the context of slave culture, became Martha's illegitimate half-sister. John Wayles died not long after Sally's birth, and Martha inherited 40,000 acres of land and 135 slaves, including Betty and Sally Hemings.

Jefferson's marriage to Martha was, by all indications, a happy one. They had six children together, although only two survived to adulthood. However, she suffered from poor health, had frequent miscarriages, and died after 10 years of marriage at the age of 33. At the time, Sally was nine years old and working as Martha's personal servant. Jefferson was extremely distraught over his wife's death and turned to public service to escape his depression. He spent two years as a delegate to the Continental Congress and then, in 1784, he left for Europe, taking his two older children with him. After a year in London, he moved to Paris, where he served nearly four years as a minister to France.

While in Paris, Jefferson received more tragic news from home. His second youngest child had died. Grief-stricken at losing yet another family member, he sent for his youngest daughter, Polly. An older slave who was supposed to accompany Polly on the long journey to Europe took ill, and a hurried decision was made to send Sally Hemings instead. Sally was then 14 years old and showing unmistakable signs of burgeoning womanhood.

Some historians believe that Jefferson began having intercourse with Sally Hemings almost immediately after her arrival in Paris. One possible indication of his growing obsession with her can be found in his journal. Prior to her arrival in Paris, Jefferson used the word "mulatto" only once in 48 pages, but shortly afterward "mulatto" appeared eight times in fewer than 25 pages. He described even the countryside of Holland as "mulatto," a curious adjective for the highly literate Jefferson to employ about the landscape.

When he was preparing to return to America in 1789, Sally Hemings announced to Jefferson that she was pregnant, presumably with his child. At that point, she was forced to decide whether to accompany Jefferson back to America or to stay abroad. She would be free as long as she lived in France, but if she returned to America she would return to slavery. Jefferson allegedly persuaded her to return with promises of material wealth and the guaranteed freedom for her unborn child.

Back in America, about 1801, Jefferson was sworn in as the third president of the United States. Some believe that he and Sally Hemings were still sexually involved, after more than 10 years since their return from Paris. She continued to live at Monticello, his Charlottesville estate, and over the years she bore five more children. Whether Jefferson fathered any or all of them became a source of national controversy. In an effort to sanitize his image, some biographic scholars have suggested that, in fact, the father of Sally Hemings' children was one of Jefferson's nephews, not Jefferson himself. A glaring contradiction to this disclaimer is that in his will, of all the slaves on his plantation, only Sally's children were allowed to go north to freedom.

A predominance of Western scholars has largely ignored the possibility that Thomas Jefferson may have engaged in sexual intercourse with a minor, and with a biracial black minor at that. Perhaps they found it hard to believe that the same person who wrote, "all men are created equal" not only owned slaves but sexually exploited at least one of the young girls among them. Several decades passed after

Jefferson's death before any of the evidence of this alleged liaison with Hemings was examined, and, by then, much of it had been lost or destroyed.

The racial heritage of Fancy Girl slaves like Hemings was the focus of much discussion per colorism as follows: a Griffe was the offspring of a mulatto and a black American; a mulatto was an offspring of a white and black American; a quadroon was from a white and mulatto; and an octoroon was from a white and quadroon American. For convenience of colorism, the word mulatto was commonly used to refer to biracial Americans, regardless of blood line or skin color (Reuter, 1969). Since free light-skinned blacks as Fancy Girls were never deemed equal to white Americans, they created a society of their own. Within this group, class lines were just as tightly drawn as among whites: the lighter the skin color, the higher the social position. Consequently, the Griffe looked down on the pure black; the mulatto regarded the Griffe as inferior and, in turn, was spurned by the quadroon while the octoroon refused any or little social intercourse with those racially below him or herself (Reuter, 1969).

Considering the aforementioned biracial categories antebellum Louisiana is notorious for Fancy Girl arrangements with white men such as Jefferson. Many such arrangements took place at the affairs of Quadroon Balls. Quadroon Ball may be interpreted as a means of prostitution carried out by white men seeking the sexual exploits of biracial Fancy Girl black women. Clientele included not only white Southerners but visiting white sailors and white Northerners as well. In the 1790s slave owners from New Orleans challenged attempts on the part of some to prohibit biracial black women from attending social gatherings popular with white male colonials. Alternatively, white slaveholders realized the potential for profit if they forced biracial black women into prostitution with white men. At some point the Louisiana Supreme Court heard cases pertaining to slave owners who "sold" or "leased out" biracial Fancy Girl black women for purposes of prostitution at Quadroon Balls. Approximately two years prior, Senator Charles Sumner addressed the Senate in a speech titled the Crime Against Kansas. According to such a speech, Senator Butler of South Carolina was introducing the Kansas Nebraska Act. The purpose included an effort not only to make Kansas a slave state, but the opportunity to sexually exploit biracial black women. Subsequently, Congressman Preston Brooks violently attacked Sumner to the point of near death. His references to slave rape made for an enraged Brooks. More and more abolitionists like Brooks resorted to accusations that the proponents of slavery wanted little more than the opportunity for white men to force sexual exploitation upon biracial Fancy Girl slaves and those who were free. Quadroon Balls were then not sponsored for purposes of romantic relationships between white men and biracial slave women. Retold by white historians the fables of Quadroon Balls merely serve as a distraction to the antebellum sex trade. In a few instances such sexual exploitation resulted in long-term relationships referred to as plaçage (The Race Card, 2016).

Not a few Fancy Girls by introduction to white men at Quadroon Balls gained access to plaçage. Plaçage was an arrangement that was extralegal in status. It pertained to couplings with white French and Spanish and later Creole men that in affect amounted to common-law marriages with women of black, Native and Creole ancestry. Plaçage derives from the French placer which means "to place with." Under such circumstances women were not considered married but were considered as places. Among free people of color such couplings were marriages or mariages de la main gauche meaning left-handed. By biracial category were quarteronnes or quadroons or the offspring of a white and a mulatto. However, plaçage was also existent between whites, mulattoes, and blacks. Such an arrangement prevailed throughout the French and Spanish colonial periods. It began to decline between 1769 and 1803. It was also quite popular beyond Louisiana, which included the cities of Natchez and Biloxi, Mississippi; Mobile, Alabama; St. Augustine and Pensacola, Florida; as well as Saint-Domingue. Despite the fact plaçage was most dramatically associated in history texts with the Southern city of New Orleans (Definitions.net, 2021).

Run 'Round Men

The biracial counterpart to Fancy Girls was Run 'Round men. Similar to Fancy Girls light-skinned biracial antebellum black men were noted for their attractiveness and romantic appeal to the opposite sex. White women were no less attracted to them for their exotic features than white men to Fancy Girl black women. However, the overt racism and rampant violence visited a type of danger upon biracial black men that Fancy Girls did not experience. If a white woman were to give in to the advances of a biracial Run 'Round man at times to save herself she might initiate his lynching. Those Run 'Round men in particular whose skin color and hair texture might otherwise define them as white might actually believe themselves to be white. They would ultimately suffer the consequences once knowledge of their biracial family heritage became apparent. To overcome their blackness and take advantage of their attractiveness Run 'Round men might elect to pass for white. For them passing for white was a better option than for Fancy Girls.

One of the foremost works on passing was written by Gunar Myrdal in the classic *American Dilemma* (Myrdal, 1944). According to Myrdal, the Southern tradition of the one-drop theory was enacted to insure that no black blood would ever get into veins of the white population. However, quadroons and other biracial Run 'Round blacks having more white blood could in affect become white. Passing was a by-product of miscegenation under circumstances of illicit white sex per Quadroon Balls. As an act passing likely began in the first appearance of Fancy Girls and Run 'Round men on the American scene. It was utilized in segmented aspects of life including the occupational or recreational. It might have been temporary or permanent; voluntary or involuntary; known or unknown on the part of the passer or without his or her knowledge. Lastly passing may have been individual or collective. For the most part, complete and permanent passing was the only version which had implications for the racial composition of the white American population.

Normally it was the light-skinned biracial Run 'Round black men who passed in the antebellum South. However, some among the darker-skinned blacks also passed as Filipinos, Spaniards, Italians or Mexicans. Research illustrates the possibility of passing for blacks who by blood were one-fourth, three-eighths, and even one-half, black ancestry and less. Given that blacks who passed usually boasted more white blood than black, it became less significant that such persons crossed over into the white population than if they were to remain within the black community. Consequently, passing in fact involved much more relative to change in social definition of the passer than it did in the racial category of the passer.

According to Webster's International Dictionary, passing is defined as "the act of identifying oneself as white used of a person having black ancestry or otherwise black in racial origin" (Woolf, 1980). Passing has been utilized in some form by a number of ethnic groups in the United States who do not fit the white Anglo-Saxon ideal. Jews, for example, have altered their noses, while Asians altered other aspects of facial features including eye-fold to appear more Caucasian. For the most part, these two groups have a phenotype at least as pertains to skin color similar to the light skin American ideal. African-Americans or blacks, are antithetical to the white ideal in that they have the darkest skin of any group among the human species. Following miscegenation in the aftermath of slavery, a nation of biracial peoples whose features ranged from the African dark to the Caucasian light emerged from antebellum circumstances. Given the racism and Jim Crow that was antebellum tradition, there came about an eventual advantage for those who had acquired enough white genes to present themselves by skin color as white (Gaudin, 2004). Except for the one-drop theory many would indeed have been classified as white. But, in America, white was defined by the notion of purity. Any infusion of black blood automatically determined the subject in question to be a member of the despised and denigrated black race who by law was forbidden the rights and privileges of ordinary white men. Thus, by introducing black blood into a family's gene pool they acquired the ethnic status of a stigmatized member of society.

Passing by Run 'Round men was a social game. It did not necessarily follow that those who played it had a preference for white skin, although this may have been the case in some instances. Most of those who passed merely had a desire to take advantage of the opportunities which their racial status prevented. The decision to pass did little to reinforce the esteem of the passer for in doing so was an admission of black inferiority. Despite such admission, passing was rationalized for its potential benefit. The individual remained clearly in touch with reality while playing the role of a white person in the eyes of the public at large (Kroeger, 2003). Passing could be temporary as in occupation or more permanent as in marriage. When marriage occurred, the consequences if the passer's race became known could have been extremely devastating.

Behavior by Run 'Round men determined a passer's success in maintaining the act. Certain patterns of speech, gestures, etc., were commonly associated with being black. As long as the passer avoided any display of such patterns, they might benefit from their light skin color and remain unnoticed among the white population. Thus, a quiet and low-keyed profile was often more than enough to succeed in selling the façade. To their advantage most biracial Run 'Round men had already acquired the social skills and mannerisms of whites so going unnoticed among them was not at all difficult. In many instances, such blacks particularly as House Negroes were reared by and lived with or near their white parent, usually a white male. Thus, behaviors attributed to being black were already foreign to them. When biracial Run 'Round men took it upon themselves to engage in the act of passing, in affect they were more likely doing what was natural to them. Often, however, this was not done without pain. A black person who passed necessarily cut themselves off from their black family and community. They necessarily cut all ties being well aware of the dangers in being discovered.

Passing was a physiological phenomenon in which the only means of detection was via family history. For this reason, it was quite difficult to detect. In fact, detection was so well guarded by passers and their black families, that marriages to whites have been consummated where the white spouse suspected nothing of "Negro" ancestry in the blood line of their mate. While researchers could not know as much about this phenomenon as they would have liked, some factors were readily apparent. The first and most obvious is that biracial blood was a necessary attribute to assume the desired light-skinned appearance. The second is the implications of gender. Although biracial blood enabled light-skinned Run 'Round men to pass, there were other mixtures which had the same potential. Native-American blood for example in the black population is an established fact. However, unlike white mixtures Native blood did not enter the black population by rape of black women but more likely under agreeable circumstances. What's more there had been such miscegenation between antebellum blacks and Native-Americans that the US government encountered great difficulty in determining who was Native and who was not (Kroeger, 2003).

Like African-Americans, Native-Americans were characterized by a wide range of skin colors. Some were as light-skinned as whites while others were much darker. Of those blacks who had some measure of white blood mixed with Native-American produced offspring whose appearance bore striking resemblance to mulattoes or biracial blacks. As a result, there emerged another opportunity for Run 'Round men via one-drop theory inspired by colorism for crossing the color line.

Communication technology during the antebellum era was less developed such that a light-skinned Run 'Round black man could escape their racial limitations by moving to a different area of the country and passing for white. In this way he could benefit from the assumed greater attractiveness which being biracial afforded him. But for light-skinned biracial black men who took advantage of their idealized light skin by passing, there was a different set of circumstances compared to light-skinned Fancy Girls. The hazards of life were much greater during the slave era, and for that reason many Run 'Round men flocked to Northern cities in order to pass the color line. They discovered early on that, unlike the South, the slave era North and West were thought of as liberal areas, at least by small town Southern standards.

The Run 'Round black male quadroons and Octoroons also benefited from their gender if they decided to pass for white. They had a number of gender-related advantages, including mobility. Any light-skinned Fancy Girl who chose to relocate without the benefit of certainty as to her background could expect negative assumptions to be made about her sexual fidelity and moral character. Men, both black and white, who faced a similar situation were afforded a means of establishing character by virtue of some accomplishment or noble deed. As more often members of the black upper-class light-skinned Run 'Round men who remained in the black community became the romantic ideal of black women for their exotic good looks. Those with less character were likely the lovers of more than one black woman who was likely not unaware of his infidelity. Such men given to their appearance gained access to any and every black woman they desired attributed to their light skin, curly hair and frequently upper-class status hence designation as Run 'Round men. Thus Run 'Round men in the old southern vernacular was reference to biracial black men known for having numerous affairs often simultaneously with black women in their community.

Due to the history of both Fancy Girls and Run 'Round men, a formidable foundation for the idealization of biracial black heritage had begun to form. The plantation social status attributed to Field Negroes and House Negroes extended to the idealization of biracial blacks by Fancy Girls and Run 'Round men. In both instances, light skin, exotic eye color, and hair texture became symbols of distinction from a despised and inferior element of humanity. Marked by their exotic features, biracial blacks more often than not were the sons and daughters of the dominant race master class (Reuter, 1969). Some were allowed to operate and own businesses denied to unadulterated blacks and/or Field Negroes. Others were sent abroad to be educated at some of the most elite academic institutions such as the Sorbonne in Paris. When biracial blacks excelled intellectually at said institutions, those whites who espoused the doctrine of white supremacy became confused. If whites were truly superior, they would contend that such an ideology could not withstand the existence of intellectually gifted via one-drop theory biracial blacks. In an effort to rescue the white supremacy ideology, the antebellum white intelligencia then constructed an ideological explanation to rationalize white supremacy. They titled it the Mulatto Hypothesis.

References

Definitions.net. (2021). Retrieved October 22, 2021, from www.definitions.net/definition/pla%C3%A7age

Duignan, B. (2016). *Loving v. Virginia, Encyclopedia Britannica*. Retrieved February 23, 2020, from www.britannica.com/event/Loving-v-Virginia

Gaudin, W. (2004). *Passing for White in Jim Crow America*. Retrieved from www.jimcrowhistory.org/resources/lessonplans/hs es passing for white.htm

Grossman, J. (2016). Race, sex, and the freedom to marry: Loving v. Virginia. *The Journal of American History, 102*(4), 1264.

Kroeger, B. (2003). *Passing: When people can't be who they are*. New York: Public Affairs.

Mitchell, M. (2016). *The young White faces of slavery*. Retrieved October 22, 2021, from https://opinionator.blogs.nytimes.com/2014/01/30/the-young-white-faces-of-slavery/

Myrdal, G. (1944). *An American dilemma*. New York: Harper & Brothers.
Rabinowitz, H. (1978). *Race relations in the urban South*. New York: Oxford University Press.
The Race Card. (2016). *Know your black history: Deconstructing the quadroon ball*. Retrieved October 22, 2021, from https://afropunk.com/2016/10/know-your-black-history-deconstructing-the-quadroon-ball/
Reuter, E. (1969). *The mulatto in the United States*. New York: Haskell House Publishers.
Russell, K., Wilson, M., & Hall, R. (1992). *The color complex: The 'last taboo' among African-Americans*. New York: Harcourt Brace Jovanovich.
Stember, C. (1976). *Sexual discrimination*. New York: Elsevier Scientific.
Woolf, H. (Ed.). (1980). Websters New Collegiate Dictionary. Springfield, MA. Merriam.

5
THE MULATTO HYPOTHESIS

The original English term "mulatto" was derived from the Spanish and Portuguese "mulato." Mulatto was a common antebellum word frequently used by whites in the American South where slavery was significant. A few scholars contend that mulatto is derived from the Portuguese mula and/or the Latin mula. Defined mula pertains to the likeness of a mule. The offspring of a mule-like horse and a donkey is the birth of a mulatto. By race a thorough bread horse was symbolic of white Americans and a donkey of black Americans. Mulatto became an official racial reference noted in the US census from 1850 to 1930 that may today be taken as offensive (Batchelor, 2011; Merriam-Webster, 2021).

As per the work of Jordan (1981) while white Americans believed they could differentiate mulattoes on the basis of observation, the truth is remote from fact. Most mulattoes—though not all—were distinguishable by their light complexions. During the antebellum anyone who was dark-skinned was assumed black and any non-white who was light-skinned and by dress and manner obviously not Native-American was assumed mulatto. Thus, some pure-blooded Native-Americans as well as their biracial black counterparts were treated differently. The challenge confronting whites about the light-skinned Native-American was one of geography and the fact that he was already in his native homeland which presented different issues pertaining to his being controlled and oppressed. Although they were light-skinned in comparison to the typical black American, Native-American skin was darker than that of most white Americans. Because Native skin color was more mulatto in appearance, it contained some element of status but being darker than that of whites was also subject to denigration.

Light-skinned mulattoes unlike unadulterated pure blood blacks were accorded some degree of status by whites for their light skin due to white beliefs. Most whites of the time took it for granted that the original skin color of mankind was light. By default, the skin of non-whites was thus representative of some form of

DOI: 10.4324/9781003302889-6

degeneration. Native-Americans and mulattoes being lighter-skinned were simply less degenerate but being darker than whites were assumed degenerate, nonetheless. Oliver Goldsmith was an influential non-scientist who proceeded to provide a scientific explanation for the issue. According to Goldsmith,

> White . . . was the natural color of man. We may consider the European figure and colour as standards . . . to which to refer all other varieties, and with which to compare them. . . . That we have all sprung from one common parent, we are taught, both by reason and religion, to believe; and we have good reason also to think that the Europeans resemble him more than any of the rest of his children.
>
> *(Jordan, 1981)*

As they had done so often in the past, whites like Goldsmith infused religion into their scientific beliefs now suggesting that Adam and Eve of the Garden of Eden were indeed white.

Goldsmith was not alone in his beliefs about people with light skin. The number of non-scientists during the antebellum willing to comment was unlimited. David Hume, a Scottish philosopher, made perhaps an even more dramatic statement regarding light skin than did his racial counterpart in Goldsmith. He was convinced that races who lived nearer the poles were much different from those in the tropics. All were inferior to whites who lived in more temperate zones. Such a notion was not new. It was also the belief of ancient Greeks who ironically had been civilized by Africans on the island of Crete (Rogers, 1967). The result of Hume's assertion was the association of superiority with light skin. That association served whites and any Native-American, or light-skinned black mulatto who looked white. But Goldsmith's work in his *History of the Earth* was most useful in application of a mulatto explanation. It determined which groups were relevant and then expounded upon the virtues associated with light skin. In reference to white people in Europe he stated the following:

> The inhabitants of these countries differ a good deal from each other; but they generally agree in the colour of their bodies, the beauty of their complexions, the largeness of their limbs, and the vigour of their understandings. Those arts, which might have had their invention among the other races of mankind have come to perfection there
>
> *(Jordan, 1981)*

These aforementioned words left little doubt as to the superiority of whites differentiated by their light skin color. Subsequently per the beginning of the 18th century in America and elsewhere light skin represented the ultimate in every way of the American and Western ideal. Perhaps more astonishing is the fact that such notions permeated ranks of the oppressed, including many among blacks, be they light-skinned or darker complexioned in hue (Jordan, 1981).

References to the black mulatto were not without criticism. Among the most dramatic and well known of criticisms pertained to notions of the "tragic mulatto." The tragic mulatto is a stereotype applied to biracial black Americans. Its origin is thought to be a product of American history most popular during the mid-19th century. Among those who speculated about mulattoes in their writings included abolitionist authors such as Lydia Maria Child, Harriet Beecher Stowe, and William Wells Brown. In their works of fiction, the tragic mulatto/a is traditionally portrayed as a biracial black American characterized as depressed, suicidal, fratricidal, and/or patricidal as a result of a lacking in their racial identity. Having both black and white heritage mulattoes became confused. They do not know if they are black or white. Therefore, according to stereotype, they do not know whether they fit racially into white society or into black society. Under the circumstances they may be coerced into making a choice to embrace their whiteness or embrace their blackness which results in depression and other psychological consequences. The most popular example of this conflict is contained in Frances E. W. Harper's Iola Leroy; or Shadows Uplifted [1892]. Those mulattoes who choose whiteness were more often punished or even put to death. Those who choose blackness were rewarded socially for their submission to white supremacy. Other dimensions of the tragic mulatto/a are portrayed as sexually depraved or weaklings, as in William Faulkner's Light in August [1932]. Ultimately, whatever character trait assumed of the tragic mulatto they were in some way degenerate, corrupt, and thus, tragic due to their biracial heritage.

The first attention to the tragic mulatto in fiction reportedly came by way of Sterling A. Brown in 1937. However, other evidence suggests that the tragic mulatto was first called to attention much earlier. Brown was to have traced the genealogy of the tragic mulatto that precedes the mid-19th-century work of Child and Wells Brown. Such works suggest that the stereotype is more than an American phenomenon. Evidence proposes it evolved from early 19th-century French colonial literature. It has been associated with an image of the Haitian Revolution that illustrates it as a family conflict. Contained in the writings of a Louisiana-born Victor Séjour was reference to the Haitian Revolution. The title of "Le Mulâtre" or "The Mulatto" was first published in French in Paris in 1837 (Daute, 2010). For the most part all such characterizations are a stereotype that permeated popular fiction. In real life perpetuated by presumed science and the white supremacy ideology in America was the concept of the mulatto hypothesis.

The Mulatto Hypothesis

The initial origin of the mulatto hypothesis is rooted in the scholarship of a Dutch anthropologist named Harry Hoetink (1967). Among all racial and ethnic groups, he contends there exists native traits perceived as ideal that suggest a direct link to intelligence via light skin and other preferred characteristics. References to ideals have been characterized by Hoetink (1967) as the "somatic norm image." The somatic norm image per mulatto hypothesis represents "the complex of physical somatic characteristics accepted as ideal" (Snowden, 1983). Skin color in the context of colorism is not irrelevant. By virtue of power white Americans set the standards for what is regarded as superior in proximity to the light skin ideal. To illustrate the global reach of this concept, Hoetink (1967) refers to a central African creation myth. In reference to this myth the African is perfectly cooked and the "white man" is underdone considering a defect existent in the Creator's oven. The same dynamic exists as a theme of Native-American culture. What's more, according to Snowden (1983) Philostratus contend that unadulterated Indians thought less of light skin because, dark skin was indicative of their kind (Snowden, 1983). Snowden (1983) further opines that among ancients Dio Chrysostom's (p. 76) treatise on idealization challenged whether or not there was an alien ideal similar to the Hellenic type. Lastly, Sextus Empiricus (p. 76) suggests that groups differ in their perceptions of the ideal. Subsequently, Africans idealized the darkest, most flat-nosed of subjects and Persians, the whitest and most "hooked-nose" in the absence of white supremacy. The fact of white supremacy has facilitated introduction of the mulatto hypothesis.

The mulatto hypothesis is a product of light skin as the ideal. In 1918, Reuter conducted a thorough investigation of the mulatto population. The contributions attributed to science and religion, under white supremacy combined to present the mulatto hypothesis as a product of scientific rigor. Succinctly put light-skinned biracial black mulattoes being closer to white were superior in every way to unadulterated, dark-skinned blacks. For this reason, rationalized in terms of the somatic norm image mulattoes were white preferred. That belief was contingent solely upon having a light complexion. Otherwise, a mulatto born of dark skin would not gain a superior status to dark-skinned blacks. Alternatively, any unadulterated black American born of light skin unless their family background be known were similarly favored (Reuter, 1969).

Given to the antebellum mulatto hypothesis dark-skinned blacks were victimized for their dark skin being selected to do the harshest of work assignments on the plantation. They were the laborers regardless of their talents or intelligence. Only on rare occasions would there be an exception if beneficial to the white slave master. Thus, via the mulatto hypothesis although not always verbalized or overtly obvious was a formidable boundary formed between those who were light-skinned and those who were dark-skinned. However, historically complicated is reference to the fact that there existed a number of dark-skinned blacks among the favored class and a few light-skinned biracial mulatto blacks victimized despite the mulatto hypothesis. Both were rare instances because their lived status was in conflict with the color of their skin (Asante & Hall, 2011).

Dark-skinned blacks, notwithstanding their victimization, were no less given to the mulatto hypothesis by their internalization of light skin as ideal. Therefore, dark-skinned blacks as similarly influenced citizens of US cultural trends contributed to sustaining the mulatto hypothesis via common belief in the superiority of light skin. Those who were light-skinned in an effort to rescue themselves from the stigma associated with dark skin frequently exaggerated their superiority. Too often as slaves they expressed little sympathy for their darker-skinned counterparts forced to labor under brutal, violent, and harsh conditions. Furthermore, mulattoes who were free were known to form private societies which denied membership to dark-skinned blacks. Particularly among free blacks living in the North the status of blacks personally having been a slave was looked down upon regardless of skin color and hence reason to distance themselves. Consequently, attributed to the mulatto hypothesis the free mulatto society of Charleston became a rather sophisticated and highly selective institution. No less true elsewhere, Southern states such as Louisiana and in Southern cities such as Mobile and New Orleans the mulatto community sustained a formidable partition between themselves and dark-skinned blacks. Said boundaries with dark-skinned blacks were so formidable that some light-skinned blacks volunteered for the Confederate army as a statement of their distinction and superiority (Russell, Wilson, & Hall, 1992).

While the mulatto hypothesis formed strict boundaries between mulattoes and dark-skinned blacks, there were those light-skinned biracial black mulattoes who committed themselves to serve the black community at large. Light-skinned mulattoes as activists advocated on behalf of all black people being in a position to take advantage of their educational and economic favor. Many assumed leadership roles by virtue of having been educated at some of the finest academic institutions in the world enabled by their middle-class standard of living (see Table 5.1).

TABLE 5.1 (Reuters, 1969)

Charles W. Anderson	*Worthy Public Official*	*Mulatto*
C. E. Bentley	Pioneer in Dental Reform	Mulatto
H. C. Bishop	Religious Organizer	Mulatto
J. W. E. Bowen	Lecturer and Teacher	Mulatto
R. H. Boyd	Captain of Industry	Mulatto
W. Stanley Braithwaite	Poet/ Interpreter of Literature	Mulatto
B. G. Brawley	Author	Mulatto
Miss H. Q. Brown	Elocutionist	Mulatto
Mrs. B. K. Bruce	Astute Leader	Mulatto
John E. Bruce	Popular Writer	Mulatto
Roscoe C. Bruce	Educational Leader	Mulatto
T. Bryant	Church Officer	Mulatto
W. H. Bulkley	Efficient Educator	Mulatto
Harry T. Burleigh	Maker of Songs	Mulatto
Nannie H. Burroughs	Organizer of Women	Mulatto
William H. Bush	Organist	Mulatto
J. S. Caldwell	Bishop of the Church	Mulatto
James L. Carr	Able Advocate	Mulatto
W. J. Carter	Able Advocate	
C. W. Chestnutt	Man of Letters	Mulatto
George W. Cook	Financier	Mulatto
Will Marion Cook	Musician	Mulatto

The Mulatto Hypothesis 55

Charles W. Anderson	Worthy Public Official	Mulatto
L. J. Coppin	Bishop of the Church	Mulatto
W. H. Crogman	Teacher/ Gentleman	Mulatto
Harry S. Cummings	Political Leader/Lawyer	Mulatto
A. M. Curtis	Surgeon and Physician	Mulatto
James L. Curtis	Minister to Liberia	Mulatto
J. C. Dancey	Public Official	Mulatto
Franklin Dennison	Lawyer and Leader	Mulatto
R. N. Dett	Composer	Mulatto
J. H. Douglass	Violinist	Mulatto
W. E. B. DuBois	Editor and Author	Mulatto
James Reese Europe	Composer/Musician	Mulatto
S. D. Ferguson	Venerable Bishop	Mulatto
J. S. Flipper	Bishop of the Church	Mulatto
T. Thomas Fortune	Founder of Negro Journal	Mulatto-Indian
S. C, Fuller	Pioneer in Psychiatry	Mulatto
Henry W. Furniss	Able Diplomatist	Mulatto
W. H. Goler	Educational Leader	Mulatto
J. M. Gregory	Veteran Educator	Mulatto
R. T. Greener	Pioneer Public Servant	Mulatto
Archibald H. Grimk6	Publicist and Writer	Mulatto
F. J. Grimke	Preacher	Mulatto
G. C. Hall	Deft Surgeon	Mulatto
W. H. H. Hart	Advocate and Defender	Mulatto
J. R. Hawkins	Church Leader	Mulatto
Mason A. Hawkins	Educational Leader	Mulatto

According to documentation among the professional and leadership ranks in the black community were dominated by biracial mulatto blacks as investigated by Reuter (1969).

Ultimately some among light-skinned biracial mulattoes may have been inspired by anger having been denied their dominant group status but for a measure of African heritage. This may have caused them to rebel against white culture and the white supremacy ideology that on one hand favored them as ideal and simultaneously among the most despised for their black heritage (Hall, 2010). Reference to their lot as noted in literature manifests the existence of the mulatto hypothesis. They were light-skinned, educated, and middle-class known as the "Talented Tenth."

The Talented Tenth

With few exceptions considering Reuter's list, light-skinned mulattoes were representative of the intellectuals of the black community. As a separate black class, they would come to be distinguished for their intellectual gifts which justified their reference as the "Talented Tenth" (Battle & Wright, 2002). The Talented Tenth was initially described as a metaphor first acknowledged by W. E. B. DuBois in his authorship of *The Negro Problem* (Washington, 1903). DuBois' effort to rescue the black community from itself and address the societal challenges he contends rested on contributions to be made by the more able and talented blacks among them. He contends that education would allow for the 10% of black Americans who were able to rescue the darker-skinned less able of the black race. Therefore, black Americans should devote themselves totally to the preparation of teachers, the training of professional men, clergy, and inspirational orators. They would commence as "talented" by uplifting the less able within the black community thereby advancing black people with each succeeding generation.

Existence of the Talented Tenth and the mulatto hypothesis in the black community imposed upon by colorism was evident in the educational process that disserved dark-skinned blacks. Their treatment can be accessed in the details of the black educational experience per dark-skinned black students and black teachers. The participation of black educators in the process merely suggests the cultural extent of colorism. The colorism experience is critical as pertains to black students who might enroll and/or aspire to a college education. A dramatic display of this issue was provided in the documentation of a white female intellectual from the state of Wisconsin who traveled South to assume a teaching position at a small HBCU institution. Her name is Dr. Ann Jones. Her book is titled *Uncle Tom's Campus* (Jones, 1973).

Dr. Jones described herself as a civil rights activist having taken part in the struggles of black folk for Civil Rights. Her institutional place of employment for reasons of confidentiality she referred to as "Thomas College." Her book detailed her experience there published in 1973. Soon after earning her PhD Thomas College had made the most serious offer for a job. She would find that HBCUs were not averse to paying white professors higher salaries than an equally qualified black scholar. As a member of the TC faculty, residing in the black community, and investigating TC's history and financial records Dr. Jones acquired the information necessary to write her book. She describes the book as a study of personalities, groups within the institutional pecking order, the role of an HBCU in a white racist society and a somewhat autobiographic account of her experience. She took issue with the school's administration of the college, funding sources and accreditation bodies that enable colorism to exist. She acknowledges that although TC disserves black students it too is a victim of colorism. The most dramatic illustration of this fact is contained in a narrative from her book of black teachers' treatment of a dark-skinned black student she once taught.

"Mr. Rogers and Mr. Hadden and a few others were at least fine teachers. Most of the professors at Thomas were not. It is difficult to say what constitutes "good teaching."" There are probably as many different definitions as there are good teachers. But if good teaching means providing students with an opportunity to grow the teacher must first believe in the possibility of growth and he must somehow communicate that belief to his students. Much more is involved that a superficial positive attitude for as people think so they behave. The ways in which teachers behave in the classroom are signals to the students invitations to respond in certain modes for most students the pattern of invitation and response is set very early in the elementary schools. Preconditioned by his IQ scores and faculty gossip the second grade teacher treats Johnny much as his first grade teacher did. Johnny quickly learns what behavior his teacher expects of him and responds accordingly.

Most of the Johnnies who grew up to come to Thomas College had long been classified as "dumb." More importantly, the faculty expected them to be "dumb." Some openly called the students "dumb" niggers while others gave more subtle cues. Ms. Washington assigned her class a few pages of the text each day to be read for the next class meeting then devoted the next class meeting to reading the assigned pages aloud to the class pausing only to define the difficult word. Her method clearly declared to the students that she considered them incapable of reading the text and looking up unfamiliar words themselves and the students knowing that she really did not expect them to do the assignments did not do them. Ms. Washington then used the fact that they did not read the assignments as evidence of their stupidity as justification for her method of teaching. Students who have learned during 12 years in the public schools that they are expected to be stupid are quick to pick up cues such as Ms. Washington offered them.

But there was at least one student who went through the most amazing transformation I have ever seen. Arnold was assigned to my remedial English class and to Mr. Haden's music appreciation class where he sat listening but pretending to be half asleep. Occasionally he tried to say something but neither Mr. Hadden nor I could understand a word uttered; he scarcely opened his mouth and the words slipped out in a jumbled blur. At least concluding that he suffered from a speech impediment Mr. Haden referred him to the speech laboratory for remedial help because he knew that Arnold had so many important things to say. Almost immediately we both noticed a remarkable improvement in his speech and as we began to understand his words we encouraged him to speak more in class. His classmates too began to seek him out for their debating and discussion teams in English class. We noticed physical changes as well: he stood up straight, threw his shoulders back and abandoned his shuffle for a long stride; we realized that he was much taller than he appeared. By the end of the semester, he had shifted gradually from the back corner of the room to a seat in the front row; there he perched on the edge of his chair alert and articulate clearly enjoying the class and himself. At the end of the semester when we congratulated the speech teacher on her work we learned that Arnold had never gone to the speech lab.

What happened to Arnold? The most obvious answer was that he was black, as black a Negro as I have ever seen. And being that color, he had been subjected to the brainwashed Negro's prejudice against the darker members of his own race. From his earliest years in school Arnold had been dismissed by his Negro teachers who favored their lighter-skinned pupils. Relegated to the back row psychologically as well as physiologically he had remained there. No one ever listened to him, so remarkable as it may seem—he quite literally lost the ability to speak intelligibly. When he at last found some people who wanted to listen to him, he learned how to speak to them. And then we discovered not only that Arnold could speak but also that he was exceptionally sensitive, intelligent, and a born leader. The most important point, was not that those of us around him discovered the real Arnold but that Arnold himself did. In three months before our astonished eyes, a wiped-out nigger had grown into a proud and beautiful black man" (Jones, 1973, pp. 144–146).

The educational experience of light-skinned biracial mulatto black Americans holds significant contrast in comparison to the aforementioned dark-skinned Arnold at Thomas College. One such dramatic illustration exists in the person of W. E. B. DuBois. Considering his light skin and brilliant intellect W. E. B. DuBois was representative of the Talented Tenth about which he spoke. At birth he was officially dubbed William Edward Burghardt DuBois on February 23, 1868. He resided in the northern city of Great Barrington, Massachusetts. DuBois' mother was not an intellectual black elite and thus not a member of the Talented Tenth. She was employed as a domestic worker in the homes of white folk. His father was not a member of the Talented Tenth as he was employed as a barber and migrant laborer. The accomplishment of their brilliant black son is a testimony to the genius of black America that goes either wasted or undeveloped. Interestingly, the Bureau of International Research located at Harvard University and Radcliffe College maintained a record of DuBois in its *Negro and Mulatto Families Questionnaire*. DuBois' biracial ancestry was reportedly comprised of "Negro," French and Dutch white heritage which accounted for his mulatto light skin. His complexion left no doubt he was mulatto. In fact, per more detail DuBois proclaimed personally that he had descended from light-skinned Bahamian mulatto slaves. They had migrated and eventually settled in the Massachusetts town of Great Barrington where he was born.

Once his family had settled in, DuBois enrolled in an integrated Massachusetts high school. There he was the first black American to graduate from its ranks. He excelled at the school academically and later was accepted at Harvard University. Unlike Arnold at Thomas College the educational system was not poised to discourage his intellectual development. Upon graduation DuBois then became the first black American to earn a Harvard PhD. His doctorate was in sociology which precipitated his later investigation of Philadelphia's black community. It was a widely read esteemed work titled *The Philadelphia Negro* (Lewis, 2009).

Despite the exceptional academic success of W. E. B. DuBois, the mulatto hypothesis cannot be held to the traditional standards of academic rigor. The lacking thereof likely extends from the impact of white supremacy born during the era of Southern antebellum. Given existence of the House Negro, the biracial light-skinned mulatto, the mulatto hypothesis, and the Talented Tenth is evidence of an intentional skew to social science investigations. In the aftermath colorism via white supremacy is reinforced by society at large manifested in the educational differentiations between Arnold and DuBois. Dark-skinned black students including non-black ethnics who aspire to academic prestige must overcome the cycle of looking-glass deficits. The deficit is a verifiable fact encouraged by prestigious "scientific" research published in the nation's most noted of academic journals (Simis, Madden, Cacciatore, & Yeo, 2016).

In 1923, a Princeton University investigator named Carl Brigham published *A Study of American Intelligence*. Proclaiming scientific rigor, Brigham insists that intelligence in America as per IQ scores was on the decline due to immigration and integration via non-whites. In an effort to rescue the country, Brigham advocated for the adoption of governmental policies to restrict non-whites by law. He was joined by others, such as Lewis Terman in 1943 who associated IQ with race. Subsequently, ethnics including Latinx and black Americans per dark skin were intellectually dull by genetic heritage. Additionally, their existence within the American population suggested a formidable threat to American stability given their prolific birth rates by active propagation. This eugenic presumption considering colorism and the mulatto hypothesis is also prevalent among modern-day psychologists. They suggest by scientific authority that "non-white" racial groups lack the ability to carry out abstract thinking as suggested by their low performance rates in mathematics. Therefore, similar to the propositions of Bingham governmental programs to educate them would be futile and a waste of tax dollars as noted in *The Bell Curve* (Herrnstein & Murray, 1994).

The Bell Curve exists as little more than a pseudo-scientific work written by Richard J. Herrnstein and Charles A. Murray in 1994. They would contend that low intelligence is the reason for disparities in the American social structure when comparing blacks to whites. Essentially *The Bell Curve* makes reference to the concept of a general factor of intelligence; accepted concepts of intelligence; the American differentiations in intelligence; job performance; the impact of IQ per societal outcomes and the factors that ultimately impact IQ. The deciding component in each of the aforementioned variables authors contend is an extension of the biologically insignificant category of traits associated with race. Therefore, American tax dollars invested in social programs are a poor investment considering the academic failures of black Americans attributed to genetics (Sternberg, 1995). Such investigations historically have overlooked facts that conflict with the white supremacy ideology as in the actuality of the black American IQ.

Colorism has necessitated a heightened interest in black performance on IQ tests. Little has been written about black Americans who have shown superior intellectual promise that more often than not is ignored. A cursory review of IQ research reveals that the highest human IQ on record belongs to a dark-skinned black American student (Theman & Witty, 1943). Such Americans as said student thought to be inferior and intellectually incapable, confused white scientists. They could not explain the intellectual brilliance of one descended from such an inferior group (Theman & Witty, 1943). Despite the fact, in 1943, the academic *Journal of Psychology* featured an article noting one such black student. Said student was described as a "Negro" girl, 9 years in age, and as being of "unmixed" African descent. Being tested at the age of 9 years the child was thought to be of such superior intellect that her IQ could only be assessed as 200. The implication implies that her IQ was so high as to be immeasurable by peer comparisons. Succinctly put, at the age of 9 this black American tested at an IQ twice her intellectual age (Theman & Witty, 1943). Her being of "unmixed" black racial heritage suggests that she was not a light-skinned biracial mulatto, Talented Tenth black, but in-deed an unadulterated dark-skinned black.

The mulatto hypothesis is the finality of colorism that has imposed upon the black community since the advent of slavery and the American antebellum. It prevailed by the emergence of House Negroes and Field Negroes that would eventually introduce racial and class divisions within the black community. Popular events such as Quadroon Balls persisted where white men forced sexual access to underaged mulatto black Fancy Girls as a means of exploitation and oppression. Not to be an exception in the black community the same dynamic of mulatto light skin prevailed as Run 'Round men by their exotic sex appeal to black women. While the plight of both disappeared from the pages of public concern a most historical of events would seem to signify an end. Foremost in consideration was Lincoln's Emancipation Proclamation of 1863 that legally abolished the institution of human bondage thereby setting free a generation of hopefuls. Unfortunately, colorism has remained immune to the inoculations of law ever present in the contemporaries of 21st-century education, occupation, and income.

References

Asante, M., & Hall, R. (2011). *Rooming in the master's house: Power & privilege in the rise of black conservatism*. Boulder, CO: Paradigm Publishers.

Batchelor, K. (2011). *The mulatto factor in black family genealogy*. Retrieved October 26, 2021, from extremeancestry.com/the-mulatto-factor-in-black-family-g. . .

Battle, J., & Wright, E. (2002). W.E.B. DuBois' talented tenth: A quantitative assessment. *Journal of Black Studies 32*(6), 654–672.

Daute, M. (2010). "Sons of white fathers": Mulatto vengeance and the Haitian revolution in Victor Sejour's "The Mulatto". *Nineteenth-Century Literature, 65*(1), 1–37.

Hall, R. (2010). Beauty and the breck: The psychology of idealized light skin vis-à-vis Asian women. *Japan Studies Review, 14*, 45–57.

Herrnstein, R., & Murray, C. (1994). *The bell curve*. New York: Free Press.

Hoetink, H. (1967). *The two variants in Caribbean race relations: A contribution to the sociology of segmented societies* (E. M. Hookykaas, Trans.). New York. Hispanic American Historical Review, 48(3), 465-467

Jones, A. (1973). *Uncle Tom's campus*. New York: Praeger.

Jordan, W. (1981). *The White man's burden*. New York: Oxford University Press.

Lewis, D. (2009). *WEB DuBois: A biography 1868–1963*. New York: Henry Holt and Co.

Merriam-Webster.com. (2021). *Dictionary Merriam-Webster*. Retrieved October 26, 2021, from www.merriam-webster.com/dictionary/mulatto

Reuter, E. (1969). *The Mulatto in the United States*. New York: Haskell House Publishers.

Rogers, J. (1967). *Sex and race*. St. Petersburg, FL: Helga M. Rogers.

Russell, K., Wilson, M., & Hall, R. (1992). *The color complex: The politics of skin color among African American*. New York: Harcourt, Brace, Jovanovich.

Simis, M., Madden, H., Cacciatore, M., & Yeo, S. (2016). The lure of rationality: Why does the deficit model persist in science communication? *Public Understanding of Science, 25*(4), 400.

Snowden, F. (1983). *Before color prejudice*. Cambridge, MA: Harvard University Press.
Sternberg, R. (1995). For whom the bell curve tolls: A review of the bell curve. *Psychological Science, 6*(5), 257–261.
Theman, V. & Witty, P. (1943). Case studies and genetic records of two gifted Negroes. *Journal of Psychology, 15*, 165–181. doi:10.1080/00223980.1943.9917144
Washington, B. (1903). *The Negro problem*. New York: Humanity Books.

Contemporary

6
COLORISM BY EDUCATION

Considering tests performed on black Americans who were world war draftees, white scientists had found a way to rationalize the black educational exceptions who excelled with regard to intelligence. Brigham, in 1923, using the Army Alpha and Beta Tests with wide samplings (a large percent of draftees of all races) found Northern blacks to be intellectually superior to Southern whites (pure-bred Anglo-Saxons). Brigham believes that biracial light-skinned mulattoes accounted for the superiority of Northern blacks. He did not take educational background and its influence on the tests into consideration. This was so despite the fact that analysis showed a high correlation (Johnson, 1930). In reality black Americans as a whole were forced to attend inferior schools if they were educated at all. Other scientists who have addressed education and the mental ability of black Americans also referred to the black mulatto class as the reason for black exceptions in education.

More serious study in the education of black Americans as pertains to skin color has been conducted in higher education at HBCUs. Hampton Institute calculated a positive correlation of only 0.09 between skin color and mental test scores. Additionally was a positive correlation of only 0.05 between skin color and a black student's academic standing (Klineberg, 1944). Other works such as that of Klineberg seemed to contradict data contained in the Hampton study (Klineberg, 1944). Klineberg's investigation is of critical significance juxtaposed with earlier studies, of which Ferguson's is perhaps the most quoted. According to data, there exists a fairly pronounced relationship between amount of white blood and black mental test scores. Thus it was discovered in one test that the unadulterated blacks who would be dark-skinned scored 73.3% as high as white Americans; three-fourths pure blacks scored 74.6% as high; the light-skinned biracial mulattoes scored 81.6% as high; and the quadroons scored 87.9% as high as white Americans. The not so subtle implication suggests a correlation between light skin and superior test performance of mulatto blacks while ignoring societal accommodations. During

DOI: 10.4324/9781003302889-8

follow-up with a second test, there were similar results. By comparison, such studies seemed to confirm the same findings.

Investigation of black Americans' educational potential as pertains to their mental ability, Gregg provides interesting results of statistics gathered in the Record Office of Hampton Institute between 1901 and 1910. At that time period, 2,404 pupils entered the school, and their previous history, school record, and history after leaving were all documented. For purposes of skin color analysis in the context of education pupils were registered under seven different shades of skin color. Variation extended from "black" up through "dark brown," "brown," etc., and eventually to pure "white." Among those tested was an abnormally high number of biracial mulattoes at more than 60%. Gregg contends that the likely reason for this disparity was due to the fact that mulattoes have been more favored by both whites and blacks regarding education. Such a view was held by such an extent as to be institutionalized. What's more, considering the scholastic records of these students, who were categorized by skin color, little difference existed between the various skin color groups. Any variations that did exist were likely due to previous schooling, or to the lack of it, as to any other cause. Therefore, the belief that these findings were the product of a rigorous and diligent scientist would conclude that there is no significance in mental ability as pertains to black Americans that would dictate to their educational potential.

Relative to the aforementioned a review of more recent history reveals that the education level for people of color including black Americans in the outcome of colorism has been quite low. Very few indeed have had the resources and, if so, often no avenue to acquire the skills necessary to succeed in the educational process. With the exception of antebellum biracial mulatto blacks by the benefit of slave master fathers or Fancy Girl concubines, black educational opportunities are no less pessimistic today. Thus, currently there remain educational advantages accrued by light-skinned black Americans not irrelevant to the fact of their descent from mulatto slaves, the mulatto hypothesis or the Talented Tenth. No doubt the descendants of dark-skinned Field Negroes have progressed. However, their minimal successes have not escaped the influences of colorism 150 years following Lincoln's Emancipation Proclamation.

The modern-day correlation between skin color and education in the black community probably owes its origin to the values of culturally dominant white Americans/Westerners. In education, the focus is consistently on white American scholars, white American ideas, white American values, and white American perspectives. Hughes states that we focused on white Americans because white Americans are the ones generally responsible for making critical educational decisions (Hughes & Hertel, 1988). They are thus more likely to decide whether blacks including people of color get into and eventually graduate from prestigious educational institutions which is critical in the quest for employment. What's more despite having produced some of the nation's foremost black scholars including Stacy Abrams, Ta Nehasi Coates, and the iconic Alice Walker, HBCUs (historically black colleges universities) are less inclined to the esteem bestowed upon

PWIs (predominantly white institutions). Not necessarily overtly intended white Americans who control the academy are predisposed to culturally normalize the less esteem of HBCU institutions. Therefore never acknowledged publicly when considered for hire an HBCU education will be an obstacle to overcome for employment at a white agency or institution just as race and skin color. In addition, when such employers observe a dark-skinned American regardless of race and ethnicity, Hughes believes they think they are seeing someone less competent and someone less like themselves which given colorism greatly influences their perspective. Subsequent to this bias in power, absent any cognitive credentials whatsoever such Americans as Herrnstein and Murray (1994) managed to acquire a major book contract to publish *The Bell Curve* describing black intellectual inferiority per IQ scores. Said publication significantly contributed to the implications of colorism not only intra-racially but inter-racially, i.e., across black and white race categories.

The white American academy in the field of social sciences has long maintained an astounding obsession with black Americans as lacking in intelligence. This obsession is no less prevalent than in the Army intelligence tests administered to black Americans during world wars of years past. Manifested by that obsession *The Bell Curve* carried forward such an obsession disguised as rigorous scientific investigation. This ability of two white authors to obtain a major book contract under the circumstances irrelevant to their credentials is in itself a rarity for scholars of color. Any content critical of white culture or the white population without white endorsement is more likely rejected as polemic or simply irrelevant to the publisher's purview. People of color who propose commentary of research less than white conducive are then prohibited from publication of their work for any number of creative reasons. Therefore, publishing establishments that immediately reject black perspective book proposals, which challenge the white academy, reveal their unspoken colorism via a hidden "white supremacy" agenda. On the other hand, blacks who propose the white supremacy narrative may experience colorism in reverse similar to the white endorsement of black conservatives. Black conservatives similar to authors of *The Bell Curve* in their suggestion of black people as less intelligent and doomed to fail in education also need not be qualified. They need not be credentialed as expert in the area of cognitive psychology. Conversely, they too may encounter rejection by the academy if they stray from the "white supremacy" position via accusations of "polemic," "controversial," or "radical." The ability of white academics to escape accusations of polemic, controversy or radical as advocates of black intellectual inferiority is likely due to what McIntosh (1989) refers to as "white privilege."

In 1989 Peggy McIntosh published the widely read paper on "White Privilege: Unpacking the Invisible Knapsack." This paper first appeared in the July/August edition of the "Peace and Freedom" commercial magazine (McIntosh, 1989). The "Peace and Freedom" magazine is an organ of the Women's International League for Peace and Freedom that at the time was located in Philadelphia, Pennsylvania. MacIntosh's paper was both widely acclaimed and controversial being the first of its kind to take ownership of the racial climate. The ability of a white American woman to subjugate her "whiteness" for purposes of acknowledging and understanding the daily benefits of light skin in a world of colorism was unprecedented. For this reason, "White Privilege: Unpacking the Invisible Knapsack" remains a milestone in the annals of modern-day American race relations.

At first thought being a feminist Professor McIntosh was inspired to address white privilege by illustrating the benefits in society that males have. Being an activist and scholar of Women's Studies MacIntosh recognized the willing privileges granted to men despite the fact that many such men acknowledge the subsequent disadvantages realized by women as a consequence of male privilege (Case, Hensley, & Anderson, 2014). Men including those men who are supportive of women's issues and who advocate for gender equality in the academy, in the details of feminist discourse as well as in the society at large must be held accountable. However, McIntosh contends that in reality they abhor any reduction in men's status privilege when doing so. In fact, much of men's status advantage is a product of women's disadvantage and amounts to a taboo estranged from polite conversations. After all the equality and empowerment of women may accrue or imply a loss of power and status which few men are willing to accept. Therefore, men's status privilege remains insulated from serious discussion as pertains to gender inequality.

At some point McIntosh experienced an epiphany considering the same dynamics as pertains to race. She realized that status privilege is multifaceted and a norm in American society that no less extends to race. In the aftermath of her epiphany as per race came a realization that white privilege is similarly insulated by white Americans from serious discussion the same as efforts to bring about equality between the sexes. As a white American woman McIntosh knew of racism but like most had overlooked its benefits. As most white Americans she had been convinced to overlook the benefits of colorism designated as race. Following dramatic analytical speculation McIntosh (1989) realized that being white in America amounts to an invisible knapsack of unearned benefits. While these privileges benefit her on a daily basis, she as all "white" Americans are unknowingly committed to remaining oblivious. Subsequently white Americans by race are not conscious of their racism in the aftermath of white race status. The most well intended among white Americans may then contribute to sustaining racism in black oppression. McIntosh then realized justly so why white Americans are so often viewed as racist regardless of the fact that they conversely view themselves as otherwise. In a pensive moment McIntosh then compiled a list of ways in which her racial status privilege enabled her quality of life (Hastie & Rimmington, 2014).

As McIntosh recalls from her educational experience and training, she was provided little content to view herself or view white Americans in general as racist. The current controversy in education relative to Critical Race Theory is the most recent example of white privilege that threatens civil evolution. In a reversal of evolution white Americans like MacIntosh are apt to be judged individually and hence free from the institutional racism standardized by white Americans collectively. In the aftermath, being white prevails as the mutual traditional American ideal. Any attempt to commit to enabling the struggles made by non-white people of color to escape racism is ultimately an attempt by white Americans to make of people of color something more "white" (Kitano, 1985). Doing so McIntosh ultimately implies that racism and race privilege are less a matter of race but more a matter of colorism. The environmental consequences visit the same privileges upon black Americans by skin color. It is such an environment that dominates society facilitating the publication of literature hostile to black educational potential.

The Bell Curve was a book hostile to black educational potential written by privileged white male authors first published in 1994 by the Free Press. Its authors were by profession a Skinnerian psychologist named Richard Herrnstein and a political scientist named Charles Murray. Neither had been trained or lettered in cognitive psychology that would enable their study of the black IQ with some validity. Despite the fact, their objective was to provide an explanation, using empirical statistical analysis, of the variations in human intelligence. The statistical evidence referred to was selectively chosen to support a "white supremacy" narrative fundamental to colorism. In other words, the outcome was pre-determined, and the statistics applied were applied commensurate with that pre-determined outcome. Authors presumed that American society should heed the consequences of an existing IQ intelligence gap that has racial overtones pertaining to black Americans. In doing so, policy makers they contend must construct a national protocol with the goal of mitigating the most challenging consequences of black Americans in education. This is advised for the benefit of American society as a whole. Absent statistical rigor, the authors conclude their findings in extensive controversy. Said controversy advocates the suggested relationships between low measured black intelligence and anti-social behavior manifested as educational failure facilitated by criminality. Following explanation, the authors attribute low black intelligence solely to race despite the possibility of other existing factors. Indicative of colorism in the academy and the society at large obsessed with black Americans as less intelligent, *The Bell Curve* sold 400,000 copies during its initial release worldwide! This would imply that the belief in black intellectual inferiority is global while any content less conducive to the intellectual reputation of white Americans such as the Cress theory is either dismissed or unknown in academic circles.

Never directly mentioned being a taboo of polite intellectual conversation was *The Bell Curve's* conformance to a "white supremacy" ideology. Conspicuously missing from the voluminous text was explanation or any reference at all to the numerous black Americans who perform at exceptional intellectual levels. The most recent in the contemporary era is a two-year-old black American girl admitted to MENSA after testing at an IQ of 142. Most dramatic as pertains to black intelligence is the case of a 9-year-old black girl reported in 1943 as having scored the highest human IQ on record. The omission of such facts from *The Bell Curve* is arguably a matter of colorism by education in that American tax dollars the book suggests would be wasted if invested in the education of black Americans.

The ability of Herrnstein and Murray to obtain a book contract for *The Bell Curve* from a major source such as *The Free Press* is not only a display of colorism by education but an imposition upon academic freedom. Therefore, the impact of colorism upon education commensurate with the "white supremacy" narrative languish in obscurity. Hence, while some challenges to *The Bell Curve* in fact do reach publication, academics associated with the most distinguished institutions in the field of social science display an inability to criticize, comment or offer an opinion on such a topic. They more often have not read such works but exhibit a keen familiarity with works such as *The Bell Curve* even when they disagree. This unfamiliarity/familiarity is no coincident or serendipity. It is in fact a deliberate function of the academy that diminishes black scholarship and educational opportunity. Evidence of the suggested disparity is given to location of *The Bell Curve* for a period of time upon the New York Times Best Sellers List. Fortunately, despite this bias the contributions of black mathematicians who operate at the elite levels of education in their fields are acknowledged owed to the efforts of black scholars (Collazo, 2017).

While Eurocentric domination of education has disserved the black community, the scientific accomplishments of black Americans via black women in particular are noteworthy. Under the most racist circumstances of colorism, they have displayed an ability to excel, as in the case of little known mathematicians Dorothy Vaughan, Katherine Johnson and Mary Jackson. Vaughan was born September 20, 1910, in Kansas City, Missouri, and died in 2008. She was educated at Wilberforce University, an Ohio HBCU for black students forced by segregation into limited educational opportunities. She graduated at the age of 19, in 1929 (Collazo, 2017).

A no less talented black woman, Katherine Johnson, was born on August 26, 1918, in White Sulphur Springs, West Virginia. Like Dorothy Vaughn, she was educated at an HBCU, West Virginia State College, where she earned bachelor's degrees in mathematics and French in 1937. Johnson was of such intellectual superiority that as a child she managed to advance several grades ahead of her peers and became a high school student at age 13; she graduated at age 15 with highest honors (Collazo, 2017).

Mary Jackson is another example of black female educational potential who displayed evidence of a superior intellect early on in her school career. Jackson was born on April 9, 1921, in Hampton, Virginia, and died on February 11, 2005. Her only educational option was an HBCU; she enrolled at Hampton Institute, earning a BS dual degree in Math and the Physical Sciences in 1942 (Collazo, 2017).

The superior intelligence of black women who excel educationally today is no less anecdotally apparent than in years past considering Vaughn, Johnson and Jackson. One such black student, Skylar Byrd, attended a Washington, DC, inner-city high school. The school Byrd attended is Banneker High School, not a private elite institution where IQ superiority would be expected. Yet, despite lacking any of the institutional advantages indicative of more privileged class students, Byrd scored a perfect 1600 on her SAT, once called the Scholastic Assessment Test. The SAT is a test similar to *The Bell Curve's* IQ technology; it measures a student's math and English language ability and is designed to project how well a student might perform in college courses. It is therefore frequently a factor for higher education college admissions. The SAT is not an IQ test per se but qualifies as a legitimate measure of intellect. College Board SAT administrators in New York City have said that, of the 1.1 million American students who took such a test, only 21 had perfect scores equal to Byrd's score. In addition to having superior test scores, while at Banneker, Byrd maintained a 3.76 grade-point average (on a scale of 4.0 as the maximum) (Horwitz, 1995).

All told, the superior intellect of a 9-year-old Negro black girl, a recent MENSA inductee and of successful black American women educated in mathematics, considering Byrd's perfect SAT score is a major contradiction to the education narrative suggested of black Americans. As assumed members of a presumed inferior race, black intellectual superiority as pertains to education in fact is perceived globally as a scientific impossibility. Therefore, absent journal publication, motion picture commemoration (Hidden Figures), and newspaper coverage, accounts of black potential in education are likely skewed. In the aftermath is "scientific fact" such as *The Bell Curve* disguised as rigorous scientific investigation. Juxtaposed to colorism by education as per black women will be informed by colorism per education and the contemporary experiences of black men.

In the course of education, the developmental process of black men is regarded as more problematic, stressful, and unpredictable than that of black women (Connell, Halpern-Felsher, Clifford, Crichlow, & Unsinger, 1995). The research of Gibbs (1992) suggests that the experiences of black male students are generally less favorable than that of black females in their family, school, and community environments. McAdoo (1982) asserts that as it is becoming increasingly laborious for black males to attain their goals, fewer of them are found in higher education than their female ethnic counterpart. Colorism either intra-racially or inter-racially is not irrelevant.

Connell et al. (1995) illustrate their results of the differences between black male students and black females as they pertain to school tendencies within an ecological context. Their longitudinal study consisted of 443 urban black seventh, eighth, and ninth graders (218 males and 225 females). Behavioral, psychological, and contextual factors were related to the likelihood that the males remained in school. The conclusions of path analysis revealed that males' reports of more familial support at home eventually influenced self-system processes of perceived competence for both males and females, perceived relatedness for black females, and perceived autonomy for black males. Those black males from familial situations that were less economically deprived per colorism were found to exhibit minimal educational risk behavior, however, they reported less support from adults in their school setting. Black males from the same economic situation residing in more affluent neighborhoods with higher concentrations of affluent neighbors sustained a greater probability of remaining in high school.

Demographic scholars have found that black fathers, in particular, live in the inner-cities where their children attend inner-city elementary, secondary, and high schools. Education administrators are cognizant of the problems of inner-city school districts such as lack of student discipline, teachers who are less competent, and poor facilities complicated by low student motivation. Such problems are recapitulated for black males who enter institutions of higher education. The politically incorrect reality is that this problem may involve a complete overhaul of the American educational system in toto to bring about a resolution of problems in inner-city Public School districts.

Although familial environmental factors such as parents' educational level and socioeconomic status are assumed to exert some impact on educational orientations, for black males there is increasing evidence in the literature suggesting that such factors in isolation do not account for variations in outcomes. Some scholars maintain that relatively weak evidence is provided as reference in support of family-background variables having a significant effect on educational outcomes for black males. Dornbusch, Ritter, and Steinberg (1991) further contend that such educational factors may indeed be more relevant in the assessment of white students and their families than for black students. Thus, theoretical and empirical research would necessitate that the analysis of unique black family processes such as colorism will provide greater insight into their educational orientation and achievement styles.

Akin to the familial rationales is the assertion that differences in educational achievement among black males may be better explained by their interpersonal relationships. Significant adult family members may have the potential to enhance academic achievement as would be required for black males. Clark (1983) considered such relationships to be the family's pivotal contribution to the ability of black males to succeed in higher education. He further contends that family background variables do not determine behavior in the school setting, but that success in higher education is grounded in family beliefs, activities, and overall cultural style. Reynolds and Gill (1994) and others suggest that parenting behaviors such as monitoring school progress, parent-child interactions, and parent involvement in school can be positively correlated to educational achievement and educational success. Datcher-Loury's (1988) exploratory investigation of the impact of parental behaviors and attitudes on academic performance revealed statistically significant relationships between parent–child interactions and long-term educational success. Similarly, Ford's (1993) research revealed that familial achievement orientations relative to perceptions of parents' attitudes and beliefs were of more significance than family demographic variables. The impact of parents' educational level and employment status on success in higher education among black males is then inconclusive and thus perhaps a matter of colorism.

The family dynamic as a significant force in the educational process has been investigated and demonstrated extensively (Billingsley, 1992). Unfortunately, the differentiations in outcomes where black males are concerned have not been substantially associated with any particular subsystem within the family environmental domain. Contemporary research has not provided any conclusive explanation as to the impact of the family environment upon the educational achievement of black males. Most scholars would attest to a lack of consensus about what is known regarding black males and the family life or the process by which adult family members influence their educational orientations. Matters are further complicated given the fact that more extensive comprehension of the impact of family on the development of males from various ethnic and racial backgrounds is necessary. Comprehension of family impact may be best served by investigating the organizational and interactive processes within a specific culture of the subjects concerned.

In the post-modern era is a limited collection of skin color data that might prove critical to the exposition of colorism in education. Therefore, existence of the issue can only be established by what is implied. According to modern-day sources, black Americans are comprised on the average of 65% African, 29% white, and 2% Native-American ancestry (Gates, 2013). As defined by the one-drop theory of racial category blacks of 50% white ancestry and of 50% black ancestry qualifies for the designation of mulatto. Mulatto by visual observation with few exceptions have been characterized as being light-skinned. Therefore, in the modern era compared to years past, black Americans over time have increasingly become lighter in skin color compared to their historical antebellum counterparts. Furthermore, in the aftermath of Loving v Virginia via biracial offspring it can be considered with confidence that the more successful in education have been light-skinned blacks similar to biracial blacks during the antebellum. Contrary to stereotypical beliefs black success in education has nothing whatsoever to do with skin color as a consequence of racial heritage. Herein it is then suggested that white blood was not the determining factor attributed to the superior intellects and educational performance of black females or black male Army recruits. More likely it was the celebration of white supremacy ideology that rationalizes superiority of blacks compared to other blacks in proximity to white American skin color. The negative educational performances of black males are then due not to any innate intellectual flaws but the societal white supremacy norms which aspire to halt their potential for success. What's more white Americans compared to black Americans being more successful in education equates with the same racial transgressions. Ultimately, in both instances colorism is evident via Field Negro dark skin among black Americans and black American dark skin via white Americans. Evidence of this colorism is apparent given to the superior intellectual performances of black Americans on IQ tests and perfect SAT scores despite societal obstacles. The fact that such accomplishments had not been discussed or acknowledged in *The Bell Curve* exposes the unspoken pathological societal objectives considering black American performance in education. That the conclusion of a link between colorism by education exists is demonstrated in a pattern where colorism no less prevails in colorism by occupation.

References

Billingsley, A. (1992). *Climbing Jacob's ladder: The enduring legacy of African-American families.* New York: Simon and Schuster.

Case, K., Hensley, R., & Anderson, A. (2014). Reflecting on heterosexual and male privilege: Interventions to raise awareness. *Journal of Social Issues, 70*(4), 722–740.

Clark, R. (1983). *Family life and school achievement: Why poor black children succeed or fail*. Chicago: University of Chicago Press.

Collazo, J. S. (2017). *NASA's hidden figures: Women you need to know*. Retrieved from www.biography.com/news/hidden-figures-movie-real-women

Connell, J. P., Halpern-Felsher, B. L., Clifford, E., Crichlow, W. & Unsinger, P. (1995). Hanging in there. Behavioral, psychological, and contextual factors affect whether African American adolescents stay in high school. *Journal of Adolescent Research*, *10*(1), 41-63.

Datcher-Loury, L. (1988). Family background and school achievement among low income Blacks. *The Journal of Human Resources*, *24*(3), 529–543.

Dornbusch, S., Ritter, P., & Steinberg, L. (1991). Community influences on the relation of family statuses to adolescent school performance: Differences between African Americans and non-Hispanic whites. *American Journal of Education*, 543–567.

Ford, D. (1993). Black Students' achievement orientation as a function of perceived family achievement orientation and demographic variables. *Journal of Negro Education*, *62*(1), 47–65.

Gates, H. (2013). *Exactly how 'Black' is Black America?* Retrieved October 29, 2021, from www.theroot.com/exactly-how-black-is-black-america-1790895185

Gibbs, J. (1992). Social indicators for young Black males. In J. Gibbs, A. Brunswick, M. Connor, R. Dembo, T. Larson, R. Reed, & B. Solomon (Eds.), (pp. 5–31). Auburn House Publishing Co.

Hastie, B., & Rimmington, D. (2014). "200 years of white affirmative action": White privilege discourse in discussions of racial inequality. *Discourse & Society*, *25*(2), 186–204.

Herrnstein, R., & Murray, C. (1994). *The bell curve*. New York: Free Press.

Horwitz, S. (1995, May 5). *Perfectly happy with her SAT*. Retrieved from www.washingtonpost.com/archive/politics/1995/05/05/perfectly-happy-with-her-sat/bb9a19ca-cedc-455a-8999-7ef2cb98d4a1/?utm_term=.715842fbd171

Hughes, M., & Hertel, B. (1988). *The significance of color remains*. Blacksburg, VA: Virginia Polytechnic Institute. Unpublished.

Johnson, C. (1930). *The Negro in American civilization*. New York: Holt and Company.

Kitano, H. (1985). *Race relations*. Englewood Cliffs, NJ: Prentice-Hall.

Klineberg, O. (1944). *Characteristics of the American Negro*. New York: Harper and Row.

McAdoo, H. (1982). Demographic trends for people of color. *Social Work*, *27*(1), 15–23.

McIntosh, P. (1989, July–August). White privilege: Unpacking the invisible knapsack. *Peace and Freedom*, 10–12.

Reynolds, A. J., & Gill, S. (1994). The role of parental perspectives in the school, adjustment of inner-city black children. *Journal of Youth and Adolescence*, *23*(6), 671–679.

7
COLORISM BY OCCUPATION

Synonymous with other aspects of society the dominant group majority of Americans in the context of occupation have been of European descent, light-skinned and/or white. Subsequently there evolved white and light skin as the occupational norm (Myrdal, 1944). However, for black and other Americans of color that norm operated in the form of colorism. The operation of colorism is further complicated given the emergence of a light-skinned biracial population descended from the antebellum mulatto (Fanon, 1965). Today as then light-skinned biracial black Americans are extended workplace advantages by the dominant white power structures (Klineberg, 1944). Intelligence, attractiveness, and overall appeal were associated with their light skin color which brought occupational advantage (Reuter, 1969).

The idealization of light skin as more attractive having been normalized by American traditions meant that it became a vehicle for occupational status. This was so despite that light skin among black Americans is still today less common than the relative dark (Huggins, 1942). As a part of black folklore value-laden terms associated with skin color have an extensive history that demonstrates colorism via terms such as high-yellow, ginger, cream-colored, and bronze (Herskovits, 1968). Terms associated with dark skin and dark skin features, such as hair, was designated "bad" if it was the kinky African type and "good" if it was the straight Caucasian type. Therefore when the term black was used and associated with dark skin, but for a few exceptions it more often implied something derogatory (Hall, 1990).

Sometime following "Negro Suffrage" and the Marcus Garvey era approaching the 60s overt verbal hostilities pertaining to the trait of dark skin largely subsided. However, light skin during the "black is beautiful" movement of the 60s remained the unspoken ideal apparent in the market place as an extension of education by black college campus traditions (Rose, 1964). Therefore, at the typical HBCU, it was all but impossible for a dark-skinned black coed to join a particular sorority.

DOI: 10.4324/9781003302889-9

In fact, some sororities catered specifically to light-skinned coeds while others to dark-skinned rejections. When social events were held such as school dances admissions might operate via the "brown-paper-bag test." Coeds in particular whose skin color was darker than a brown paper bag were assessed a fee for their skin color as compensation to be admitted. Those who were light-skinned might be admitted free of charge (Hall, 1990). This curious aspect of black American culture necessitated theoretical explanations that would rationalize the existence of unspoken colorism by occupation that prevails as a universal American social tradition.

Theoretical Explanations

Numerous theories have been conceptualized to elucidate the problems encountered by black Americans as pertains to occupations. Initial attempts at conceptualization have been categorized as "deficiency" theories. So-called "deficiency" theories contend that there exists a group lacking among black Americans attributed to dark skin. The purpose of such theories are an attempt to utilize black inferior economic, social, and political status in society as an explanation (Greeley, 1977). When couched in the context of biology so-called race "deficiency" theories then assumes to scientifically rationalize the fact of racial inequality. That inequality is advocated as a manifest function of genetic endowment in occupational disparities extended from the presumption of an inferior gene pool as suggested in publications such as *The Bell Curve*.

Among the more noted among biological deficiency advocates is white psychologist Arthur Jensen (1969). According to Jensen's research, inferior genes including for skin color, biologically fixed at birth, are responsible for the IQ differential between black and white Americans. He would contend that the subsequent intelligence differentiation is a consequence of biological inheritance directly impacting occupation. Unfortunately, Jensen's research is without merit and scientific rigor given its inconsistent scholarship and tendency toward serious methodological flaws. Most apparent his speculation distorts the variables of contrived race and reference to class. Said distortion is credited to the difficulty of isolating the impact of biological inheritance and the environment upon "inherited" intelligence. In the aftermath per research, biological deficiency theories have been all but dismissed by serious scholars unless they are practicing extremists.

Social structure as deficiency theory relative to colorism by occupation is less flawed methodologically than the biological rationale. By social theories black Americans are assumed members of an inferior culture. These inferior cultural norms have occupational implications and negative prospects for hire. Jensen (1969) would add that even if the social structural deficiency theories could be substantiated, it would make no difference in the outcome. The essential causes of racial inequality in the work force would remain the same.

Cultural deficiency theories as an occupation explanation are grounded in a model which trivializes the complexity of diversity among black Americans and other people of color. Such theories advocate that occupational immobility of certain ethnic groups is not a matter of skin color but solely a matter of culture that includes family background, and parental attitudes (Stevenson, Chen, & Uttal, 1990). This suggestion can be gleaned from the research of Stevenson et al. (1990). Contained in such works is the idea that Latinx people of color are highly traditional and non-adaptive. This produces a language handicap, fatalism, attitude, and a present rather than future orientation not conducive to American occupational norms. In fact, the aftermath is reinforcement of a "blame the victim" rationale for workplace disparities.

The eventuality of deficiency theories facilitated "bias" theories prevalent during the 1960s. Bias theories simply attribute occupation inequality in the workplace to common prejudice and discrimination (Quinnan, 1997). According to bias theories, black Americans experience occupational difficulty as a result of discrimination brought by racial prejudice. Therefore bias theories emphasize discrimination experienced by black workers as an extension of racism, and lack of opportunity as major impediments (Quinnan, 1997). Additionally, as a matter of logical conclusion bias theories of racial inequality would assign the source of black disadvantage to the social structure of society at large. That social structure then permeates occupational patterns of social interaction that exist in workplace institutions and serves to deter black progress.

Other alternative theories produce what has been labeled as "discontinuity" theories. Discontinuity theories profess that it is not prejudiced individuals who are responsible for inequality, but in fact that inequality is a product of social patterns indicative of the larger society (Hallinan, 1997). Discontinuity theories then focus on the existing cultural differentiations between black Americans and the mainstream white population. They ascribe racial differentials when significant to the degree of discontinuity between black American culture and white American culture (Ogbu, 1982). In other words, differentiation problems are due to cultural values, style of interaction, communication, and social competence. This would impair the ability of black Americans by skin color to successfully navigate the unspoken social terrains of occupation. In the aftermath that difference will impede the attitudes, aspirations, and expectations of otherwise qualified and highly motivated black job applicants. The results suggests that for success black Americans unlike white Americans must become bicultural in every sense (Williams, 1992). W. E. B. DuBois acknowledged this requirement of black Americans as "double consciousness" (Black, 2007). Norton (1993) refers to the same phenomenon as "dual perspective."

DuBois (Black, 2007) constructed double consciousness to explain the ability of black-Americans and other people of color to navigate more than one cultural environment. Due to white as standard white Americans lack this ability with few exceptions. Norton (1993) borrowed DuBois' concept calling it "dual perspective" in a social work context. By double consciousness and dual perspective relative to occupation and the US job market white Americans as dominant population are more likely to exhibit a myopic view as their life circumstances do not require otherwise (Sagi & Dvir, 1993). This becomes critical not only in hiring and job performance reviews but may determine failure for people of color assigned to white occupational authority. As a theoretical construct double consciousness/dual perspective are invaluable for assessing an otherwise complex and stealth social phenomenon as are other useful theories.

Similar to discontinuity theories is the "caste" theory. Caste theories suggest that occupational disparities are given to black American relationships with the white American mainstream (Ogbu, 1982). This assumption is a matter of membership in one of three minority group paradigms: autonomous minorities, voluntary immigrant minorities, and involuntary minorities. When defined, autonomous minorities have a distinct ethnic, religious, linguistic, or cultural identity. Therefore, they are most likely to encounter prejudice and discrimination. However, unlike black Americans the typical autonomous minority is not necessarily economically, socially, and politically subordinate. Among autonomous minorities in the United States include Jewish-Americans. Jewish-Americans may escape colorism, have light skin or otherwise appear white. In deed some are known to embrace a white identity. What's more relative to black Americans, voluntary immigrant minorities may have migrated voluntarily to the United States often for economic reasons. Many have maintained a distinct group identity less stigmatized than that of black Americans. Considering autonomous minority groups who differ as people of color by skin color from the white mainstream include Asian-Americans. Most immigrated voluntarily to the United States also searching for greater economic opportunities. They vary extensively by skin color from the very darkest to the lightest such as to equate with a black or white American. Finally, there are the involuntary minorities. Involuntary minorities include those populations who did not migrate by choice to the United States. Their circumstances require that they arrived by slavery, conquest, or colonization for purposes of exploitation (Kitano, 1985). The involuntary paradigm subsequently includes Native-Americans who were conquered, black Americans who were brought by way of the Atlantic slave trade and Latinx-Americans who came by way of both slavery and colonization. The ability of all such Americans to achieve occupational success is grounded in colorism and the implications of dark skin for their settlement status. To some degree all of the aforementioned theories such as deficiency, bias, caste, and discontinuity may be fashioned as a viable explanation of colorism by occupation.

Research Investigations

Imposed upon by colorism relative to occupation among black Americans as a group has been historically limited to those jobs that carried little or no prestige. In a post-modern era of advanced technologies many are relegated to jobs that are menial in task and require little to no skill to perform. When there are exceptions to this explanation, those exceptions usually come by way of light-skinned biracial black Americans. Therefore, education and personal ingenuity alone does not always provide a means for occupational success as colorism would suggest.

The issue of colorism by occupation is a powerful inter-racial factor that has intra-racial implications for dark-skinned black Americans. However, "most telling," says Hughes, are the percentages for both racial groups as pertains to who is employed in professional and managerial occupations. Among the noted include high-status jobs (Hughes & Hertel, 1988). When skin color is not a necessity despite the fact it may make a difference. Therefore, in occupations contingent upon intellectual ability and professional competence, light skin may offer advantages, according to Poussaint. As a result high status occupations that employ light-skinned black Americans may be similar in percentage to those held by white Americans (Poussaint, 1975). The results are similar in that nearly 29% of all white Americans hold such jobs, compared to black Americans holding the same jobs at about 15%. "That's nearly a 2-to-1 ratio," proclaims social scientist Hughes. By comparison, the same ratio exists intra-racially where light-skinned black Americans hold 27% of such jobs compared with 15% of dark-skinned black Americans (Hughes & Hertel, 1988). The exact same advantage is reflected in the health status differential between light- and dark-skinned black Americans in that those who are lighter-skinned may live a better quality of life given to better health care via occupation. In a follow-up study supporting the implications of skin color for colorism by occupation includes reference to the Charleston Heart Study. One of the investigators was impressed by the lack of hypertension and excellent health and low mortality among black Americans correlated to skin color (Beckett, 1983).

Black Americans frequently deny that there is any truth to such assumptions about colorism due to the taboo of colorism in public discourse. However, they are not averse to at least submit partially. "I don't believe in color; but there are advantages to pass for white." This comment was made some time ago by a black American during an interview. Many of the old Southern black American families admit to the implications of skin color as an age-old tradition. Such families are responsible for the continued emphasis on the significance of light skin for success in one's occupation combined with a good income as being of more importance (Frazier, 1966). Relative to income they labor under false beliefs of what a successful family-owned business can do for them. Although black-owned businesses have always been few compared to the great industrial and commercial structure of the nation, the black middle class was obsessed with the illusion that being in business for self will not only provide a means to earn for the black community but that it would also become a solution to the elimination of inter-racial colorism as in racism. Influenced perhaps by the philosophy of Booker T. Washington, this light-skinned middle-class black community belief insisted upon income and occupation via colorism as having close ties. Proof of this alliance is evident in that as a family's income increases, the tendency of its members is to enter professional occupations. These expectations were dramatized by those who gained access to white collar jobs. Unfortunately, such a belief was compromised by those who made good incomes but were not employed in the most prestigious of occupations.

Within the upper echelons of black American occupations not irrelevant to colorism, was a constant infiltration of ex-ball players, musicians, ministers, and part-time movie actors. These occupations provided experience in entertainment as a form of public performance and mass persuasion (Hare, 1965). For the most part, however, these occupations were by black exception rather than the rule. The light-skinned biracial black American class was much like any other to be engaged in business enterprises, white collar occupations, and public service from which they could earn a considerable income and thereby progress in life. This may be due to the fact that the light-skinned black American class has historically maintained an occupational advantage over the dark-skinned masses. Early on in the black American experience was that of occupational specialization advantages light-skinned biracial blacks as mulattoes dominated. In Charleston, South Carolina, for example, most of the fashionable tailors and shoe manufacturers of skill were light-skinned blacks including a few descended from families who were never enslaved. Some authorities would contend that their educational advantage made for their early start in skilled or prestigious occupations. The difference in educational attainment is assumed as being the reason for their occupational success. Alternatively, others contend that skin color is the reason for the differential. As more black Americans made occupational gains the entire group was said to have advanced. The overall expansion of the black middle class inspired growth in professional, technical, clerical, and sales occupations. Still the identifying characteristics assessed light skin that put its members in contact with either white Americans or professionals and business trained people as critical (Kronus, 1971). Eventually, the black middle class included non-manual service and professional employees. By this time many in the black American middle class began to vary by skin color and viewed themselves despite colorism as the equal to white Americans and required the same occupational rewards. They were demanding the right to share in the status symbols of personal success including a good quality of education for their children, and greater access to managerial or executive jobs (Clark, 1965).

Colorism by occupation is not limited to light-skinned biracial black Americans. Some such evidence is contained in the issue of phenotypic discrimination against Mexicans who work in the US labor market. Social scientists attempted to explain such an issue by investigating the Puerto Rican and Cuban populations in the US labor market. They used ranking scores calculated by R. M. Hauser and J. R. Warren (1996) combined with statistics from the 1990 Latino National Political Survey (LNPS). Occupational rankings are a reflection of the level of labor market discrimination that individuals are confronted by. Conclusions reached suggest that darker-skinned Mexicans and Cubans earn significantly lower occupational prestige scores compared to their lighter-skinned counterparts. This finding is consistent even when controlling for elements that impact performance in the labor market. However, as it pertains to Puerto Ricans there was no conclusive evidence that skin color of the worker had an impact on the occupational prestige scores. Referring to earlier data, some investigators concluded in evidence that explained the difference in labor market performance for Mexican-Americans. That difference was a function of "phenotypic variations" indicative of Mexican-Americans. Currently, dark-skinned Mexican-Americans and Cuban-Americans consistently confront higher levels of discrimination in the labor market. Dark-skinned Puerto Ricans do not. This could be due to regional differences across each of the three groups that investigators failed to control for (Espino & Franz, 2002).

Investigations of the black American community per skin color is no less significant than that of the Latinx-American community. A study was thus conducted to determine the relationship between occupational aspirations and skin color. It utilized subjects from a 1988/89 self-report instrument consisting of 200 black American college students located in south Georgia. The results conclude that light-skinned black American students aspire to more prestigious occupations than their dark-skinned counterparts (Hall, 1990). This finding may be attributed to colorism as per the psychological advantage and self-confidence experienced by those who are light-skinned. It also highlights the potential for unconscious color discrimination that is evidence of colorism. Acknowledgment of this fact is a serious psychosocial issue that behavioral scientists have not adequately addressed (Hall, 1996).

Evidence of colorism by occupation specific to women further establishes the significance of colorism. Subsequently, data compiled from the 1998 to 2005 waves of the Panel Study of Income Dynamics were applied to assess the particularistic mobility thesis. This thesis suggests that considering women there is a color by racialized continuum. This continuum is associated with the determinants of two "upper-tier" occupational categories. Evidence supports this theory in that racial gaps arranged by the continuum are more pronounced for professional/technical compared to managerial/administrative positions. In more exact terms, the means of mobility for black Americans is more often limited and structured considering traditional stratification causal factors. That includes human capital, background status, and job/labor market characteristics. On the other hand, compared to whites, the route to mobility is broad and less structured as per stratification-based causal factors. Therefore, they experience mobility with the least hesitation. As a product of colorism, Latinx-Americans occupy a position mid-way between black and white Americans. By skin color Latinx-Americans display a range of complexions from white to black which may explain their mid-way status (Wilson, 2012).

The sociological research as pertains to occupational inequality has been direct as per racial disparities and persistent vulnerabilities to current structural biases. However less is known, about the impact of age per people of color employees and their susceptibilities to downward mobility. Combining research about race with employment-based age discrimination Wilson and Roscigno (2018) assessed blacks and whites aged 55 and older. They considered the extent to which members of each group experienced a loss of employment over time. Upon investigation results suggested displayed a pattern for higher- and lower-level status managers and professionals pertaining to men and women. Patterns observed in the data from the Panel Study of Income Dynamics illustrate the consistency of significant inequalities. Compared to older whites, older black Americans encounter higher rates of downward mobility. Said downward trend cannot be explained by traditional rationales such as human capital credentials, job/labor market characteristics. This problem is most pronounced for men and for those employed in higher status white-collar managerial and professional jobs compared to technical/skilled professional and blue-collar "first line" supervisors. Researchers aligned their results not only with contemporary concerns regarding ageism but the skin color vulnerability of people of color in the workplace (Wilson & Roscigno, 2018).

Public Opinion

The conclusions of the aforementioned rigorous research are recapitulated by public opinion. Upon the conduction of interviews respondents concur that "You're more likely to get a 'good' job if you're white, compared to someone with exactly the same education level who is black or Latino." Respondents contend that this is a matter of fact, regardless, if you hold a high school diploma, have workforce skills, or have a college degree. In support of this opinion is "The Unequal Race for Good Jobs," compiled by Georgetown University's McCourt School of Public Policy Center on Education and the Workforce. Their findings describe a good job as one that compensates workers at least $35,000 a year and for more senior workers at least $45,000 a year. As pertained to median salaries good jobs paid $65,000 a year in 2016 as reported by the Center.

The Georgetown report established the existence of colorism by occupation considering that white American workers are paid higher salaries than their black and Latinx-American counterparts. This is a fact regardless of equality in skill and educational level. According to Klein (2019), a white employee holding a bachelor's degree, or more is compensated a median income of $75,000 a year in 2016. The same salary for black and Latinx-Americans was $65,000. When considering white middle-skilled workers who are those workers holding some post high school credentials absent a bachelor's degree are paid $60,000 a year versus $53,000 for black workers and $55,000 for Latinx-American workers. In this instance colorism is never more dramatically displayed as Latinx-Americans defined by mixed race tend to be lighter in skin color. Finally, considering white American workers whose education is limited to a high school diploma or less earned a compensation median salary of $56,000 a year. The same earnings for equally qualified black and Latinx-Americans was reported as $50,000 a year.

As reported by Klein (2019) during an interview with Wil Del Pilar who is the vice-president for higher education at the Education Trust "It confirms a lot of the things we know about society generally and how education does not pay out the same for everyone." However, this contention is more likely an assessment by race and action by skin color as race is determined by color. It is then by skin color that American workers improved their chances for getting a "good" job between 1991 and 2016. Still white American workers acquire the most significant share. The data for that larger share grew from 50% to 58% despite the rhetoric of diversity that would appear to produce an environment of more balanced competition.

Unfortunately, for people of color, black Americans increased their share from 33% to 41%. Latinx-American workers increased their share from 30% to 37%.

White workers also hold a disproportionate share of good jobs when considering their overall share of available jobs. The results are less than desired in that people of color are inclined to a lesser share of the good jobs. Therefore, white Americans held 77% of the good jobs when tabulated for the United States while holding 69% of all American jobs collectively. The same comparison for black Americans was 10% of the good jobs while overall they held 13% of all jobs. A slightly better outlook existed for Latinx-Americans in that they held 18% of all jobs and also 18% of good jobs. Once again, such data for Latinx-Americans may be a reflection of colorism where light skin is a dominant factor (Klein, 2019).

Considering the aforementioned data as pertains to good jobs the findings were likely begun well before adulthood. Certain good jobs are accessible by science education. When questioning high school seniors in the United States, most responded that they enjoy the subject of science as reported by 44% of respondents. Their belief is that they would elect to have a job in science as reported by the Pew Research Center which conducted an analysis of the 2015 National Assessment of Educational Progress (NAEP). In conformity to the colorism by occupation hypothesis student responses tended to vary by race. This variation was no less apparent in American students' science test scores. Therefore, collectively, 71% of twelfth-grade high school students state in agreement, "I like science." This agreement was coupled with race groups who reported a "fondness for science." By ethnicity Asian and Pacific Islanders were most likely to report fondness and black Americans the least in a colorism pattern.

The most telling findings relative to good job outcomes are suggested in the racial and ethnic differences of students by science as a career. When questioned 60% of Asian and Pacific Islanders as high school seniors report that they would like a job in science. Another 64% report the significance of doing well in science to get a good job in science. When race is a factor, 45% of whites, 40% of Latinx, and 39% of black Americans report they want a science-related job. A maximum of 50% of these racial groups report the need to do well in science for a good job in science.

More recent investigations of student attitudes toward science overall are diverse as pertains to student response. Aside from high school seniors fourth- and eighth-graders, are evidence of progress made since 2009. Unfortunately, test scores involving twelfth-grade seniors have stagnated as reported by the NAEP. What's more, progress made by black and Latinx-Americans while evidence of improvement remain significantly lower compared to Asian and Pacific Islander and white students. This is a fact regardless of the grade level reported.

Investigators who study the lower representation of black and Latinx-Americans in science occupations refer to the age of exposure to the subject matter. For students who do well in science and aspire to science occupations may be initiated at the high school level or sooner according to NAEP statistics. The evidence is couched in data where 37% of black-American eighth graders aspire to a science job. However, 44% of white American students and 55% of Asian and Pacific Islander students have the same aspirations.

The statistical evidence pertaining to student differentiations in science occupations is not a simple matter of group membership. Race, skin color, and colorism by occupation are relevant associated with other less obvious phenomena. Included are input from higher science test scores, parental support, parental educational level and poverty level which may play a significant role. As pertains to poverty in particular the availability of advanced science courses is less likely at poorer, inner-city high schools (Anderson, 2017).

Colorism by occupation can be gleaned from a considerable body of research evidence. While the bulk of relevant data refers to racial and ethnic categories these categories are distinct by skin color giving race category less significance. In the aftermath deficiency, bias, caste, and discontinuity, theories which explain minorities such as Jewish workplace discrimination are incomplete. What's more the same theories which explain black American workplace discrimination are equally incomplete. Jewish-Americans may include traditional white members and biracial black Americans that by virtue of white heritage are exceptions. In both instances such Americans may be characterized by white-light-skin that allows them to escape being identified. If they conceal their identity stigma they may access good jobs, higher salaries, successful hires, and any other advantages available to their non-stigmatized white counterparts. The significance brought by such advantages are critical to their eventual quality of life. In reference to quality of life is then access to wealth by education and occupation culminating in colorism by income.

References

Anderson, M. (2017). *Among high school seniors, interest in science varies by race, ethnicity*. Retrieved November 2, 2021, from www.pewresearch.org/fact-tank/2017/01/04/among-high-school-seniors-interest-in-science-varies-by-race-ethnicity/

Beckett, A. (1983). *The relationship of skin color to blood pressure among Black Americans*. AUSSW. Unpublished.

Black, M. (2007). Fanon and DuBoisian double consciousness. *Human Architecture, 5*, 393–404.

Clark, K. (1965). *Dark ghetto*. New York: Harper and Row.

Espino, R., & Franz, M. (2002). Latino phenotypic discrimination revisited: The impact of skin color on occupational status. *Social Science Quarterly, 83*(2), 612–623.

Fanon, F. (1965). *Black skin, white masks*. New York: Grove.

Frazier, E. F. (1966). *The Negro family in the US*. Chicago: University of Chicago Press.

Greeley, A. (1977). Anti-Catholicism in the academy. *Change, 9*(6), 40–43.

Hall, R. E. (1990). *The projected manifestations of aspiration, personal values, and environmental assessment cognates of cutaneo-chroma (skin color) for a selected population of African Americans* (Doctoral dissertation). Dissertation Abstracts International, 50, 3363A. Atlanta University, Atlanta.

Hall, R. E. (1996). Occupational aspirations among African Americans: A case for affirmative action. *Journal of Sociology and Social Welfare, 23*(4), 117–128.

Hallinan, M. (1997). The sociological study of social change: 1996 presidential address. *American Sociological Review, 62*(1), 1–11.

Hare, N. (1965). *The Black Anglo Saxons*. New York: Marzani Munsell.

Hauser, R., & Warren, J. (1996). *Socioeconomic indexes for occupations: A review, update, and critique*. CDE Working Paper 96–91. Madison, WI: Center for Demography and Ecology, University of Wisconsin-Madison. Retrieved from ftp://elaine.ssc.wisc.edu/pub/hauser/paper/96-1.pdf

Herskovits, M. (1968). *The American Negro*. Bloomington: Indiana University Press.

Huggins, N. (1942). *Key issues in the Afro-American experience*. New York: Harcourt Brace Jovanovich.

Hughes, M., & Hertel, B. (1988). *The significance of color remains*. Blacksburg, VA: Virginia Polytechnic Institution. Unpublished.

Jensen, A. (1969). How much can we boost IQ and scholastic achievement? *Harvard Educational Review, 39*(1), 1–123.

Kitano, H. (1985). *Race relations*. Englewood Cliffs, NJ: Prentice-Hall.

Klein, A. (2019). *White workers more likely to get good jobs at every level of education*. Retrieved November 2, 2021, from www.edweek.org/leadership/white-workers-more-likely-to-get-good-jobs-at-every-level-of-education/2019/10

Klineberg, O. (1944). *Characteristics of the American Negro*. New York: Harper & Row.

Kronus, S. (1971). *The Black middle class*. Columbus, OH: Merrill Publishers.

Myrdal, G. (1944). *An American dilemma*. New York: Harper & Row.

Norton, D. (1993). Diversity, early socialization, and temporal development: The dual perspective revisited. *Social Work, 38*(1), 82–90.

Ogbu, J. U. (1982). Cultural discontinuities and schooling. *Anthropology and Education Quarterly, 13*, 290–307.

Poussaint, A. (1975, February). The problems of light skinned blacks. *Ebony, 30*, 85.

Quinnan, T. (1997). *Adult students "at-risk": Culture bias in higher education*. Westport, CT: Bergin & Garvey.

Reuter, E. (1969). *The Mulatto in the United States*. New York: Haskell House.

Rose, A. (1964). *The Negro in America*. New York: Harper & Row.

Sagi, A., & Dvir, R. (1993). Value biases of social workers in custody disputes. *Children and Youth Services Review, 15*, 27–42. https://doi.org/10.1016/0190-7409(93)90051-A

Stevenson, H., Chen, C., & Uttal, D. (1990). Beliefs and achievement: A study of Black White and Hispanic children. *Child Development, 61*(2), 508–523.

Williams, B. (1992). Changing demographics: Challenges for educators. *Intervention in School and Clinic, 27*(3), 157–163.

Wilson, G. (2012). Women's mobility into upper-tier occupations: Do determinants and timing differ by race? *Annals of the American Academy of Political and Social Science, 639*(1), 131–148.

Wilson, G., & Roscigno, V. (2018). Race and downward mobility from privileged occupations: African American/White dynamics across the early work-career. *Social Science Research, 39*(1), 67–77.

8
COLORISM BY INCOME

The term "income" refers to money or some equivalent of money as compensation for labor, interest, or profit acquired from money invested. This may include the rental of property such as residential or land. Income derived from labor is traditionally assessed by wage or a salary. Therefore, any income including worker, company, investor, charity, or organization can be described as having been earned. In other references such as accounting, income pertains to an excess of money accumulated beyond expenses over a specific period of time as in a quarter or fiscal year. Income may also be described as an increase in the value of total assets during an accounting period. In the United States, this is a matter of profit in the context of companies. Considering other nations in the Western hemisphere, it is simply revenue (Mourre & Reut, 2019).

As per the aforementioned terminology, income may be described and/or defined contingent upon the situation involving an individual, a company, a household, or the national economy. Subsequently, this involves the consumption and savings opportunity in profit by any source per a specific frame of reference that is expressed in financial terms. Relative to the aforementioned individual and their households, income is most likely the totality of the wages, salaries, profits, interest payments, rents, and other earnings obtained during the prescribed period of time.

Scientists who study the origin of words trace the modern English term of "income" historically to the year c. 1300. It pertained by meaning to "arrival," "entrance," or "a coming in." Consequently, the old English verb "incuman" pertained to "come in" or "enter." During this time as pertains to "income" in the old English language was reference to "that which comes in as payment for work or business" during c. 1600. The relevant income tax evolved as a common term sometime later around the Napoleonic wars, declined from usage then re-emerged in 1842. Globally, the concept of income is quite common: ingresos (Spanish), renda/receita (Portuguese), le revenu (French), reddito (Italian), and Einkommen (German).

The term income is also a component of relevant concepts expressed in common societal transactions. In per capita income, income combines with a second word to refer to the total GDP or gross domestic product of a sovereign country, a city or a particular region divided by its population. As defined the combination of income and "per capita" extends from Latin and means "per head." The "per head" pertains to the relevant population. The GDP considering per capita income is then an approximation of how many wealthy or poor the residents of one country are in comparison to those of another country.

"Income" in combination with "effect" signifies the impact that a change in taxes, prices or wages has or might have on individuals' spending or saving behavior. For example, a reduction in the amount of taxes that workers have to pay on their wages usually results in greater consumer spending across a nation. While there are a number of other "income" combination concepts the aforementioned are most relevant to the individual where colorism by income is concerned. The US Census data contains an extensive account of individual incomes in the national data of what is earned (Market Business News, n.d.).

Income by Skin Color

The 1990 US Census reports that the mean earnings of adults in the United States as a whole was $15,105 per year. The same account of earnings for Native-American adults was $11,949; for Latinx-American adults it was $11,219. Lastly, for black Americans the mean adult earnings were $10,912 (Ramos, 1994). Assuming white Americans generally to be the lightest-skinned and people of color progressively darker, a pattern of colorism emerges. According to that pattern, the US Census would then suggest a positive correlation between light skin color and higher income. For dark skin the same correlation is suggested in the negative. Contingent upon the cultural significance of that correlation, the income levels of individual black Americans including other people of color is then most likely put at risk.

In a study of incomes by Akee, Jones, and Porter (2019), linked data examined income inequality and mobility over racial and ethnic populations in the United States. For their population analysis investigators accessed the entirety of income tax filers in the United States beginning in 2000 and ending in 2014. They linked individual-level race and ethnicity information collected from various census data and American Community Survey data. What was documented pertained to both income inequality and mobility patterns regarding a particular period of time. The end results illustrated a significant stratification relative to average incomes organized by racial/ethnic category and distinct intra-group differences relative to income inequality. While this study did not intend to address colorism, colorism is a plausible element in the outcome of income differentiations.

As determined by the collection of data in the aforementioned study those groups having earned the highest incomes were white and Asian-Americans. What's more, both groups as colorism might suggest also had the highest levels of intra-group inequality in addition to having the lowest levels of intra-group mobility. In reversal of this trend was a factor of the lowest-income groups. Such groups included black, Native-, and Latinx-Americans who maintained lower intra-group inequality and immobility. What's more, low-income groups are likely immobile overall, as opposed to intra-group mobility. Additionally, these same groups may have a higher likelihood of encountering downward mobility when compared to white and Asian-American subjects. In the final analysis, investigators also discovered that intra-group income inequality increased for all study populations from 2000 to 2014. As expected, this increase was particularly significant for white Americans. Thus, in consideration of conclusion, researchers suggest the existence of a rigid income structure. Coincidently by evidence is the existence of whites and Asians located at the top and blacks, Native-, and Latinx-Americans the likely darker-skinned assigned to the bottom (Akee et al., 2019).

Other investigators also conducted significant research on income and demographic factors such as that implied by colorism. They reviewed a systematic analysis of residential segregation and spatial interaction associated with incomes. They determined that as income level rises, people of color gained more access to integrated neighborhoods, and had more interaction with white Americans. In addition to this they had more affluent neighbors as a consequence. Unfortunately, indicative of a colorism pattern, the income advantages were much less for black Americans overall. The reverse was especially true as pertains to interactions with Asian-Americans. While Latinx-American and Asian-Americans have additionally shown declining levels of white non-white dissimilarity coupled with increased levels of minority-white interaction per income increase, income differentials per these outcomes for black Americans did not appear until 1990. Since 1990 improvements have occurred at a very reduced pace for black Americans. Ultimately as per higher overall levels of segregation and income's limited impact on the residential attainment, black Americans incur decreased integration, and increased neighborhood poverty regardless of income when compared to other non-white groups. These factors are exacerbated in location of the nation's 21 hyper-segregated metropolitan areas (Intrator, Tannen, & Massey, 2016). Therefore, as evidence would suggest political efforts were activated to address income disparities implied by colorism. Without specific reference to skin color, colorism was addressed by reference to race and racism resulting in the politically controversial policy of Affirmative Action.

Affirmative Action

Among the most charged and salient revelations of colorism by income, brought to the US Supreme Court, pertains to Affirmative Action. Despite opposition from white conservatives who contend that the policy is racially biased, rigorous scientific investigations such as the aforementioned substantiate the opposite. As a result of considerable research, the Affirmative Action policy was originally adopted by Congress. It is a most salient phenomenon because it offers the modern-day Supreme Court a means to advance a racist status quo via the elimination of race-based criteria, i.e., colorism. Much like traditional racism the outcome of Affirmative Action restores white racial advantage. It disrupts policies intended to address societal transgressions of the past, the present and insures a more equitable access to future opportunity irrelevant to race category.

According to the 1935 Congressional Records, the origin of Affirmative Action was adopted for the benefit of non-unionized white males who sought redress for discrimination at the hands of employers. The most visible among its advocates and primary sponsors was a New York Senator named Robert F. Wagner (US Congress, 1935). During a session of Wagner's seventy-fourth Congress, it was declared that discrimination against an employee by an employer shall require "such person to cease and desist from such unfair labor practices and to take such affirmative action, including reinstatement of employees with or without back pay, as will effectuate the policies of this act" (US Congress, 1935). Formally referred to as the National Labor Relations Act and occasionally the Wagner Act, Affirmative Action was initially approved by the US Congress on July 5, 1935. The language omitted terms pertaining specifically to black Americans, and other people of color today taken as members of an oppressed population. The traditional oppression characteristic of this earlier era made opposition to racism moot when it involved employees of color. "Employee" was assumed for all practical purposes to refer to "white males" exclusively and preferably of "non-Jewish stock." Congressional modern-day legislation marked the beginning of the Affirmative Action controversy which stoked the most intense fears from white workers. Its central theme was that it is not enough to cease and desist discriminatory acts directed at people of color. It should extend to address the consequences of historical injustices that ultimately require deliberate action to be corrected. Eventually passed by Congress, the original Wagner Act of 1935 was an attempt to correct prior injustices due to oppression. It posted notices in 1935 of a new policy and in affect reinstating white workers to good standing who were terminated for union activity (US Congress, 1935). Had Congress not done so, the future impact of previous physical and financial intimidation by employers would have imposed upon the democratic elections which the Act warranted. Therefore, the original Affirmative Action benefited white males who had been discriminated against and eventually eliminated their problem entirely. Critics of the day dissimilar to today did not attack Affirmative Action as "preferential treatment" or "reverse discrimination" often heard in modern-day political debates. Most Americans recognized the inherent value to society that would come as the result of its enactment because hiring practices pertained to the preferences for whites while ignoring the implications of race and/or skin color.

The 1964 Civil Rights act was a failed attempt to redress income inequality that the 1935 Affirmative Action policy was assumed to have corrected. To compensate for that failure, Affirmative Action was one of a number of economic policies designed to enable equality of opportunity particularly for black Americans and other oppressed populations (Karger & Stoesz, 1990). However Affirmative Action as an economic policy advocated today may be passively enforced by Conservative political administrations. Those opposed contend that it violates equal protection under the law and sets up a process of reverse discrimination that is biased in favor of the so-called oppressed (Wilson, 1980). Those in opposition further contend that it will benefit people of color who are not victims of discrimination in the workplace and because of hiring practices punish whites who are "innocent" of any wrongdoing. If the implications of light skin are correct some among people of color including black Americans may indeed profit in a way that violates the spirit of the policy. However, such an assumption may be naive and merely reflect the spoils of power. While true to some extent, the same critics of Affirmative Action ignore the complex web of workplace disadvantage met by people of color that are not only irrelevant to "innocent" whites, but in some cases create an advantage (Hiskey, 1990). A culture that values light skin as the ideal regardless of race relative to income may in fact be one such example.

The legal and political assaults occurring on US college campuses against Affirmative Action efforts inspire efforts to impede the ability of black Americans to acquire income security. Indirectly higher education represents a gateway to higher incomes. Subsequently, the state of Texas suspended several scholarship programs suspected of Affirmative Action bias. In one instance its law school was barred from utilizing racial preferences as admissions criteria and awarding financial aid to potential students. What's more in the state of California a three-judge panel of the US Court of Appeals for the Fifth Circuit undercut the State Supreme Court's decision regarding the 1978 Bakke case. It determined that Affirmative Action programs were in fact illegal (O'Neille, 1985). Those in opposition to Affirmative Action insist their objective does not pertain to impeding black progress but to see to it that whites are not discriminated against in the process. Ironically upon initiation of Affirmative Action in 1935 no such concern was expressed as the policy was directed at white males exclusively and preferably of non-Jewish stock.

Despite federal policies such as Affirmative Action and other legislative efforts to attain income equality for black Americans, the issue of skin color continues to influence income level (Jenkins, 1993). A society that values workers for their physical attributes such as skin color via race will impact income level as well as income security (Hall, 1990). Such an impact relative to colorism by income undertaken to offer empirical evidence could be used as a basis for defending economic policies such as Affirmative Action in a depressed economic era. By analyzing the impact of skin color upon the income projections of a selected population of black American students located in the area of south Georgia, results suggest that skin color should be the basis for redress. Laws inspired by Bakke and others can be dissolved by evidence and eliminate accusations of "reverse discrimination." The social environment is rife with research evidence that equates with skin color as a dictate to income level.

Skin Color and Income

Brothels in the United States provide evidence of a skin color bias for services rendered. Income differentials are illustrated according to the amount of extra consumers agree to pay for light-skinned versus dark-skinned employees. To conduct investigation skin color was measured using photographs of women advertised on escort websites in Mexico. Price differentials per skin color were documented as a means to answer the research question. Conclusion revealed that employees characterized by darker skin were found to be underrepresented. Additionally, lighter-skinned employees were documented as costing more than darker-skinned employees. Considering factors such as age, weight, hair color, and body type, it was calculated that a one standard deviation increase in dark skin reduced an employee's cost relative to income by approximately 10% (Campos-Vazquez, 2021). This example of colorism by income is not an anomaly to the brothel industry but extends no less to the physiology of child adoptions (Fenster, 2002).

McRoy and Grape (1999) are employed as social work practitioners. They investigated the child adoption process to assess the process as manifested in the United States. The focus of their research aimed at the historical, social, and political dynamics associated with skin color. They were particularly interested in the process as pertains to black Americans. The sample chosen for the project consisted of adults who had been adopted intra-racially and trans-racially. Intra-racial adoptions by black American families exposed the existence of colorism in that light-skinned black children were preferred over their dark-skinned counterparts.

> Zena Oglesby, founder and executive director of the Institute of Black Parenting in Los Angeles, for example, has found that as many as 40% of the African-American couples who seek to adopt a child from his agency express a preference for a light-skinned or mixed-race child, regardless of their own complexions.
>
> *(McRoy & Grape, 1999, p. 679)*

Trans-racial adoptions involving black children by white families revealed a similar preference for those characterized by light skin. Therefore, those who desired adoption of a child of color preferred said child be biracial in hopes light skin would be among their traits. These families as per McRoy and Grape (1999) were convinced that a light-skinned child might be more commensurate with the family's ideals, the family's neighbors and the family's friends. In the aftermath, it was assumed by social workers that light-skinned children would be more socially acceptable which for income-based adoption agencies would bring increased profits. This assumption is reflected in duration of adoption time statistics (Hjelm, 2007).

Data documented in 2004 contained 51,993 adopted children taken from the public child welfare authority. In totality 43% were determined to be white (light-skinned) and 33% were determined to be black (dark-skinned). In conclusion of the data black children displayed the longest mean duration of time between termination of parental rights and adoption of the child whose parents' rights had been terminated. When all races were assessed black American children spent a mean of 15.3 agency months before being adopted. White children spent a mean of 12.3 months. For the most part over time agency means declined relative to a child having light skin.

When confronted by prospective parents, black social workers employed at white adoption agencies are queried about a newborn or anticipated child's skin color. The objective is to assess how dark-skinned the child might be which could impact their placement potential and thus ultimately income profit. This concern is not limited to white Americans but includes light-skinned, brown, and dark-skinned black Americans equally (McRoy & Grape, 1999). This practice is widespread not limited by race or agency location. In view of such colorism by income, the American Civil Liberties Union (ACLU) conducted a court-authorized review of 50 adoption case files. It also conducted interviews with social workers in New York City. As the investigation concluded findings suggested that social work practitioners "engaged in placement practices which result in favored treatment for children who have more Caucasian features" (McRoy & Grape, 1999). Therefore, when potential adopting families asked for light-skinned children, social workers acted according ultimately commensurate with profit. While social workers contend that their primary aim was to protect dark-skinned children from the psychological pain of rejection their actions contribute to profit motives and aspirations for income enhancement (McRoy & Grape, 1999). That profit motive per income enhancement is not exclusive to the adoption agency or potential American parents. The issue extends to immigrants where income level via colorism is associated with skin color.

Among the world-renowned scholars who investigate the implications of skin color and income of immigrant populations in the United States is Dr. Joni Hersch (2007). Dr. Hersch is employed as a professor of law and economics at Vanderbilt University in Tennessee. In a recent study she reviewed a government file containing 2,084 legal immigrants in the United States. They migrated from various locations around the world. After calculating the data her conclusion revealed that those having the lightest skin were compensated an average of 8%–15% more compared to immigrants characterized by dark skin. "On average," Dr. Hersch explains, "being one shade lighter has about the same effect as having an additional year of education." Further revealed by Dr. Hersch via societal emphasis upon the physiological was that those immigrants distinct by greater height were compensated higher incomes compared to their shorter counterparts. Statistically, for each inch of height there was a 1%increase in the amount of income compensation. Additional investigations concur with that of Dr. Hersch suggesting a "skin-tone prejudice" that has income implications that exceed racial boundaries. In an effort to ensure the validity of her work Dr. Hersch took into consideration the impact of extraneous variables including English-language proficiency, education, occupation, and race or country of origin. After considerable analysis she determined that skin color remained a significant factor for income level. Subsequently, by comparison if two immigrants from the same ethnic group such as Bangladesh, migrated to the United States simultaneously, employed in the same occupation and command the same English-speaking ability, those characterized by lighter skin would on average be compensated higher incomes. "I thought that once we controlled for race and nationality, I expected the difference to go away," according to Dr. Hersch, "but even with people from the same country, the same race, skin color really matters" (The Associated Press, 2007).

When immigrants are located abroad in their home countries the same dynamic of colorism by income applies. According to Bailey, Saperstein, and Penner (2014), there is a relatively linear relationship between skin color perceptions and per capita household income. In specificity, lighter skin is associated with higher incomes, and darker skin is associated with lower incomes. The populations where this conclusion was established include Paraguayans. Paraguayans distinct by the lightest skin color realized incomes 47% higher on average. Those Paraguayans having the darkest skin colors have incomes that are 36% lower. In general, these findings are commensurate with a traditional skin color hierarchy existing nationwide. However as pertains to nations globally the degree to which particular skin colors are associated with advantage or disadvantage may differ significantly. Therefore, the most significant gaps between the lightest and darkest color (mid-range) exists in the Dominican Republic and Guatemala. Conversely, in El Salvador and Colombia exists significant disadvantages for dark-skinned residents. What's more in the United States and Bolivia there is clustering at different points in the skin color distributions. This would imply that at each particular step per the color scale consequences may differ (Bailey et al., 2014).

No doubt the implications of skin color have been established by the rigorous calculations of statistical evidence. The history of income as defined in the old English language and per statistical evidence has not changed dramatically to any extent. Affirmative Action policies originally brought in 1935 and reactivated in the sixties have had little impact on income disparities. Governmental efforts in general continue to standardize the concept of race while society operates via the concept of color (Billinger, 2007). Race is a contrived concept void of objective, mathematical measure other than subjective estimates. Statistical calculations are then limited to nominal data that has no mathematical significance. The less standardized skin color is objective and mathematically measurable that provides a more secure foundation for income investigations. Income cannot be overstated as critical to quality of life regardless of race, color, or any other demographic factor. Various scholars have established the impact of skin color upon income level that dictates quality of life. Less income relative to quality of life equates with a reduced access to healthy nutrition, social stability, and viable health care most encountered by those having dark skin. In the aftermath, a reduced quality of life is dramatically illustrated by women of color victimized in the event of stillbirth colorism (Thomas, 2006).

References

Akee, R., Jones, M., & Porter, S. (2019). Race matters: Income shares, income inequality, and income mobility for all U.S. races. *Demography, 56*(3), 999–1021.

The Associated Press. (2007). *Study of immigrants links lighter skin and higher income.* Retrieved December 10, 2021, from www.nytimes.com/2007/01/28/us/28immig.html#:~:text=Study%20of%20Immigrants%20Links%20Lighter%20Skin%20and%20Higher,reason%20appears%20to%20be%20discrimination%2C%20a%20researcher%20says

Bailey, S., Saperstein, A., & Penner, A. (2014). *Race, color, and income inequality across the Americas.* Retrieved November 6, 2021, from www.demographic-research.org/volumes/vol31/24/31-24.pdf

Billinger, M. (2007). Another look at ethnicity as a biological concept: Moving anthropology beyond the race concept. *Critique of Anthropology, 27*(1), 5–35.

Campos-Vazquez, R. (2021). The higher price of whiter skin: An analysis of escort services. *Applied Economics Letters, 28*(1), 1–4.

Fenster, J. (2002). Transracial adoption in Black and White: A survey of social worker attitudes. *Adoption Quarterly, 5*(4), 33–58.

Hall, R. E. (1990). *The projected manifestations of aspiration, personal values, and environmental assessment cognates of cutaneo-chroma (skin color) for a selected population of African-Americans* (Doctoral dissertation). Dissertation Abstracts International, 50, 3363A. Atlanta University, Atlanta.

Hersch, J. (2007). *Study of immigrants links lighter skin and higher incomes.* Retrieved November 5, 2021, from www.nytimes.com/2007/01/28/us/28immig.html

Hiskey, M. (1990, February 1). Boss: Skin hue, firing unrelated. *The Atlanta Journal-Constitution, 1,* 4.

Hjelm, R. (2007). *Transracial adoption and the multiethnic placement act.* Child Welfare League of America. Retrieved April 22, 2016, from http://thehill.com/images/stories/whitepapers/pdf/MEPA_Final_IB.pdf

Intrator, J., Tannen, J., & Massey, D. (2016). Segregation by race and income in the United States 1970–2010. *Social Science Research, 60,* 45.

Jenkins, S. (1993). *The socially constructed meaning of skin color among young African-American adults* [CD-ROM]. Abstracts from ProQuest file: Dissertation abstracts item: 453. University of Michigan, Ann Arbor.

Karger, H. J., & Stoesz, D. (1990). *American social welfare policy.* New York: Longman.

Market Business News. (n.d.). *What is income? Definitions and meaning.* Retrieved November 5, 2021, from https://marketbusinessnews.com/financial-glossary/income-definition-meaning/

McRoy, R., & Grape, H. (1999). Skin color in transracial and inracial adoptive placements: Implications for special needs adoptions. *Child Welfare, 78*(5), 673–692.

Mourre, G., & Reut, A. (2019). Non-tax revenue in the European Union: A source of fiscal risk? *International Tax and Public Finance, 26*(1), 198–223.

O'Neille, T. (1985). *Bakke and the politics of equality.* Scranton, PA: Wesleyan University Press.

Ramos, D. (1994). Losers. *The New Republic,* p. 24.

Thomas, J. (2006). Blacks have a greater risk of stillbirth than whites following a cesarean, and higher stillbirth recurrence. *Perspectives on Sexual and Reproductive Health, 38*(2), 115–116.

US Congress (74th) Session I CH. 372. US Statutes at Large, Wash. GPO. (1935, July 5).

Wilson, W. J. (1980). *The declining significance of race.* Chicago: University of Chicago Press.

9
HEALTH RISKS IN STILLBIRTH COLORISM

Recent trends in beauty cosmetics have spurred an escalation of industry profits inspired by colorism. Enabled by the colonial histories of Asia, Latinx America, and Africa, monies generated by industry profits were attributed to the colonial idealization of light skin. Commensurate with Hitler's WWII era and the ensuing eugenics of racial superiority the Aryan traits of blonde hair and blue eyes relative to feminine beauty was idealized accordingly (Harvey, 2014). By turn of the 21st century the colonial ideal of light skin in feminine beauty is no less the preferred representation of racial superiority that has once again been projected on to women of color. Said projection perpetuates the colonial myths associated with light skin dramatically illustrated in the behaviors of dark-skinned women who risk stillbirths as an aftermath of their skin bleaching (Harper & Choma, 2019).

Skin bleaching by dark-skinned women is a modern-day social phenomenon that began with euro domination. Cosmetics companies originally marketed bleaching creams as a way to give dark-skinned women access to feminine beauty by light skin otherwise unavailable. Recent sales of such creams reached double-digit growth in India where skin color remains a most significant physical attribute (Dorman, 2011). Those who are characterized by a light complexion are immediately presumed the most beautiful and superior in every way. Subsequently by default dark skin is denigrated and as such perpetuates the notion of human hierarchy extended from the colonial myths of racial superiority. This "Hitlarian" propaganda ploy originally associated with light skin in the assessment of feminine beauty has now been realized in the quest for light skin by women who bleach.

Skin bleaching is a far more global phenomenon than modern-day social science has been willing to acknowledge (Fritsch, 2017). Not irrelevant to women of European descent women of color who bleach their dark skin include Asian, Latinx, and African descent to become the mainstay of industry profits. In India the practice of skin bleaching is no less apparent among women of Asian descent. As one of the most potent bleach cream markets in the world India witnessed a striking growth in the bleach cream business in 2005 (Kukreja, 2021). No doubt skin bleaching in India and Southeast Asia was an aftermath of the WWII Aryan myth but in fact the history of Asian skin bleaching long preceded the Aryan myth and the Western colonial hegemony associated with it. In a 2008 social science investigation it was determined that in India, Hong Kong, Japan and Korea: "An absence of freckles and scars have been preferred since the first dynasty in Korean history" (the Gojoseon Era, 2333–108 B.C.E.). Skin bleaching was practiced in Korea by applying miansoo lotion and dregs of honey (Jeon, 1987). Well known in Japan is the application of white powders to the facial area to enhance beauty in Japanese women which contributed years later to a predisposition among other women of color to idealize light skin (Ashikari, 2005). Said idealization proved critical to stillbirth events among pregnant women of color.

Stillbirths by expectant mothers are frequently confused with miscarriages. However, there exists significant differences between the two. When death of the fetus occurs prior to 20 weeks of gestation merits the definition of a miscarriage. When death of the fetus occurs in excess of 20 weeks of gestation merits the definition of a stillbirth (Star Legacy Foundation, 2021). The causes of stillbirth are numerous and vary extensively. Subsequently, many stillbirth events remain completely unresolved as pertains to cause or explanation. Their statistical proportion is approximately 33 1/3% of all stillbirth events reported globally. This necessitates a challenge that the assorted social scientific and/or medical institutions are bound to resolve. Alternatively, those stillbirth events given to an explanation by statistical proportion account for 66 2/3% of stillbirths globally as suggested in the following (Murphy & Botting, 1989).

In developed nations, maternal obesity is among the most preventable causes of infant stillbirth. However, the circumstances relative to this association remain unknown. Bodnar et al. (2015) estimated the relationship between maternal pre-pregnancy body mass index (BMI) relative to stillbirth may present risks of pathophysiologic factors. They utilized a case-cohort design in which they randomly sampled 1,829 single deliveries from a cohort of 68,437 deliveries. The location took place at Magee-Women's Hospital in Pittsburgh, Pennsylvania during 2003–2010. This set was amplified with additional remaining cases. Classification of stillbirth cases were assessed by probable cause(s) of death including maternal medical conditions, obstetric complications, fetal abnormalities, placental diseases, and infection. Select clinical experts reviewed medical records, placental tissue slides and pathology reports, and fetal postmortem reports of all stillbirth cases involved. Considering the causes of fetal death investigators employed the Stillbirth Collaborative Research Network Initial Causes of Fetal Death protocol. It was obtained from the Eunice Kennedy Shriver National Institute of Child Health and Human Development. According to results, stillbirths of lean, overweight, obese, and severely obese women was 7.7, 10.6, 13.9, and 17.3 per 1,000 liveborn and stillborn infants, respectively. The results of data per adjusted stillbirth HRs (95% CIs) were 1.4

(1.1, 1.8) for overweight, 1.8 (1.3, 2.4) for obese, and 2.0 (1.5, 2.8) for severely obese women, respectively when compared with lean women. Considering obesity and severe obesity relative to stillbirth revealed placental diseases, hypertension, fetal anomalies, and umbilical cord abnormalities. However, BMI was irrelevant to stillbirth caused by placental abruption, obstetric conditions, or infection. A considerable number of variables linked obesity to stillbirth (Bodnar et al., 2015).

Ngoc et al. (2006) investigated stillbirth and early neonatal mortality. Their objective was to quantify the relative significance of various primary obstetric causes of perinatal mortality in 171 perinatal deaths. Their population consisted of 7,993 pregnancies that concluded following 28 weeks in nulliparous women. The process for investigation utilized all stillbirths and early newborn deaths reported for the WHO calcium supplementation trial. The location included cooperating centers in Argentina, Egypt, India, Peru, South Africa and Viet Nam. Investigators applied the Baird-Pattinson system by which they could assign primary obstetric causes of death. They then classified causes of early neonatal death by application of the International Classification of Diseases and relevant health problems. Subsequently, stillbirths were measured at 12.5 per 1,000 births and early neonatal mortality rate was 9.0 per 1,000 livebirths. What's more, preterm delivery and hypertensive disorders appeared to be the most common obstetric events associated with perinatal deaths by 28.7% and 23.6% (Ngoc et al., 2006).

As per the aforementioned, is an ample research explanation extending from 66 2/3% of stillbirths in toto. The remaining 33 1/3% in need of explanation is hereby suggested as being caused by colorism. Colorism is a form of discrimination that inspires a quasi, social-psychological assimilation strategy exemplified by people of color and/or women in particular. Where stillbirths are concerned colorism pertains specifically to having fewer options compared to men of color. In an effort to enhance their beauty and quality of life, women of color internalize alien ideals including reference to light skin which necessitates the use of bleaching creams. Bleaching creams contain toxic substances ingested by frequent cutaneous application. When women of color are pregnant said toxins enter the fetus via the placenta resulting in death by stillbirth. In an effort to facilitate resolution and explanation of a contributing factor to the remaining 33 1/3% of unexplained stillbirths will be suggested as commensurate with colorism.

The Biology of Colorism

In the biology of colorism melanin is a natural product of human cells referred to as melanocytes. Melanocytes are located in the epidermis of human skin. Visually it is commonly assumed that the level of melanin in human skin will determine what for the most part accounts for skin color. Therefore, lesser melanin encourages lighter skin; modest amounts of melanin, encourages medium dark skin; and significant amounts of melanin encourages the darkest skin. Significant amounts of melanin in human dark skin, according to Jablonski (2006), are a human trait in the origin of man.

The quality of melanin may also account for light or dark skin. Said quality pertains to eumelanin and pheomelanin. Eumelanin is a critical ingredient for the darkest in skin color consisting of black or brown pigmentation. Pheomelanin is a critical ingredient for a more medium complexion consisting of red or yellow pigmentation. Those who by genetic heritage acquire pheomelanin are considered Mongoloid, i.e., Asian, etc. Those who by genetic heritage acquire eumelanin are considered Negroid, i.e., African descent. Thus, regardless of racial heritage eumelanin content may impose social consequences by virtue of associations with stigma which impact health status as the stillbirth rates of black women illustrate accordingly.

Geneticists including Cheng (2008) have investigated the genes attributable to the dark skin of non-white people. Their research led to one such gene called melanocortin 1 receptor (MC1R). If this gene is functioning, it will direct melanocytes to convert pheomelanin to eumelanin. Failures of such conversion will result in an excess of pheomelanin. Those persons characterized by red hair and/or light skin may suffer from MC1R gene dysfunction. In the aftermath they maintain an excess of pheomelanin resulting in lighter skin.

Investigations of fish by geneticists have helped in study of the biology of skin color with the discovery of two skin color genes. One was discovered in stickleback fish and the second was discovered in zebrafish (Cheng, 2008). Those who investigated the first found that the stickleback fish's kit ligand gene (kitlg) differed dependent upon whether the fish was light or dark in color. By inference these investigators concluded that mankind may possess different manifestations of the same gene which accounted for lighter or darker skin in members of the human species. The function of the kit ligand gene is to enable melanocytes. Subsequently among fish as well as mankind where the kit ligand gene fails, the melanocytes succumb to dysfunction. The end results of fewer melanocytes necessitate reduced pigment resulting in lighter skin.

Investigators who researched zebrafish similar to those who investigated stickleback fish made significant discoveries about skin color and the SLC24A5 gene. The lighter fish were found to have a dysfunction of this gene. This finding was similar to that among women as per humanity. Unfortunately, unlike comparisons with kitlg, investigators are uncertain as to the function of the SLC24A5 gene. Some suggest that the gene may operate to distribute calcium where calcium may be required for melanin distribution into cells. Therefore light-skinned East Asians acquire their skin complexions from a dysfunction of kitlg. Those from Northern Europe and who are light-skinned may have an SLC24A5 dysfunction. Other light-skinned Europeans may suffer from an MC1R gene dysfunction as well.

Little acknowledged in Western academe is the biological dysfunctions of non-African descended peoples. African descended populations characterized by dark skin display not a dysfunction but a human genetic function. The crux of their function is attributed to dark skin relative to sunlight. The role of sunlight as a function of dark skin conforms to the ecological perspective. Thus, racial groups such as Northern Europeans and Asians harbor a tendency to lighter skin compared to those racial groups rooted in the tropics. The significance of sunlight to their dark skin is given to the impact of UV rays. UV rays pose a considerable threat to human existence if not addressed properly. Overexposure can destroy folic acid or facilitate mutations in the DNA of human skin cells that produce melanoma. Therefore, dark skin is functional for health reasons in geographic locations where the human species is exposed to ample sunlight.

Dark skin may serve additional functions as pertains to sunlight. Sunlight is critical for the manufacture of vitamin D. Vitamin D can be found in numerous animal products such as milk and cheese critical to bone health. The diseases associated with deficiencies in vitamin D include rickets and/or osteoporosis. Thus, UV rays which emanate from the sun are instrumental in the processing of vitamin D. In considering the functions of dark skin melanin serves as a filter for protection from UV rays and as a means of long-term survival in tropical locations (Conklin, 2016). Therefore, unlike light skin where less melanin is associated with dysfunction, dark skin associated with more melanin is a product of evolutionary human function. Both are historical events attributable to the human species as a whole. Unfortunately, more melanin is also a product of human dysfunction in the rate of stillbirths irrelevant to evolution of the species. It is a societal construct contrived in the social dynamics of Western society which encourages women of color to partake in the use of toxic bleaching creams not irrelevant to stillbirths.

Toxic Bleaching Creams

Toxic bleaching creams are a critical function of stillbirths. The toxicity of bleaching creams is apparent in consideration of its ingredients. The use of such creams is also functional in the outcome of stillbirth events. The various toxic substances contained in bleaching creams include mercury, arsenic and hydroquinone. Most recently glutathione has become an additional substance thrust into the controversy. Trade names often confuse the purchasing public. For example, mercury by other terms may be designated as calomel, mercuric, mercurous, or mercuriom. In chemical science mercury is designated according to symbol by Hg. If referenced in Greek translation, mercury is designated hydrargyrum. Hydrargyrum means "liquid silver." The meaning of "liquid silver" was inspired by mercury's shiny, metallic appearance. It is also referred to as "quicksilver" given to its active mobility. That mobility associated mercury with the fastest moving planet in the earth's solar system. Unfortunately, the utilization of mercury as a bleaching cream ingredient may factor in stillbirth events among women of color. The toxic qualities of mercury may be ingested by breaks in the skin, lung ingestion via inhalation or oral consumption. Aside from stillbirths, women of color who ingest mercury via bleaching cream usage may damage their nerves and kidneys.

No less potent than mercury, arsenic is a natural element of the environment. It exists in measurable quantities of water, air, food, and soil. Arsenic also exists in cosmetic products for women such as eye shadows, lotions and lipsticks. In bleaching creams, arsenic may contaminate the raw materials used in the manufacturing of the products little known by women of color who purchase them. Therefore, contamination that may not be intended is spread from the metal machinery utilized in the bleaching cream's manufacturing process (Reay, 1972). When arsenic is consumed in lower levels over time, its toxic impact may damage skin, liver and kidneys. It may also cause a reduction in red and white blood cells, which can precipitate fatigue and an increased risk of infections that ultimately encourage stillbirth events (Jordaan & Van Niekerk, 1991).

Fewer bleaching creams contain mercury and arsenic than hydroquinone. Hydroquinone is the most common of toxic substances contained. Arsenic and mercury are natural toxins that occur in the environment. Hydroquinone is an artificial toxin manufactured solely for specific use in commercial bleaching creams. Its reference in chemical science is $C_6H_4(OH)_2$. Application of hydroquinone containing bleaching creams by women of color is supplemented in occasional use by dominant group women who apply it to eliminate "freckles," "age spots," and "liver spots." Ingesting hydroquinone can also cause "ochronosis." Ochronosis is a skin condition identified by its thickening and discoloration (WebMD, 2017). The critical toxic factor of hydroquinone is perhaps its designation as a category C carcinogen linking it to cancer. Category C pertains to research linking toxins to animals often assumed to be human relevant. For such reasons bleaching creams are limited by law to contain a maximum of 2% ingredients of a bleaching cream product.

The aforementioned mercury, arsenic and hydroquinone are commonly known toxins contained in bleaching creams. Glutathione is a less known agent that has stoked controversy among investigators. The skin lightening properties of glutathione are known to enhance tyrosinase activity. Tyrosinase activity of the skin prevents melanin from synthesizing natural sunlight. In the aftermath is an impact on skin color. Glutathione has developed into a major health risk given to its potential for adverse sequelae. Aside from skin bleaching properties glutathione is prescribed for various alcoholic liver diseases and adjunctive treatment in cisplatin chemotherapy. The FDA has not officially approved glutathione for use as a skin lightening product (Sonthalia, Jha, Lallas, Jain, & Jakhar, 2018). However, as oral and intravenous ingestions of glutathione have increased in popularity no known safe dose currently exists (Sonthalia et al., 2018). Therefore, as pertain to stillbirths, the toxic properties of glutathione can only be assumed associated with hepatic, neurologic, and renal toxicity, Stevens Johnson Syndrome, and air emboli that in spite of the fact manages a profitable bleaching cream market (Dadzie, 2016).

Bleaching Cream Market

Regardless of toxicity, a global bleaching cream market has emerged spurred by women of color. This bleaching cream market is viable and increasingly popular with women of color. In fact, Nigeria as a nation of 180 million residents in West Africa leads the continent in sales. What's more Nigeria not only leads Africa but is foremost globally reporting a total of 77% of its female population who daily use bleaching creams to lighten their skin. Contributing to robust sales are the endorsement of Nigerian celebrities and socialites who contribute to market share by selling bleaching cream products online. In November 2018, the African-American socialite Blacc Chyna travelled to Nigeria by invitation from Dencia to promote a bleaching cream product called Whitenicious. While some Nigerians resort to commercial agents endorsed by celebrities, others rely upon various pills or cosmetic surgeries to lighten their dark complexions (Johnson, 2019).

Additional African communities are equally committed to the bleaching cream market. Among members of the Francophone African population in Europe there exists a formidable bleaching cream sales component. Any cursory review of market participants and it becomes immediately apparent that in addition to Nigeria, major bleaching cream purchasers also include other African nations such as Togo, Cameroon, Congo, Burkina Faso and the Ivory Coast. Subsequently, according to the World Health Organization approximately 59% of the female population in Togo bleach their dark skin for a lighter complexion. The applications and concoctions they resort to frequently escape the legal limits of toxic ingredients. In the aftermath, a number of women in Togo reported contracting severe skin disorders, cancers and some have even died in their efforts to acquire light skin by bleaching (Johnson, 2019).

South Africa is among the more developed of African countries on the continent. Unfortunately, it is no less given to the use of bleaching creams than those previously mentioned. Bleaching creams in South Africa are more often used by African women in hopes that a lighter complexion will enhance their quality-of-life chances brought by beauty and/or sex appeal. Investigators have compiled empirical evidence to substantiate the fact. Dlova, Hamed, and Tsoka-Gwegweni (2014) administered a cross-sectional survey of 579 black African and Indian women in Durban, South Africa. They ranged in age from 18 to 70 years. The investigation was carried out at two large public hospitals located in Durban. Subjects who took part in the study consisted of 292 black Africans and 287 African Indians. Considering combined totals of both groups 32.3% contributed to the bleaching cream market by their purchase of bleaching cream products. Assessed separately 60% of Africans and 40% of Indians were participants in bleaching cream purchases. A substantial number of purchasers who had used skin lighteners did not deny being informed of bleaching cream health risks. A total of 85% of Africans and 76% of Indians admitted to such. Another 90% of Africans then expressed satisfaction with bleaching cream results. However, 32% admitted to adverse results (Dlova et al., 2014).

By the year 2024 the projected bleaching cream market is expected to reach sales of US$31.2 billion globally. Africa joined by Asia represents one of the fastest-growing bleaching cream markets in the world. The combination of both poses an additional US$5.7 billion in market share occurring over the next four years. Africa and Asia are not alone contributing to the profits of bleaching cream sales. European nations where African and Asian peoples reside are also a potent bleaching cream market. Considering that today there exists between 1 and 5 million French citizens who confess some element of African descent creates an additional market for the industry. Thus in 2007 there were 170,363 immigrants who left Africa to settle in France. By that number, 38,530 were relocated from Cameroon and just as those who remained in Cameroon they enabled stillbirths in contributing to making the bleaching cream market stillbirth profitable (Hall, 2018).

Stillbirths and Women of Color

The toxic substances known to be contained in bleaching creams have spurred a robust market among women of color not irrelevant to their stillbirth events. While the United States remains a multi-racial, multi-cultural society the most glaring stillbirth descriptive statistical contrast exists between dark-skinned African-Americans (black) and light-skinned Euro-Americans (white). As per data compiled by the CDC (Center for Disease Control) the rate of stillbirth events per 1,000 livebirths pertaining to white mothers was 4.89. In consideration of comparable data for dark-skinned black mothers the count was a dramatic 10.32 per 1,000 livebirths. As pertains to light-skinned Asian and Pacific Islander mothers was a count of 4.29 stillbirths per 1,000 livebirths. What's more, the same descriptive statistics for light-skinned Latinx women in the United States is 5.22. In addition, for light-skinned Native-American women of color was a rate of 7.22 stillbirths per 1,000 livebirths. Therefore, when considering the likelihood of bleaching cream use the rate for dark-skinned black women who experience stillbirth events is more than twice that of light-skinned white women (CDC, 2020). A comparable pattern is produced for lighter-skinned Asian, Pacific Islanders, Native-American, and Latinx-American women of color relative to darker-skinned African-American mothers. Furthermore, this same domestic pattern of stillbirth events is reproduced by pregnant women of color globally. As a result, those women of color having the lightest of skin regardless of their race or nationality display lower rates of stillbirths compared to those darker-skinned.

As documented publicly, international stillbirth information provides significant statistical data. Its source can be gleaned from the International Stillbirth Alliance (2009). That alliance contends that considering African countries populated by dark-skinned women of color where stillbirth rates reached double-digits per 1,000 total births the calculated mean was 23.96. When reporting of African countries that were consulted the highest number of double-digit stillbirths per 1,000 total births, Nigeria was highest documenting 41.7. This statistic is commensurate with Nigeria as the leading African country in the sale and use of bleaching creams internationally. In contrast the African country reporting the lowest number of double-digit stillbirths per 1,000 total births is Tunisia at 10.1. Tunisia per light skin of a mixed-race Arab ancestry population is less inclined to bleaching cream use.

Global data sets attest to the high number of stillbirth events reported by women of color globally that provides an ample market. According to Saleem, Tikmani, and Goldenberg (2018), some statistical variations from Africa exists considering the mean stillbirth rates pertaining to select locations were 21.3 per 1,000 births for Africa, 25.3 per 1,000 births for India, 56.9 per 1,000 births for Pakistan, and

19.9 per 1,000 births for Guatemala. Data collection for 2010 to 2016 for the same select locations consisted of a mean stillbirth rate that declined from 31.7 per 1,000 births to 26.4 per 1,000 births. This accounts for an average annual decline of 3.0%. Considering risk factors for stillbirth brought commonality to selected locations. The ages of the women of color who took part in this investigation were ideal for bleaching cream usage resulting in a profitable market (Saleem et al., 2018).

As contained in data is an illustration of skin color via race and/or ethnicity. It purports that the rates of stillbirth are differentiated according to documented tendency to bleaching creams. Therefore, among the lightest complected non-Hispanic white women who evidence lesser use of bleaching creams the stillbirth rate was 4.89 per 1,000 livebirths. Said rate is approximate to that of Asian/Pacific Islander women at a stillbirth rate of 4.29. A slightly higher rate pertained to American Indian/Alaska Native women of color which was 7.22 per 1,000 livebirths. Lastly considering women of color the stillbirth rate for Latinx mothers was 5.22 per 1,000 livebirths. The most conspicuous statistic was reported for non-Hispanic black women which totaled 10.32 per 1,000 livebirths. Their rates almost doubled that of the mean total of 5.89 (Hoyert & Gregory, 2016).

Conclusion

Stillbirths via colorism are a global health risk for women who experience some aspect of an abnormal pregnancy. Said abnormality may be due to inherent physiological traits or exposure to health risk substances located in their environment. While modern medicine has addressed and resolved many of the causes of stillbirth not a few causes of stillbirth remain unresolved. Their pathologies are a product of the social environment and often subject to personal control by the mother's decision-making processes. Stillbirths under such circumstances are primarily attributed to women of color in their succumbing to the use of bleaching creams known to be toxic as a significant contributing factor to the 33 1/3% of stillbirth events yet resolved. The existence of colorism while more than a century of years in longevity is all but unknown to social science and medical personnel given to the Eurocentric publication trends of the Western academy (Helber, 2012).

The excessive rates of stillbirth among women of color are a product of colorism. Colorism prevails in the aftermath of colonization, the Atlantic slave trade, white supremacy ideologies and other forms of non-white denigration. The ideals extended from non-white denigration were then dramatically illustrated by the biology of melanin in skin color. Light skin evolved as the ultimate ideal associated with its dominant group characteristics. In a social environment orchestrated by dominant group participation non-white people of color were no less given to dominant group ideals. Subsequently, they accepted the denigration of their dark skin by default seeking by whatever means available to acquire light skin (Xie & Zhang, 2013). Attributed to colorism women of color then resorted to the daily application of bleaching cream products to bleach their dark skin light. In this way they might satisfy the requirements of dominant group ideals and thereby enhance their quality-of-life chances based on a belief in the beauty of light skin. Unfortunately, the frequent application of bleaching creams by women of color introduced toxic substances into bodies of their unborn and thereby commencing to stillbirth.

Toxic bleaching cream substances are critical to the function of colorism. Women of color who apply them in many instances are little aware of their toxic ingredients. Medical personnel while cognizant of mercury, arsenic and hydroquinone as toxic bleaching cream ingredients and its potential life threatening risks to an unborn fetus are less aware of the colorism circumstances that inspire toxic bleaching cream use (Alharbi, 2021). The end result is a contributing factor to the 33 1/3% of stillbirth events lacking explanation. The significance of human life would necessitate the immediate introduction of colorism into required academic content that no stillbirth event would exist lacking an explanation.

The significance of colorism in the perpetuation of stillbirths is a global health risk to women of color residing in both developed and undeveloped nations (London, 2016). The extent of its threat risk can be measured in proximity to light skin. Therefore, those countries in Africa where Arab or other mixed-race populations exist by light skin report lower stillbirth statistics. In the more developed Western nations such as those in Europe where significant black African populations reside, the statistical contrasts between white and non-white stillbirths merit the ultimate intolerance (Thomas, 2006). The initiation of such intolerance may begin by educating both the lay and professional public.

The risks for stillbirths brought by the toxic substances contained in bleaching creams are not unknown by every faction of society. Indeed, various branches of local and federal governments have enacted legislation to limit the amount of hydroquinone contained in bleaching cream products. However, the general public may be unaware of such laws or what to do when they encounter a violation. Cigarettes contain similar toxic substances that are stated very clearly on the warning label of every pack purchased. The women who use toxic bleaching creams might prevent a stillbirth if each tube of bleaching cream carried a similar such warning label as that found on a pack of cigarettes.

Women in Western societies and indeed the world are valued for their physical attributes (Duke, 2002). Subsequently, the ideal of light skin may have an impact on women of color less relevant to men of color who may have options of fame, wealth and power as alternative status enhancers. However, although the bleaching cream market has introduced bleaching creams such as "Fair & Lovely" for women of color, "Fair & Handsome" has been marketed for use by men. Such a product may in fact be a testament to the power and influence associated with having light skin. Having such a trait in observable qualities may enhance their attractiveness regardless of wealth or other physiological attributes. To reduce the impact of skin color upon women of color including men will ultimately require diversification of feminine beauty standards where a range of complexions may be idealized. In this way the use of toxic bleaching creams in colorism will decline. Attributed to this decline will accrue a 33 1/3% explanation and rescue the unborn from the unnecessary tragedies of stillbirth.

References

Alharbi, M. (2021). 1927 nm thulium laser successfully treats post inflammatory hyperpigmentation in skin of color. *Dermatology Research and Practice*. doi:10.1155/2021/5560386

Ashikari, M. (2005). Cultivating Japanese Whiteness. *Journal of Material Culture, 10*(1), 73–91.

Bodnar, L., Parks, W., Perkins, K., Pugh, S., Platt, R., Feghali, M., . . . Simhan, H. N. (2015). Maternal pre-pregnancy obesity and cause-specific stillbirth. *The American Journal of Clinical Nutrition, 102*(4), 858.

Center for Disease Control. (2020). *Data and statistics*. Retrieved August 19, 2021, from www.cdc.gov/ncbddd/stillbirth/data.html

Cheng, K. (2008). Demystifying skin color and "race". In R. Hall (Ed.), *Racism in the 21st century: An empirical analysis of skin color*. New York: Springer Science.

Conklin, J. (2016). *Where do different skin colors come from?* Retrieved May 9, 2016, from http://genetics.thetech.org/ask/ask288

Dadzie, O. (2016). Unethical skin bleaching with glutathione. *British Medical Journal*. Retrieved August 30, 2021, from www.sciencedaily.com/releases/2016/08/160831223742.htm

Dlova, N., Hamed, S., & Tsoka-Gwegweni, J. (2014). Women's perceptions of the benefits and risks of skin-lightening creams in two South African communities. *Journal of Cosmetic Dermatology*. Retrieved September 5, 2021, from https://onlinelibrary.wiley.com/doi/abs/10.1111/jocd.12104

Dorman, J. (2011). Skin bleach and civilization: The racial formation of blackness in 1920s harlem. *The Journal of Pan African Studies, 4*(4), 47–80.

Duke, L. (2002). Get real!: Cultural relevance and resistance to the mediated feminine ideal. *Psychology & Marketing, 19*(2), 211–233.

Fritsch, K. (2017). 'Trans-skin': Analyzing the practice of skin bleaching among middle-class women in Dar es Salaam. *Ethnicities, 17*(6), 749–770.

Hall, R. (2018). *Bleaching creams are by-products of colonialism: A view from French history*. Retrieved September 5, 2021, from https://theconversation.com/bleaching-creams-are-by-products-of-colonialism-a-view-from-french-history-83692

Harper, K., & Choma, B. (2019). Internalised white ideal, skin tone surveillance, and hair surveillance predict skin and hair dissatisfaction and skin bleaching among African American and Indian women. *Sex Roles: A Journal of Research, 80*(11–12), 735–744.

Harvey, D. (2014). The lost civilization: Jean-Sylvain Bailly and the roots of the Aryan myth. *Modern Intellectual History, 11*(2), 279–306.

Helber, P. (2012). Ah my Brownin' Dat!": A visual discourse analysis of the performance of Vybz Kartel's masculinity in the cartoons of the Jamaica observer. *Caribbean Quarterly, 58*(2–3), 116–128.

Hoyert, D., & Gregory, E. (2016). *Cause of fetal death: Data from the fetal death report, 2014*. National Vital Statistics. Retrieved September 5, 2021, from www.cdc.gov/nchs/data/nvsr/nvsr65/nvsr65_07.pdf

International Stillbirth Alliance. (2009). *The partnership for maternal, newborn and child health*. Retrieved May 22, 2017, from www.who.int/pmnch/media/news/2011/stillbirths_countryrates.pdf

Jablonski, N. G. (2006). *Skin: A natural history*. Berkeley: University of California Press.

Jeon, W. (1987). *The cultural history of make-up in Korea*. Seoul, Korea: Yeolhwadang.

Johnson, E. (2019). *Top 5 African countries where women bleach their skin to look white*. Retrieved September 5, 2021, from https://face2faceafrica.com/article/top-5-african-countries-where-women-bleach-their-skin-to-look-white

Jordaan, H., & Van Niekerk, D. (1991). Transepidermal elimination in exogenous ochronosis: A report of two cases. *The American Journal of Dermatology, 13*(4), 418–424.

Kukreja, R. (2021). Colorism as marriage capital: Cross-region marriage migration in India and dark-skinned migrant brides. *Gender & Society, 35*(1), 85–109.

London, S. (2016). Global burden of stillbirth has declined in recent years, but remains generally high. *International Perspectives on Sexual and Reproductive Health, 42*(1), 51.

Murphy, M., & Botting, B. (1989). Contrasts in the multiple causes of stillbirth, neonatal death and postneonatal death. *Journal of Epidemiology and Community Health, 43*(4), 343.

Ngoc, N., Merialdi, M., Abdel-Aleem, H., Carroli, G., Purwar, M., Zavaleta, N., . . . Villar, J. (2006). Causes of stillbirths and early neonatal deaths: Data from 7993 pregnancies in six developing countries. *Bulletin of the World Health Organization, 84*(9), 699–705.

Reay, P. (1972). The accumulation of arsenic from arsenic-rich natural waters by aquatic plants. *Journal of Applied Ecology, 9*(2), 557–565.

Saleem, S., Tikmani, S., & Goldenberg, R. (2018). Trends and determinants of stillbirth in developing countries: Results from the global network's population-based birth registry. *Reproductive Health, 15*(100). Retrieved September 5, 2021.

Sonthalia, S., Jha, A., Lallas, A., Jain, G. & Jakhar, D. (2018). Glutathione for skin lightening: A regnant myth or evidence-based verity? *Dermatol Pract Concept, 8*(1), 15–21. doi:10.5826/dpc.0801a04

Star Legacy Foundation. (2021). *About stillbirth*. Retrieved August 19, 2021, from https://starlegacyfoundation.org/about-stillbirth/

Thomas, J. (2006). Blacks have a greater risk of stillbirth than whites following a cesarean, and higher stillbirth recurrence. *Perspectives on Sexual and Reproductive Health, 38*(2), 115–116.

WebMD. (2017). *Hydroquinone skin bleaching cream*. Retrieved May 21, 2017, from www.webmd.com/drugs/2/drug-87530-9198/hydroquinone-skin-bleaching-cream/details

Xie, Q., & Zhang, M. (2013). White or tan? A cross-cultural analysis of skin beauty advertisements between China and the United States. *Asian Journal of Communication, 23*(5), 538–554.

10
THE BLEACHING SYNDROME

As a function of Western civilization, colorism in the United States has been consistently portrayed on the basis of race as if racial prejudice were a legitimate category of transgression. In fact, race is little more than a contrived concept from which consequences are derived. In the aftermath is a belief in the sanctity of race as if it were the essential resolution ingredient for the elevation of society to the next level of civilization. Subsequently, the dynamics of interactions between people of color and white Americans have suffered totally unnecessary consequences. In fact, transgressions in the United States and elsewhere West extend beyond the various categories of race. Therefore, race is less relevant necessitating skin color as crux of the problem. This is due to the fact that commensurate with skin color all so-called race groups adhere to US transgression as much as white Americans although significantly nuanced. Therefore, seldom discussed are the nuances of skin color, i.e., colorism relative to previously enslaved, colonized, or otherwise dominated populations among people of color. As a legacy of slavery, colonization, and domination the history of prejudice between the "black," the "yellow," and the "brown" man has then been omitted from public discourse relegated by social taboo. Because colorism has been subjugated by race its intra- and inter-group manifestations have long been discouraged from annals of the Western academy (Hall, 2002).

No doubt, the single issue of colorism does not exist without participation by people of color. Furthermore, the current unspoken myth of "white supremacy" for the most part is no longer fashionable in society or the academy at large. Despite the fact, such a myth though shattered in the scholarly literature and banished from the circles of polite society, remains largely intact on the basis of skin color: the lighter the skin, the greater likelihood of assumed superiority that has also been assumed by people of color. The subsequent behaviors are most apparent in the actuality of everyday life in the United States among its great masses of relatively dark-skinned people of color. In addition to participation by white Americans, those of African, Asian, Latinx, and Native decent skin color has become an unspoken prescript of colorism. Skin color then figures—however tacitly-in their daily behavior and will clearly continue to do so until the pathological psychological residue of Western civilization is completely dissipated (Hall, 2003). Until then people of color by colorism will act out the transgressions of their victimization due to influences of the dominant Western model of societal assimilation.

Assimilation is a critical sociological concept that has been studied by several scholars such as those at the University of Chicago during turn of the 20th century. At the time Chicago was an industrial center that attracted numerous immigrants looking for work having migrated from eastern Europe. Their arrival caught the attention of Chicago sociologists whose interest were peaked by the process of immigrant assimilation. Shortly thereafter William I. Thomas, Florian Znaniecki, Robert E. Park, and Ezra Burgess became leaders in the field of such study. They conducted scientifically rigorous ethnographic research with both immigrant and racial minority populations residing within the Chicago geographical spaces. Their works produced theoretical concepts as pertains to assimilation that moved assimilation science forward.

As described by the aforementioned sociologists, assimilation is a linear process that encourages similarity between culturally differentiated groups over the course of time. This process is apparent over generations of immigrant families. Upon arrival, immigrants differ culturally but eventually become culturally similar to the dominant group. This according to Kitano (1985) is due to the dominant model of Western assimilation. Subsequently, the first-generation of immigrant children will grow up socialized to a culture dissimilar to that of their parents' home country. That initially foreign culture will then be native to first-generation immigrant children. They may maintain the values and traditions of their parents' culture at home or in a community environment where the parents' culture dominates. However as pertains to the second-generation of immigrant children the cultural traditions of the dominant group are more pronounced. By language and other norms said children may be culturally indistinguishable from the dominant group. Sociologists have termed this phenomenon in the United States as "Americanization" where immigrants are eventually "absorbed" resulting in the emergence of a "melting pot" society.

Assimilation of immigrants may involve populations differentiated contingent upon race, ethnicity, and religion. Such differentiations may dictate a smooth, linear process for some, and for others it will be quite challenging via institutional and interpersonal obstacles. Such obstacles may take the form of racism, xenophobia, ethnocentrism, and religious prejudice. One such obstacle includes residential "redlining." Redlining pertains to the prevention of immigrants from purchasing homes in predominantly white American communities. This practice existed throughout much of the 20th century. It enabled residential and social segregation which disrupted the successful assimilation of minority groups. In addition to minority groups was the experience of religious groups such as Sikhs and Muslims.

In addition to skin color, they might be identified by the religious inspirations of their dress and then socially excluded from mainstream of the dominant group society.

Wealth is an attribute that will facilitate the ability of immigrants to assimilate in the United States and elsewhere. When an immigrant family arrives in poverty, they face additional obstacles that might be overcome by financial means. Otherwise, those such as day laborers or agricultural workers may encounter food and housing challenges that the host nation may ill afford or lack provisions. The response of immigrants in poverty to this challenge may contribute to difficulty. In banning together to share food and other resources is a form of immigrant self-segregation that does not encourage dominant group assimilation. Immigrants enabled by wealth do not encounter such challenges and thus are less confronted by dominant group dismay. Their ability to access shelter, consumer goods and services, educational resources, and leisure activities will significantly assist their assimilation into the mainstream of the United States and other Western societies (Cole, 2019). The one obstacle immune to immigrant exception per colorism is complexion, i.e., so-called race.

Assimilation by Race

As per assimilation of immigrants into a white America necessitates their status as "minorities" (Kitano, 1985). The most salient feature of this minority in contrast to white Americans is skin color (Hall, 1990). Skin color may have an impact on every phase of life for all people of color, including mate selection, stereotype, treatment by the judicial system and most importantly for the Bleaching Syndrome self-concept (Vontress, 1970). Skin color is a "master status" which distinguishes non-whites from the dominant white mainstream as an inferior element of society (Farhard, 1988). So potent is this "master status" that it has recently served as grounds for legal action between persons of light and dark skin color but belonging to the same ethnic group (Hiskey, 1990). A resort to legal tactics is an indication that for black Americans, assimilation has been particularly stressful given the psychologically conflicting implications of dark skin. That is, they have internalized much of white American culture but unlike members of the "white" mainstream are prohibited from assimilation into it (Rabinowitz, 1978). Their willingness to assimilate regardless reflects an effort not to become white but to improve their quality of life and live the "American Dream." In so doing, black Americans may develop a disdain for dark skin because the disdain is an expectation of assimilation. It is regarded by the various societal institutions as an obstacle that might otherwise afford them the opportunities necessary to succeed. For those black Americans who labor, unaware of the inherent limitations of being endowed with dark skin, stressful conflict is the end result. In order to reduce such stress and at the same time enable assimilation, some have opted in various ways to alter themselves. Furthermore, since degree of assimilation closely correlates with having a color approximate to the white population, light skin has emerged as a critical ideal relative to the aspirant's ability to assimilate (Reuter, 1969). It is acted out by aspiring black Americans as an ideal point of reference in a dominant mainstream white society.

In understanding the dominant group white American model of assimilation, mode of entry of a minority group such as black Americans is exacerbated by skin color. Mode of entry is critical for a number of reasons. If entry is by warfare and conquest, the bloodshed of the original conflict will remain in the consciousness of both groups imposing upon their personal and institutional interactions (Hacker, 1992). Such entry will make it difficult for structural assimilation and the two groups to coexist peacefully. For those groups who immigrate and enter the country voluntarily, there are no antagonisms to impose upon their dominant group interactions (Smolicz & Lean, 1979). The immigrant is hopeful about improving his or her socioeconomic status per locale of assimilation. Additionally, the mode of entry will affect the size and distribution of the minority group. If the mode of entry is by conquest the conquered group can be a powerless majority in their own land. That will make them more cohesive and enhance segregation. The conquerors are likely to be scattered in geographically small but strategic areas of the land which they have conquered. If the mode of entry is voluntary immigration, the minority will be small because it is not likely that a society will permit itself to be overwhelmed by an outside group. It is also unlikely that after voluntary immigration an immigrant group will arrive in such numbers that they take over a large area of land. Rather they tend to settle in pockets adjacent to the dominant society (Kitano, 1985).

Mode of entry may also impact the cultural distance between the conquerors and the conquered. When groups are conquered in their own land, the land itself may keep the influence of culture and history potent. Thus, conquered groups are not as likely to change their ways as an immigrant group traveling to a new country. Lastly, and perhaps at the risk of controversy, via colorism mode of entry will be affected by skin color differences. White populations, for quite some time, have taken to conquering and colonizing people of color the world over. Recent history fails to give any account of people of color having conquered their white counterparts for purposes of colonization. Therefore, the most dramatic products of assimilation pertain to people of color including black Americans.

The Products of Assimilation

The American antebellum period offers a dramatic illustration relative to the products of assimilation. Black Creoles in culture and physiology are derived from nearly three centuries of interaction between African slaves, French and Spanish colonists, gens libres de couleur (free people of color), Cajuns, and Native-Americans. In the modern era, this biracial African-French population displayed a diversity of ethnic styles and associations considering their residence, family history, economic status, and perceived racial heritage. In the aftermath of assimilation some Creole populations provided evidence of folk Catholicism via voodoo, and traiteurs, or "traditional healers," language use such as French Creole, music/dance like New

Orleans jazz and zydeco, celebrations in Mardi Gras, and ethnic foods such as congris, jambalaya, and gumbo. Given to the extent of internal cultural diversity and overlapping boundaries, Creole ethnic identity is quite fluid and situation-derived. As black Creoles interacted with black Americans, Cajuns, and other whites, they displayed pride in their diverse heritage. The term "Creole" itself is quite fluid and given to the context of interpretation.

Marital events are critical to the individuality and assimilation potential of ethnic groups. Creoles tended to be Catholic. Their marital events traditionally occur between partners' teen and early 20s years. As pertains to colorism upper-class Creoles in particular aspire to marriage into a similar status family or to a white American as a form of hypergamy. While marriage to a black American does occur on occasion it is normally under the circumstances of exchange theory. According to exchange theory, intermarriage of a low status group member to a higher status group member is possible if the lower status partner is a socioeconomic superior.

Relative to assimilation Creoles normally reside within or near Creole communities or Creole neighborhoods. In rural Creole communities, families may make a gift of land to a newly married Creole couple. Childbearing is traditionally valued and rural families engaged in agriculture are adjacent to American standards. These extended families living in close proximity enable child rearing cooperation frequently involving older females. When older Creole females are widowed, they are found to reside with their children and grandchildren.

The Creole patriarch is not as restrictive as in the dominant group culture in that considerable respect is accorded to Creole women and Creole elders. They accentuate the values of self-improvement via church attendance, education, and hard work. Young Creole males may take issue with these values when they frequent bars and dance halls where they act out liberal sexual attitudes. However, they eventually settle into a respectable Creole home life. All considered the Creole community especially as pertains to their cultural attitude toward dark-skinned or black American are a white American product of assimilation (Spitzer, 2019).

Despite being victims black Americans are no less a product of white American assimilation than the Creole community. Ironically scholars contend that there has existed a black American middle-class product of assimilation prior to the Emancipation Proclamation. However, as pertains to colorism that class was negatively impacted by colorism which extended from the traditions of slavery. Said colorism was a matter of light-skinned slaves being favored by the master class who assigned them indoor work. They were considered less of a threat. Dark-skinned slaves on the other hand being more of a threat were limited to hard labor. Unlike light-skinned slaves they had no white blood or white kinship. Due to assimilation criteria light-skinned black slaves could be scorned or isolated from dark-skinned members of the black community. In response many developed separate institutions, businesses, and places of worship. The black colleges attended by DuBois's "Talented Tenth" were thus known to require a photograph with their applications before admission could be approved. In this way dark-skinned students could be flagged and rejected upon sight.

Modern-day middle-class black Americans regardless of skin color were still red-lined to inner city neighborhoods where they resided among impoverished often dark-skinned black Americans. Improvements followed the Civil Rights movement. Subsequently, following the sixties middle-class black Americans have increased in numbers. Many have been promoted into more white-collar jobs and are more educated than previously. Some managed integration into previously segregated white middle-class neighborhoods while others cooperated in the formation of their own exclusive communities no less commensurate with light skin and the dynamics of assimilation (Black Demographics, 2021). Hare (1991) refers to this black middle-class product of assimilation as "black Anglo Saxons" and Frazier the "black bourgeoisie."

Originally published in 1965 and re-released in 1991 Dr. Nathan Hare authored *The Black Anglo-Saxons*. In describing black Anglo Saxons Floyd McKissick opines:

> Dr. Nathan Hare has neatly defined the black Anglo Saxons, those members of the black middleclass who have lost all sense of identity and responsibility for the black masses. These black Anglo Saxons are the product of a history of oppression and deception by whites. They are in many ways mutants—white minds inside black bodies. But this middle class did not spring up automatically from the slave population. They are the result of miseducation and forced assimilation.
>
> *(Hare, 1991)*

E. F. Frazier (1957) more accurately describes this black Anglo Saxon middle class of today by reference to the black bourgeoisie. The black bourgeoisie are America's modern-day black upper class as defined by their wealth and financial income. They consist of black Americans employed as engineers, lawyers, accountants, doctors, politicians, business executives, venture capitalists, CEOs, celebrities, entertainers, and entrepreneurs. Some are heirs to considerable wealth joined by those who are employed earning annual incomes of $200,000 per year or more.

As a group, the modern-day black American middle class at times are called the black upper class, the black upper middle class or simply the black elite. Statistically they account for less than 1% of the total black American population. In the context of assimilation, they maintain a history of organizations and activities that distinguish them from other black Americans and the white American upper class as well. They are evident in talented-tenth-like black neighborhoods, black fraternities, and black sororities. They have a long history of traditions documented in Lawrence Otis Graham's 2000 book: *Our Kind of People: Inside America's Black Upper Class* (AAREG, 2021). This black upper class is a dramatic illustration of assimilation in the resulting human social products. They remain culturally and racially black aliens unto themselves by the prescripts of colorism. In order to survive and adjust to their existence within a pathological social environment they like Creoles have become predisposed to the psychological proposition of the Bleaching Syndrome.

The Bleaching Syndrome

As pertains to the aforementioned process of assimilation and the denigration of dark skin via idealization of light skin is a vehicle of pathology. It compromises the normalization of ideals conducive to psychological self-preservation among dark-skinned particularly black American citizens. The influence of dominant group forces motivated by somatic assimilation paradigms has extended this pathology most critically to dark-skinned women in a patriarch that values women for their physical attributes. Their attempts to escape into psychic calm comes by way of the Bleaching Syndrome.

As defined by the authority of Webster's Dictionary (Mish, 1989), "bleach" is a verb which pertains to the removal of color which in the case of the Bleaching Syndrome is to make one's appearance and hence identity less native and more alien contingent upon the dominant group denigration of dark skin. A "syndrome" in case of the Bleaching Syndrome consists of a compilation of symptoms, i.e., behaviors which include skin bleaching that occur in conjunction with other applications and make up a recognizable pattern (Mish, 1989). In both instances it is not limited to skin color but may include a host of stigmatized characteristics. These literal definitions provide a context for comprehension of the Bleaching Syndrome dramatized in skin color that incorporates a somatic assimilation paradigm containing three basic components. Said basic components are contained in the following criteria: (a) psychological according to internalized ideals; (b) sociological according to the behavioral reactions to those ideals en masse; and (c) physiological according to the extent of personal somatic alterations applied by the victims. Such examples include dark-skinned or African descended women of color in their efforts to reduce the content of melanin contained in their dark skin. As a result, the Bleaching Syndrome herein is then defined succinctly as the internalization of physiological and/or sociological pathogens relative to the denigration of dark skin and other stigmatized qualities which disrupts the normal development of a conducive psychological frame of reference.

For dark-skinned and/or African descended people of color worldwide the Bleaching Syndrome begins with what they perceive about Caucasian light skin in the process of dominant group Western assimilation. Their acceptance of a stigmatized negative connotation denigrating dark skin is not compulsory to their psyche but merely a manifestation of the post-slavery, post-colonial or post-dominant group assimilation experience (Ortega & Verdugo, 2015). Unlike members of the dominant group white-American mainstream characterized by light skin, this causes among dark-skinned members of a population existential conflict. Psychologically, the negative implications of the denigration of dark skin via idealization of light skin having been internalized by victims create obstacles to their self-esteem. What they perceive as necessary for preferred quality-of-life assimilation paradigms then takes hold of their preferred, conducive self-concept. In an effort to reduce the psychic conflict caused and be simultaneously enabled by a preferred quality-of-life assimilation, those people of color impacted by the Bleaching Syndrome make a conscious decision to act out various forms of otherwise destructive self-alterations. This behavior is manifested in a sundry of psychological, sociological and physiological objectives as they resort to submission to a pathological somatic assimilation paradigm (Hall, 2001).

The Bleaching Syndrome is also the conscious awareness in this case colorism of the cognitive and attitudinal levels of the similarities and differences between the light skin ideal and the denigration of dark skin. The objective is to negate for African descended and other people of color their native "self" for the purposes of preferred quality-of-life assimilation. The quality of life that this may infer commensurate with the hierarchy of Maslow (1999), include the fulfillment of such physiological needs as food and shelter, such safety needs as protection and security. The need to satisfy belongingness, self-esteem, and self-actualization needs are irrelevant from victim perspective in the context of pathological somatic assimilation paradigms. This ultimately means that the Bleaching Syndrome prevents those impacted from advancing beyond the base of Maslow's hierarchy of needs. The process in toto then requires substantive knowledge and empathic appreciation of alien norms of Western Eurocentric culture at the expense of the native non-Eurocentric culture (Jandt, 2014). Subsequently, the Bleaching Syndrome is also a metaphor not limited to skin color but may include a broader, more inclusive range of native identity characteristics such as surnames, hair texture, geography, eye shape, speech patterns, marital patterns, dress styles, social preferences, religious persuasion, political preference, and culturally significant pastimes. Ultimately the Bleaching Syndrome prevails as a quasi-functional societal assimilation strategy that eventually leads to emotional and/or psychological dysfunction extended from various pathogens pertaining to self-acceptance. This pathology enables a compromise of the normal psychologically conducive assimilation experience (Hall, 2010). Such a critical existential feature encountered by dark-skinned people of color and African descent has been mainstream-subjugated. The end result is a perception of academic trivia or academic exotica and hence all but dismissed by the academy in its exchanges of significant intellectual discourse. The fact of this dismissal in the exchanges of intellectual discourse is verified by the popularity of bleaching creams despite their apparent toxicity per stillbirths of dark-skinned women.

The largest population of people of color conflicted by the Bleaching Syndrome via assimilation reside in the locales of Western influence. Similar to that of black Americans, their skin color varies greatly from the European light to the African dark. This variation has contributed to a belief on the part of some, that people of color are not very distinct in skin color unless subjected to comparisons with Europeans (Korzenny & Schiff, 1987). But much like black Americans their experience with assimilation may be generally associated with severe forms of Bleaching Syndrome stress (Boyle, 1970). Consequently, it is a well-established fact extending to the previous colonial era that with the arrival of European explorers necessitated a pathological confrontation with people of color (Montalvo, 1987). The ability of colonists to impose their ideals upon the indigenous people they encountered was long lasting and not without psychological consequence. The colonial legacy is continued by colorism in the standard of living, and the frequency of Bleaching Syndrome depression often experienced in association with skin color. That fact was recently corroborated quite by coincident (Relethford, Stem, Gaskill, & Hazuda, 1983).

A team of scholars assembled to study diabetes among people of color. They used a spectrophotometer to measure the skin color of their subjects. Their research revealed that the color of those in the sample became progressively lighter as the team moved from the low-income housing to the more affluent metropolitan suburbs (Relethford et al., 1983). In a later study, Arce, Murgia, and Frisbie (1987) found a correlation between light skin among people of color with higher levels of income and education. Additionally, the same researchers discovered that those who had darker skin reported significantly more instances of discrimination than their lighter-skinned counterparts implying increased Bleaching Syndrome stress. Those who had darker skin were reportedly perceived as more sinister and less attractive on that same basis. Particularly for minority males, this would imply that the experience of Western assimilation is not only stressful but a threat via Bleaching Syndrome to mental and emotional health of victims.

Those who succumb to severe forms of the Bleaching Syndrome may experience depression. As per the stress of assimilation, depression increases with the incidence of darker skin (Codina & Montalvo, 1994). This is a fact regardless of education, family income or internalization of Western culture (Codina & Montalvo, 1994). But perhaps what is most striking in consideration of the Bleaching Syndrome is that there is a gender component visited upon women of color in particular. In the aftermath are accounts of suicide committed by women of color consumed by depressive circumstances.

Karyn Washington was a dark-skinned 22-year-old black American woman who founded an organization in the United States to combat colorism called "For Brown Girls." She used the hashtag: #DarkSkinRedLip following a Rapper's insistence that dark-skinned girls not wear red lipstick. The objective of Ms. Washington's organization was to create a space where dark-skinned women of color could salvage their self-esteem or otherwise celebrate their beauty. It has not been substantiated as fact whether the skin color issue imposed upon the dark-skinned Washington personally, but critics are confident that it did. In 2012, the 22-year-old dark-skinned founder of "For Brown Girls" committed suicide (Bell, 2014).

According to research, a certain class of women of color born in the United States are not psychologically conflicted by the ideal of light skin in the same way as are males (Maldonado & Cross, 1977). This is especially peculiar given the fact that females in society tend to be valued for the way they look as opposed to males who may be more valued for their ability to earn. A possible explanation for this phenomenon may have to do with the greater likelihood of males having to interact with the mainstream in the role of "bread-winner." However, consistent with the ideal of light skin, Vargas-Willis and Cervantes (1987) found that of women of color who were accorded position and status at "home," assimilation stress led to depression after they immigrated to the United States. Their depression brought about by assimilation is evident, but for different reasons. If they are light-skinned such females once they immigrate may be associated with the dark-skinned "minority" class because of their immigration status and language. Due to their light skin and other features characteristic of the mainstream, they may be rejected particularly by employers as not dark enough to receive "minority" status. Their depression then, unlike that of males who are darker may be borne out of ambiguity indicative of the Bleaching Syndrome. They may be privy to the racial slurs and ethnic jokes of mainstream society while at the same time expected to be loyal to the darker-skinned communities of color. Additionally, many members of that same community express some resentment that such persons seem to overcome their "minority" status with greater ease than should be expected. This notion is further cause for depression and similar to that experienced by black Americans who claim "bi-racial" heritage. For both, the experience of assimilation is impacted by the implications of colorism in reference to skin color and the Bleaching Syndrome.

According to the aforementioned, there is reason to suspect a relationship between skin color and the incidence of stress and depression. It may exist among both the light-skinned and dark-skinned victims albeit for different reasons. The inability of people of color to experience normal assimilation makes them susceptible to pathology. For some, the Bleaching Syndrome may enable a temporary relief brought by some measure of function. Such Bleaching Syndrome circumstances are less striking and dramatic. Unlike people of color who succumb to more severe forms of the Bleaching Syndrome, those by a measure of function impact the evolution of familial and other systems vital to group preservation. Their indiscriminate internalization of alien ideals is ultimately anti-people of color and will insure a continuation of the Bleaching Syndrome and domination as prerequisite into the mainstream of society. The outcome will prove increasingly devastating for the overall emergence of diversity within today's population. Absent deliberate interruption of colorism and afflictions of the Bleaching Syndrome will encourage what Washington (1990) refers to as "brown racism."

References

AAREG. (2021). *The American black bourgeoisie, a story*. Retrieved November 9, 2021, from https://aaregistry.org/story/the-american-black-bourgeoisie-a-brief-story/

Arce, C., Murgia, E., & Frisbie, W. (1987). Phenotype and the life chances among Chicanos. *Latino Journal of Behavioral Sciences, 9*, 19–32.

Bell, T. (2014). For Brown girls, Karyn Washington, light skin vs. dark skin, low self-esteem. *The ReadyWriter*. Retrieved September 21, 2016, from https://conversationsofasistah.wordpress.com/2014/04/11/she-committed-suicide-because-of-her-skin-color/

Black Demographics. (2021). *The African American population*. Retrieved November 9, 2021, from https://blackdemographics.com/households/middle-class/

Boyle, E. (1970). Biological patterns in hypertension by race, sex, body weight, and skin color. *American Medical Association Journal, 213*, 1637–1643.

Codina, G., & Montalvo, F. (1994). Chicano phenotype and depression. *Hispanic Journal of Behavioral Sciences, 16*(3), 296–306.

Cole, N. (2019). *How different cultural groups become more alike*. Retrieved November 9, 2021, from www.thoughtco.com/assimilation-definition-4149483

Farhard, D. (1988). Jung: A racist. *British Journal of Psychotherapy, 4*, 263–279.
Frazier, E. F. (1957). *Black bourgeoisie*. New York: Collier Books.
Hacker, A. (1992). *Two nations: Black and white, separate, hostile, unequal*. New York: Maxwell Macmillan International.
Hare, N. (1991). The Black Anglo-Saxons. New York: Marzani & Munsell.
Hall, R. (1990). *The projected manifestations of aspiration, personal values, and environmental assessment cognates of cutaneo-chroma (skin color) for a selected population of African-Americans* (Doctoral dissertation). Dissertation Abstracts International, 50, 3363A, Atlanta University, Atlanta.
Hall, R. (2001). *Filipina eurogamy: Skin color as vehicle of psychological colonization*. Manilla: Giraffe Books.
Hall, R. (2002). Pseudo-racism among Chicano(a), Asian and African Americans: Implications of the Black/White dichotomy. *The Social Science Journal, 39*, 109–112.
Hall, R. (2003). *Discrimination among oppressed populations*. Lewiston, NY: Mellen Press.
Hall, R. (2010). The bleaching syndrome in the context of somatic norm image among women of color: A qualitative analysis of skin color. *European Journal of Social Sciences, 17*(2), 180–185.
Hare, N. (1965). *The black Anglo-Saxons*. New York: Marzani & Munsell.
Hiskey, M. (1990, February 1). Boss: Skin hue, firing unrelated. *The Atlanta Journal-Constitution, 1*, 4.
Jandt, F. (2014). Review of the global intercultural communication reader, 2nd ed. *European Journal of Communication, 29*(4), 507–509.
Kitano, H. (1985). *Race relations*. Englewood Cliffs, NJ: Prentice-Hall.
Korzenny, F., & Schiff, E. (1987). Hispanic perceptions of communication discrimination. *Hispanic Journal of Behavioral Sciences, 9*, 33–48.
Maldonado, B., & Cross, W. C. (1977). Today's Chicano refutes the stereotype. *College Student Journal, 11*, 146–152.
Maslow, A. (1999). *Toward a psychology of being*. New York: Wiley & Sons.
Mish, F. C. (Ed.). (1989). *Webster's ninth new collegiate dictionary*. Springfield: Merriam Webster.
Montalvo, F. (1987). *Skin color and Latinos: The origins and contemporary patterns of ethnoracial ambiguity among Mexican Americans and Puerto Ricans* (monograph). San Antonio, TX: Our Lady of the Lake University.
Ortega, J., & Verdugo, G. (2015). Assimilation in multilingual cities. *Journal of Population Economics, 28*(3), 785–815.
Rabinowitz, H. (1978). *Race relations in the urban South*. New York: Oxford University Press.
Relethford, H., Stem, M., Gaskill, S., & Hazuda, H. (1983). Social class, admixture, and skin color gradation in Mexican Americans and Anglo-Americans living in San Antonio, Texas. *American Journal of Physical Anthropology, 61*, 97-103.
Reuter, E. (1969). *The mulatto in the United States*. New York: Haskell House.
Smolicz, J., & Lean, R. (1979). Parental attitudes and cultural linguistic pluralism in Australia: A humanistic sociological approach. *Australian Journal of Education, 23*(3), 227–249.
Spitzer, N. (2019). *Black creoles of Louisiana*. Retrieved November 9, 2021, from www.encyclopedia.com/humanities/encyclopedias-almanacs-transcripts-and-maps/black-creoles-louisiana
Vargas-Willis, G., & Cervantes, R. C. (1987). Consideration of psychosocial stress in the treatment of the Latina immigrant. *Hispanic Journal of Behavioral Sciences, 9*, 315–329.
Vontress, C. (1970). Counseling Black. *Personnel and Guidance Journal, 48*, 713–719.
Washington, R. (1990). Brown racism and the formation of a world system of racial stratification. *International Journal of Politics, Culture, and Society, 4*(2), 209–227.

11
BROWN RACISM AS PRE-COLORISM

The genesis of Western racism begins with the speculated origins of mankind and is purely a matter of conjecture. As recorded in numerous history texts, human origin in terms of the earth's existence began quite recently considering the earth's longevity. The first appearance of homo-sapiens was in fact as determined by scientists to have taken place on the continent of Africa. Although the entirety of the continent is now inhabited, it is in the Southern region of Africa that is thought to be the birthplace of human beings (Rogers, 1967). According to Charles Darwin, human being as intelligent organism represents the final link in a succession of primates who would eventually come to dominate the earth. Whether one is inclined to accept this notion of human origin is a matter of intellectual preference. However, few if any scholars or scientists alike will take exception to Africa as the birthplace of humanity. Therefore, every human being alive today, French, English, Chinese, Puerto Rican, Japanese, Native-American, Latinx, etc., is at some point on the scale of human evolution the biological descendants of Africans! Ironically it is to the most despised by skin color that they owe their very existence.

Life in the south of Africa proved to be the perfect incubator in which the human organism could thrive and develop. The air was conducive being fresh and clean. The water was equally conducive being pure and plentiful. Abundant sources of available game and plant life allowed for nourishment almost without effort. Additionally, the climate in all of Africa was so favorable to human evolution that it was not an obstacle to be reckoned with in the sustenance of life. These nourishing factors no doubt arguably impacted the psychological pre-dispositions of early mankind. For thousands and thousands of years, the newly evolved species existed in relative isolation brought by the geographical distance between groups. Variations in phenotype was then of much less consequence. Therefore, at least in Africa skin color was synonymous with dark (Rogers, 1967). Thus, any distinguishable characteristics among the original human beings in Africa were likely

DOI: 10.4324/9781003302889-13

based on some factor other than skin color making skin color less of a vehicle for antagonism. A conducive climate, the availability of food and other nourishing elements for thousands of years fostered within early man a sense of vitality which facilitated a propensity toward survival.

The ability of early Africans to satisfy basic physiological needs with relative ease provided for the eventuality of fulfilling higher needs. According to Maslow, such needs included the fulfillment of "self-actualization" which suggests maximum evolution of the human species (Rogers, 1967). Thus, humans in Africa per ecological perspective not having been threatened by their environment were predisposed to group harmony versus the need to impose environmental control. This environmental theory accommodated a social system less aggressive despite strong territorial instincts that conflict with civil ideals (Windsor, 1988).

Until recently the ecological perspective of Western civilization was given little if any recognition as a critical factor in the psychological predisposition of various human groups. Perhaps disinterest on the part of behavioral scientists allowed such information to remain dormant while being obsessed with the "survival of the fittest" prescripts like those of Charles Darwin. Fortunately, a number of social science authors began to move beyond Darwinism. They acted to analyze the environment per ecological perspective as a means of comprehending the genesis of modern-day racism per colorism. Simply put, the ecological theory of racism is that its origins are attributed to experiences with a hostile environment. Survival of human populations situated in a hostile environment required their exercising control for the provision of food, shelter, and other necessary resources for sustaining life. When encountering others external to the group, the same need for control precipitated immediate violence and aggression. Whether this scenario resulted in the concept of a superior or inferior being remains a matter of considerable debate (Bradley, 1978). However, the defining difference between a conducive and a hostile environment for human beings is not only physiological in nature but psychological. That difference facilitated a mindset fertile to the evolution of Western racism. The premises that the environment can be a powerful force in the behavior of mankind is perhaps a new way of thinking, but it looms scientifically verifiable nonetheless (Welsing, 1970).

Just as hostile environments proved fertile ground for the perpetuation of racism, the conducive environment eventually proved fertile ground for the victimization of those granted the fortunes of a conducive experience. The calm and relative ease with which groups were able to sustain themselves in a conducive nurturing environment encouraged peace but also docility. The business of satisfying higher needs for some encouraged intellectual discourse as ancient history would suggest. Thus, at one point in time Africa was the center of civilization and all learning in the world (Rogers, 1967). African universities had been internationally renowned for their scholarship. Intellectuals from around the globe would meet on the African continent to rendezvous with knowledge and civil ideas. In fact, Africa was indeed an area of the world devoted solely to the development of knowledge and intellectual discourse.

By the eventual decline of Africa as a center of knowledge and civilization the differences between the so-called races had been exaggerated. The idea put fourth, by those who advocated the race concept was that three racial groups comprised a difference in humankind and not human variation. In actuality, "race refers to a differential concentration of gene frequencies responsible for traits which, so far as is known, are confined to physical manifestations such as skin color or hair form" (Rogers, 1967). Hence by these criteria there may be as much or as little physiological differences between the various race groups as there is within them. While there exists no hard scientific evidence as pertains to physiological differences being brought about by regional location such conjecture is an equally valid theoretical perspective compared to other theories. Succinctly put, if it is true that the original skin color of man being African was dark and that there is no genetic difference between the so-called races of man then any differences that do exist can arguably be attributed to differences extended from geographical region (Bradley, 1978).

According to legitimate research, some among anthropologists contend that there exist three contrived races of mankind which include the Caucasoid, the Mongoloid and the Negroid. The Caucasoid as pertains to dimensions of race is found to be indigenous to Europe, North Africa, the Middle East, and Northern India. Considering the dimensions of physical stature, Caucasoids are medium to tall and have long to broad head shapes. What's more, where Caucasoid hair is concerned, color ranges from the lightest pastel blond to a darker brown. In addition to this Caucasoid hair texture may range from straight strands to wavy strands upon observation. In other features such as Caucasoid eye color is a range from light blue to dark brown that is accentuated by a high-bridged nose shape. Most significantly as pertains to racism, Caucasoid skin color is a dramatic contrast that ranges from a pale reddish white to an olive brown. In comparison to other so-called races, the Caucasoid race is then by observation dramatically distinguishable by light skin. Consequently, given to the aforementioned physiology, the Caucasoid racial category represents a potent opportunity for purposes of racism (Peregrine, Ember, & Ember, 2003).

Next to Caucasoid, Mongoloids are a distinct racial category. Mongoloids include reference to populations known to be native to East Asia, South America, and North America. Their skin color is somewhat similar to that of Caucasoids being in approximation to Caucasian light. Therefore, upon visual observation, Mongoloid skin color can be described by viewers as saffron to yellow or reddish brown. Their physical stature may be determined when carefully measured as medium height and their head shape as broad. In hair texture, Mongoloids range from strands that are straight to strands that are course and consistently dark in color. Such strands sparsely cover the entire body. Mongoloid eye color upon observation is also more likely to be dark. Perhaps, the most salient feature among certain Mongoloid groups is their distinct eye-fold and nose shape that has a low to medium bridge. While they are somewhat similar to Caucasoids in having light skin, the typical Mongoloid membership are actually darker in complexion (Lynn, 2000).

By observation, compared to the Caucasoid and Mongoloid race categories, the Negroid is darkest in skin color. Their appearance may overlap with some among modern-day Mongoloids such as the ethnic group Latinx. Otherwise, the unadulterated Negroid group member being darkest in complexion will have a long head shape. In their measure of stature, the Negroid may also vary from Caucasoid to Mongoloid in height characterized by a dark color and usually kinky hair texture. The unadulterated Negroid eye color is also dark by observation and their nose shape a consistently low bridge with wide nostrils. Geographically, Negroid populations are known to be native to Africa, Indonesia, and New Guinea (Wilson, 2016). Distinguished by their dark skin, and facial features Negroid is the most visible race category in contrast to the typical Caucasoid and Mongoloid populations. Attributed to these race-based characteristics of the aforementioned racial groups, skin color is perceived as the most salient and dramatic feature conducive to racism. Therefore, considering those who advocate the legitimacy of race, skin color has evolved as a status hierarchy implied by the various race categories (Maxwell, Brevard, Abrams, & Belgrave, 2015).

Status hierarchy in reference to race allowed for the classification of humanity into distinct biological divisions that began during the Enlightenment period. Race categories were advocated in a scientific context which conveyed legitimacy to the lay public. Some among the most respected of scholars contributed reams of documentation to accrue the validation of race. Among initial proponents and the first universal classification was contributed by a Swedish naturalist named Carolus Linneaus (1707–1778). In his groundbreaking published work *Systema Natura (1758)*, Linneaus classified mankind into four distinct races. They included American, European, Asiatic, and African. Each category in addition to physical characteristics Linneaus contends were distinct by emotional and behavioral criteria. Similarly, Johann Blumenbach (1752–1840), credited as being the founder of the field of physical anthropology, divided humanity into five race categories. They consist of Caucasian, Mongolian, Malayan, Ethiopian, and American. He is also given credit in his scientific field for coining the term Caucasian which he used in his doctoral dissertation. The title of that dissertation is *On the Natural Varieties of Mankind (1755)*. Of particular note when reading *On the Natural Varieties of Mankind* is that each of Blumenbach's races includes peoples who were recently colonized by European forces. In response, the author contends that the purpose of his categorical system of human classification is then to identify those subjected to European colonization.

Of considerable concern is that while a hierarchy of behavior is implicit in the work of Linneaus and Blumenbach neither scholar focused their efforts on human behavior. Fortunately, Samuel Morton (1799–1851), a Philadelphia physician, was credited with being the first scholar to explicitly link the race construct with behavior and additionally intelligence. To validate his contention, Morton collected and then measured the skulls of American Indians. In his published scientific research titled *Crania Americana* (1839) he suggests that not only were American Indians qualified to be a separate race category but that their behavioral differences compared to white Americans was grounded in the physical structures of their brains. Expanding his study, Morton additionally examined the skulls of ancient Egyptians. That published work was titled *Crania Aegyptiaca* (1844). In this investigation Morton concluded that the so-called racial differences he investigated appeared to be ancient and unchanging.

Morton's work in the context of science eventually became critical for establishing the assumed inferiority of American Indians and dark-skinned Africans. Thus, given his status, Morton influenced a generation of white scholars who would proceed him. Evidence of this influence was provided by Josiah Nott and George Glidden. They contend that "[i]t is the primitive organization of races, their mental instincts, which determine their characteristics and destinies, and not blind hazard. All history, as well as anatomy and physiology, prove this" (Nott, 1854, p. 460). From their perspective as legitimate scientists, it is apparent that anatomical differences are the rationale as to why some peoples are the victims of conquest as are those subjected to colonization, and others the victors as are those who impose colonization.

The content essence of earlier works has been sustained over time. Among modern-day advocates of the race concept include the Canadian Philippe Rushton. Rushton contends in his book *Race, Evolution, and Behavior* (1995) that humanity may be divided into three distinct races that he labels Mongoloid, Caucasoid, and Negroid. Each group according to Rushton maintains a reproductive strategy that upon investigation is commensurate with the unique environmental conditions by which it is influenced. He purposely avoids the ecological perspective per racism in his racial discourse. Under the pretense of rigorous analysis Rushton's work appears to be no less erroneous as per the evolutionary theory and the data methodology he applies. Despite the fact of methodological challenges, Rushton maintains a significant following and is widely published in academic journals. The popularity of Rushton's questionable work is evidence of Western civilization having been consumed in the modern era by the race ideology. Said ideology facilitates the longevity of transgression and the universal validation of white supremacy in the perpetuation of Western racism (Encyclopedia.com, 2019).

White supremacy as suggested by Banton, refers to the assumed rights of a dominant race group to find means to exclude a dominated race group from sharing in the material and symbolic rewards of status and power (Kitano, 1985). This concept differs from ethnocentricity in that one's superiority is based on the heretofore reference to race category (Wilson, 1992). Ethnocentricity is an aspect of normality and may contribute to self-esteem associated with group membership. The racial category of the dominant elements when expressed as an exaggeration of ethnocentricity is then corrupted via white supremacy. In Western standards of white supremacy however unspoken is then assumed a natural order of the human biological universe (Minor & McGauley, 1988). The most zealous advocates of white supremacy contend that Caucasians are superior to non-Caucasian race groups, i.e., black and other people of color (Welsing, 1970). They postulate that Caucasians have been endowed with the intellectual capacities necessary to bring about the advancement of mankind and hence the advancement of civilization. The so-called "advancing of civilization" was initially a thinly veiled version of colonization committed to rationalizing the right of Caucasians to undertake a worldwide mission aimed at the exploitation of non-Caucasians (Daly, Jennings, Beckett, & Leashore, 1995). Given to white supremacy Caucasian race groups left no terrain or societal institution untouched by supremacist views. Following centuries of what McIntosh (1989) refers to as "white privilege" white supremacy prevails in political discourse as a natural explanation of consequences (Hyde, 1995).

In the opinion of celebrated social scientist William Julius Wilson (1980), author of *The Declining Significance of Race*, while race exists as a social fact its importance in the dynamics of society is obviously on the decline. Similar to the crude conceptions of earlier scientists, Wilson is limited by intellectual challenges that impede his perception of a skin color reality. Much to the contrary, white supremacy remains a potent force in political discourse perpetuated by suspicious political operatives. Considering these operatives white supremacy has been institutionalized by stealth efforts on the part of advocates to sustain the preferred white supremacist race status quo. Their preference not obvious in intellectual discourse is to sustain white supremacy as a customary tradition. Thus, in the history of white supremacy current era operatives will be no less inclined to black subjugation than their antebellum predecessors (Blee, 1991). Their illusions in antiracist rhetoric and equal opportunity are little more than a convenient façade. Therefore, in law, in rhetoric and in social activism, political discourse remains an extension of white supremacy. White supremacy in all forms will then ensure that white racism prevails and is thus ultimately sustained in non-white racism.

Non-White Racism

Assisted by the racial rhetoric of intellectually challenged social scientists, white racism in America has managed to sustain itself as arguably the most malignant and tenacious of unnecessary social problems (Banton, 1992). By social impacts, it is frequently regarded as an extension of white supremacy. In the Western world including the US racism is also a dynamic of the assimilation process. Scholars of the social sciences study in great detail the implications of white racism resulting in various forms of discrimination against "inferior" race people of color. They trace the origins of drug addiction, hypertension, stress, family disjointure, and other societal ills to its continued existence (Boyle, 1970). Fresh theoretical perspectives and civil alternatives have not been forthcoming. Perhaps an attempt to add insight can be gleaned by ignoring for the moment, the white supremacy model and addressing the role played by non-white immigration in sustaining the existence of white racism by which they are victimized.

As a result of mass migrations from Europe and other locations West, most Americans have been of European descent, i.e., "white" (Hyde, 1995). In an increasingly heterogeneous society in both the United States and Europe their most salient feature as previously suggested is light skin. Having migrated to the United States in largest numbers enabled a white supremacist white power structure. This white power structure generated what evolved as an accepted traditional ideal (Clark & Clark, 1980). On the basis of that ideal a false racial dichotomy was postulated which prevailed as the genesis of symbolic and/or covert white racism (Disch & Schwartz, 1970). In the aftermath light skin, without exception was standardized as the Western ideal (Arce, Murgia, & Frisbie, 1987). That ideal has remained unchallenged due in part to white power and the racist implications it implies about miscegenation (Edwards, 1973). This ideal is a dramatic remnant of the American antebellum (Garcia & Swenson, 1992). Early on, the antebellum light-skinned offspring of the plantation class were granted a privileged status (Hall, 1992). Black beauty, black wealth, and overall black attractiveness were associated with black physiological proximity to the white power structure attributed to light skin.

White racism as a dynamic of Western civilization whether overt or covert has been a concern of conscientious activists throughout the history of its existence (Hacker, 1992). Activist members, both black and white, red and yellow as well as brown, dominated the leadership of the Civil Rights Movement. Theirs was an effort generated in the traditions of the earlier Suffrage and Settlement House movements that took place in England and Chicago (Shapiro, 1978). However, recent manifestations of white racism by non-whites have begun to surface as an issue requiring further activism and investigation (Stoddard, 1973). Although its existence was not previously allowed into public discourse, existence of non-white participation was not previously unknown (Russell, Wilson, & Hall, 1992). This version of racism and white supremacy by non-whites is a direct result of European conquest, colonization or other forms of domination. In an effort to assimilate for quality-of-life reasons, non-white ethnic groups internalized a white racist skin color hierarchy. Under the circumstances the uppermost in status became those whose skin color most approximated that of the dominant race power structure (Mirande & Enriquez, 1976). This arrangement eventually fostered a tradition whereby those, regardless of race, whose dark skin was an extreme opposite of the ideal were relegated to become the focus of discrimination (Welsing, 1970). Dark skin was used to deny their rights and privileges (Cheung, 1989). That denial is also the basis of a system that was not only alien prior to colonization and slavery but in many ways sustaining of white racism. For a population as diverse and heterogeneous as that in the West, the ethnic terrain made fertile grounds for coming generations. Efforts on their part to assimilate were in affect pathological and a conducive element of white racism. The end result of this white racism perpetuated in part by non-white operatives is a non-white version of racism referred to as brown racism.

Brown Racism

Perhaps the most dramatic demonstration of white racism perpetuated via skin color among people of color is referred to as "brown racism." According to Washington (1990), "brown racism" involves people of color and their racist attitudes toward darker-skinned persons of African descent. Washington prefers the term "brown" to emphasize racism distinct from the black/white dichotomy. Subsequently it may be acted out by populations that include Mestizos (mixed race), Chinese, Filipinos, and South Asians among others. It is considered a variation of white racism that probably occurred as a result of European imperialism, colonization or otherwise white domination. This non-white version of racism is quite obvious and recently reflected in violent confrontations.

"In Shanghai, during the same period, several African students were surrounded by "thousands" of Chinese on the Textile University campus in what one student called a "terrifying night" of stoning and abuse. Several years later in May 1986 at Tianjin University, a skirmish between African and Chinese students occurred. It was a five hour long rock and bottle throwing brawl between 300 and 500 Chinese students and approximately 18 foreign (mostly African) students" (Washington, 1990).

Such violent events as the aforementioned are not exclusive to Chinese but unfortunately pertain to any and all known non-white people of color otherwise conquered or dominated by Western power structures. Said domination is suggested in the following:

> In India, in addition to the widespread prejudices exhibited against dark skinned Indians, there have been many reports of discrimination against African students, who often find themselves socially ostracized and treated as a pariah group. In Eastern and Southern Africa, where there exist large Indian communities, dating back to the early years of British colonialism, Indians typically avoid fraternization with Africans, whom they view as racially inferior. In Puerto Rico, in Mexico, in the Philippines, in Korea and in Saudi Arabia-indeed throughout the brown societies of the third world- the majority populations evidence an aversion to people with dark skin. Similarly, in the United States, in England, in Canada, in France and in other Western countries where brown and black groups from the third world live as minorities, brown communities avoid association with blacks.
>
> *(Washington, 1990)*

Perhaps the most dramatic expression of brown racism is when Africans direct the same brown racism disdain against Africans as occurred in Egypt.

> Several years ago, in Egypt, for instance, a scheduled telecast of an American movie dramatization of Anwar Sadat's life was cancelled because a public outcry arose when it was learned that the slain Egyptian leader would be portrayed by a black American actor.
>
> *(Washington, 1990)*

Essentially the ideal of Egyptian leadership could only be portrayed by a white American as dictated by racism and white supremacy.

Critics of the brown racism phenomenon as an extension of white racism contend that people of color cannot exhibit racism nor that skin color any longer exists as an issue of disdain (Holtzman, 1973). Most are either uninformed or perhaps harbor some personal or familial agenda that limits their perception of social reality (Atkins, 1992). The fact that brown racism presents a significant issue is now a matter of judicial record. In litigation the first case involving black Americans was brought by Morrow vs the IRS (1990). Tracey Morrow, the plaintiff, alleged that her supervisor commenced to discriminate against her due to the implications of her light complexion (Hiskey, 1990). The plaintiff being light-skinned was attributed to the skin color of the defendant, who by comparison was dark. Although the light-skinned plaintiff did not prevail, the court determined that indeed civil litigation on the basis of skin color was actionable.

According to the findings of DuBois, the American Dilemma is the dilemma and no doubt an extension of the color line (Yellin, 1973). That assertion is no less apparent and relevant some 60 years later today. However, as Stember (1976) suggests the issue of racism considering the various groups have never been resolved. What exists is merely construed as an inappropriate topic of assimilation not permissible for polite conversation. As Hall (1996) further notes the issue of transgression among people of color is even less amenable to public resolution. The denial of a victim role in transgression would hardly serve the efforts of same who seek resolution. Despite that the issue has been addressed to a limited extent by Ethnic Studies scholars, for the most part brown racism has been all but ignored by the legitimate mainstream of academic institutions (Codina & Montalvo, 1992). Unfortunately, in the outcome of denial, pathology is no less stressful and thus no less a reality. For example, in Nicaragua skin color has an influence upon the manner in which common Latinx folk once interacted. Mestizos who are considered the racially mixed majority refer to the darker-skinned Costenos who are persons of African descent in denigrated terms (Lancaster, 1991). In the Latinx country of Cuba skin color has been an issue of denigration historically despite the attempts of Castro's Revolution to eliminate it. In such a country, status is continually based on gradations of skin color and affects all aspects of Cuban life both covertly and overtly during social interactions (Canizares, 1990). In a nation dominated by people of color vehement forms of brown racism are carried out by those who migrate to the United States and other locations West. Hence, Chinese, Indians, Egyptians, Western immigrants, and Africans alike are driven by white domination manifested in colorism.

Colorism

At the heart of colorism is a significant measure of melanin in human skin (Stephen, Coetzee, & Perrett, 2011). As documented by Morison (1985), melanin pertains to the biological ingredient responsible for differentiating dark skin from light or Negroid from Caucasoid. Among Caucasoid populations, in general melanin content while existent is less pronounced in Caucasian light skin (Harrison & Buttner,

1999). Conversely, those of Negroid descent are characterized by a considerable concentration of melanin in their skin as well as throughout the body. Other locations include the eyes, the ears and the brain. At various points where melanin is concentrated such as in the dramatic location of Negroid skin consists of three varieties: neuromelanin, eumelanin, and pheomelanin. Neuromelanin is less relevant because it cannot be visually observed. It is found only in the human brain where its functions are not clearly understood. On the other hand, there exists general agreement as to eumelanin and pheomelanin pertaining to the thermoregulation functions of dark skin (Morison, 1985).

Scientifically melanin as operative of skin color aside from colorism is quite effective in the regulation of body heat. This ability allowed dark-skinned populations throughout ancient Africa and other humid areas an advantage of protection from harmful UV rays. Scientists who study melanin have recently suggested that dark skin per melanin content will also provide supplementary energy (solar heat) that can also facilitate thermoregulation in the human body. Melanin content furthermore functions as a means of replacing body hair indicative of lower primates. In the absence of body hair, early man as an African was still no less given to the maintenance of a core temperature documented as thermoregulation (Ibraimov, 2012).

Unfortunately, the early members of humanity while having access to an abundance of food did not consistently have access to food sources that meet energy demands, including those for thermoregulation. Therefore, early man compensated for this energy deficiency by reference to the use of solar radiation. While such energy is presumed by scientists to enter the body via human skin, it did not serve a practical purpose in manual work performance. What's more, it is not known to have a function in cellular metabolism. Considering this, solar energy, simultaneous to the heating of blood found in the skin was a useful tool in the conduct of thermoregulation. Such use was ultimately a critical advantage. The presence of melanin then allowed mankind to sustain maximum physiological health (Ibraimov, 2012). Unfortunately, in the racism and white supremacy what initially prevailed as a physiological advantage had been reduced to a trait of inferiority. As a by-product of the Western academy colorism emerged.

Due to the limited attention paid by the social science academy the details of colorism have been attributed to black/Negroid populations exclusively. In fact, colorism spurred by Caucasoid participation is a social pathology relative to all non-white race populations. By succinct definition, colorism therefore pertains to an immoral transgression commensurate with racism and the ideology of white supremacy (Snell, 2017). Although colorism has existed over an extended, period of time, its absence from the mainstream literature gives the appearance that it is little more than a recent modern-day social phenomenon.

The term "colorism" was first introduced into documentation by the iconic Alice Walker. According to Walker, colorism was first mentioned in 1982 and then a year later in 1983 in *Essence* magazine (Webb, 2019). During both years, colorism was addressed by this icon as being similar to racism. As such it pertained to an immoral act that operates not on the non-scientific subjective basis of race, but on the more objective basis of melanin content in skin color. Therefore, by virtue of complexion attributed to the measure of melanin contained in human skin, denigration and accusations of inferiority may be directed at Negroid and all other dark-skinned non-white populations. What the members of said dark-skinned populations encounter consists of discriminatory behaviors acted out as a consequence of the light skin Caucasoid ideal. In the aftermath is colorism as increased levels of discrimination and denigration in proximity to Caucasoid light skin (Churchill, 2003). What's more according to Walker and others, unlike racism manifested across racial boundaries, colorism is manifested both across and within racial boundaries. Succinctly put, colorism may be acted out both intra-racially as in brown racism and inter-racially as in white racism hence the whole of humanity (Snell, 2017). However, most distinctly, colorism is not contingent solely upon biological attributes of racial heritage, but the mere observation of skin color. Subsequently, given to advocates of racial diversity and increased levels of racial miscegenation, which distorts distinct racial features, racism will prevail into the 21st century and perhaps beyond as colorism.

References

Arce, C., Murgia, E., & Frisbie, W. (1987). Phenotype and the life chances among Chicanos. *Hispanic Journal of Behavioral Sciences, 9*, 19–32.

Atkins, E. (1992, November 22). Skin color peels away Black on Black prejudice. *Detroit News and Free Press*, p. A1.

Banton, M. (1992). The nature and causes of racism and discrimination. *International Sociology, 7*(1), 69–84.

Blee, K. (1991). *Women of the Klan: White supremacy and gender in the 1920s*. Berkeley: University of California Press.

Boyle, E. (1970). Biological patterns in hypertension by race, sex, body weight, and skin color. *American Medical Association Journal, 213*, 1637–1643.

Bradley, M. (1978). *The ice man inheritance*. Toronto: Dorset.

Canizares, R. (1990). Cuban racism and the myth of the racial paradise. *Ethnic Studies Report, 8*(2), 27–32.

Cheung, M. (1989). Elderly Chinese living in the United States: Assimilation or adjustment? *Social Work, 34*(5), 457–461.

Churchill, W. (2003). An American holocaust? The structure of denial. *Socialism and Democracy, 17*(1), 25.

Clark, K. & Clark, M. (1940). Skin color as a factor in racial identification of Negro preschool children. *Journal of Social Psychology, 11*, 159–169.

Clark, K., & Clark, M. (1980). What do Blacks think of themselves? Ebony 36, (V) Nov pp 176-82.

Codina, E., & Montalvo, F. (1992). *Chicano phenotype and depression*. San Antonio, TX: Our Lady of the Lakes University, Worden School of Social Services. Unpublished Manuscript.

Daly, A., Jennings, J., Beckett, J., & Leashore, B. (1995). Effective coping strategies of African Americans. *Social Work, 40*(2), 40–48.

Disch, R., & Schwartz, B. (1970). *White racism* (2nd ed.). New York: Dell.

Edwards, O. (1973). Skin color as a variable in racial attitudes of Black urbanites. *Journal of Black Studies, 3*(4), 473–483.

Encyclopedia.com. (2019). *Racial hierarchy: Disproven*. Retrieved November 14, 2021, from www.encyclopedia.com/social-sciences/encyclopedias-almanacs-transcripts-and-maps/racial-hierarchy-overview

Garcia, B., & Swenson, C. (1992). Writing the stories of white racism. *Journal of Teaching in Social Work, 6*(2), 3–17.

Hacker, A. (1992). *Two nations: Black and White, separate, hostile, unequal*. New York: Maxwell Macmillan International.

Hall, R. E. (1992). Bias among African Americans regarding skin color: Implications for social work practice. *Research on Social Work Practice, 2*(4), 479–486.

Hall, R. E. (1996). Impact of skin color upon occupational projection: A case for Black male affirmative action. *Journal of African American Men, 1*(4), 87–94.

Harrison, S., & Buttner, P. (1999). Do all fair-skinned Caucasians consider themselves fair? *Preventive Medicine: An International Journal Devoted to Practice and Theory, 29*(5), 349–354.

Hiskey, M. (1990, February 1). Boss: Skin hue, firing unrelated. *The Atlanta Journal-Constitution, 1*, 4.

Holtzman, J. (1973). Color caste changes among black college students. *Journal of Black Studies, 4*(1), 92–101.

Hyde, C. (1995). The meanings of whiteness. *Qualitative Sociology, 18*(1), 87–95.

Ibraimov, A. (2012). Evolution of human skin color and thermoregulation. *International Journal of Genetics, 4*(3), 111–115.

Kitano, H. (1985). *Race relations*. Englewood Cliffs, NJ: Prentice-Hall.

Lancaster, R. (1991). Skin color race and racism in Nicaragua. *Ethnology, 30*(4), 339–353.

Lynn, R. (2000). Race differences in sexual behavior and their demographic implications. *Population and Environment: A Journal of Interdisciplinary Studies, 24*(5), 73–81.

McIntosh, P. (1989, July–August). White privilege: Unpacking the invisible knapsack. *Peace and Freedom Magazine*, pp. 10–12, Women's International League for Peace and Freedom, Philadelphia, PA.

Maxwell, M., Brevard, J., Abrams, J., & Belgrave, F. (2015). What's color got to do with it? Skin color, skin color satisfaction, racial identity and internalized racism among African American college students. *Journal of Black Psychology, 41*(5), 438–461.

Minor, N., & McGauley, L. (1988). A different approach: Dialogue in education. *Journal of Teaching in Social Work, 2*(1), 127–140.

Mirande, A., & Enriquez, E. (1976, Fall). Chicanas: Their triple oppression as colonized women. *Sociological Symposium, 17*, 91–102.

Morison, W. (1985). What is the function of melanin? *Archives of Dermatology, 121*(9), 1160–1163.

Morrow vs the Internal Revenue Service, 742 F. Supp. 670 (N.D. Ga). (1990).

Nott, J. (1854). *Types of mankind*. Philadelphia, PA: Lippincott, Grambo & Co.

Peregrine, P., Ember, C., & Ember, M. (2003). Cross-cultural evaluation of predicted associations between race and behavior. *Evolution and Human Behavior, 24*(5), 357–364.

Rogers, J. (1967). *Sex and race*. St. Petersburg, FL: Rogers.

Rushton, J. (1995). *Race, Evolution and Behavior*. New Brunswick, N.J.: Transaction Publishers

Russell, K., Wilson, M., & Hall, R. E. (1992). *The color complex*. New York: Harcourt Brace Jovanovich.

Shapiro, E. (1978). Robert A Woods and the settlement house impulse. *Social Forces Review, 52*(2), 215–226.

Snell, J. (2017). Colorism/neo-colorism. *Education, 138*(2), 205–209.

Stember, C. (1976). *Sexual racism*. New York: Elsevier Scientific.

Stephen, I., Coetzee, V., & Perrett, D. (2011). Carotenoid and melanin pigment coloration affect perceived human health. *Evolution and Human Behavior, 32*(3), 216–227.

Stoddard, E. (1973). *Mexican Americans*. New York: Random House.

Washington, R. (1990). Brown racism and the formation of a world system of racial stratification. *International Journal of Politics, Culture, and Society, 4*(2), 209–227.

Webb, S. (2019). Everyday colorism: Reading in the language arts classroom. *English Journal, 108*(4), 21–28.

Welsing, F. (1970). *The Cress theory of color confrontation and racism*. Washington, DC: CR Publishers.

Wilson, M. (1992). What difference could a revolution make? Group work in the new Nicaragua. *Social Work with Groups, 15*(2–3), 301–314.

Wilson, P. (2016). *Eugenics*. Retrieved November 7, 2016, from www.britannica.com/science/eugenics-genetics

Wilson, W. (1978). *The declining significance of race: Blacks and changing American institutions*. Chicago: University of Chicago Press.

Wilson, W. J., (1980). The Declining Significance of Race. Chicago: University of Chicago Press.

Windsor, R. (1988). *From Babylon to Timbuktu*. Philadelphia: Windsor.

Yellin, J. (1973). Documentation: DuBois' crisis and women's suffrage. *Massachusetts Review, 14*(2), 365–375.

Future

12
COLORISM AS RACISM IN THE 21ST CENTURY

Prior to the 17th century, what is today America was little more than an isolated continent apart from the rest of the world. The few inhabitants known today as Native-Americans occupied the Gulf Coast, the Pacific Coast, and the later state of Alaska. There were those who occupied the interior but were scattered and less concentrated. By the 17th century, Europeans began to migrate to what came to be called the New World. Among those most represented in numbers coming to the New World were all white and/or Caucasian British, French, Irish, German, Scandinavian, Dutch, Russian, and Italians.

Among Europeans, the British were the largest group to immigrate to the New World prior to the American Revolution. They also settled in Upper Canada at a steady pace that continued following the Revolution. Many of these British immigrants followed Protestant Christian sects. They separated from the Roman Catholic church in a period that came to be known as the Reformation. History credits this group with starting what would become Boston, Providence, Hartford, Philadelphia, and Baltimore. By race the arrival of the British brought the arrival of Caucasians to the New World.

The French who immigrated to the New World settled in what is today known as Quebec. It was originally known as Lower Canada, and a part of Nova Scotia, first known as Acadia. Most of the French immigrants were dispersed elsewhere by the British. Some immigrated to the French owned islands of Miquelon and Saint-Pierre. By the 1800s, French immigrants left Canada for the United States due to economic hardships there. The French in Canada numbered approximately eight million citizens. Additionally following the Louisiana purchase there now exists a large French population in the state of Louisiana. They are located in cities such as New Orleans and Baton Rouge. Similar to the British, the French are Christian and Caucasian.

DOI: 10.4324/9781003302889-15

Joined with the Scotch, the Irish amounted to the largest European immigrant group coming to the New World from the 1790s following the American Revolution up to the 1810s. This was also in the time of the war of 1812 and the Napoleonic Wars. The Irish made up the largest number of European immigrants in the early 1800s who arrived seeking escape from famine at home. Most were practicing Roman Catholics whose arrival continued well into the 20th century. Approximately 1.5 million entered the New World by Canada. Those who chose the United States often settled in the Appalachian Mountains in such places as Kentucky, Tennessee, and southeast Ohio. They might arrive as indentured servants to work off debt. Others settled in the Southern states, including North and South Carolina. As were other Europeans, the Irish are Christians and by race Caucasian.

The migration of Germans to the New World is historical dating back to the colonial period. Their arrival was quite active throughout the early 1800s as they were second only to the Irish in numbers. In religion most tended to be Roman Catholic while not a few identified as Lutherans. By the American Civil War Germans prevailed as the largest immigrant population arriving in North America. Similar to the Irish many Germans immigrated to escape famine and a desire for freedom. They made their way to the Midwest attracted by the available farmland. By states Germans often settled in Kentucky, Indiana, and Illinois. Canada also welcomed Germans evident along the south shore of Nova Scotia, Southern Ontario, and at some point, later the Canadian prairie provinces. Germans too are Caucasian and Christian. The operative word for German as well as for all European immigration is "welcomed."

Scandinavian immigrants were fewer than their Irish and German counterparts. They were actively arriving to the New World during the early part of the 1800s. They are credited with helping to tame the prairie provinces of Canada—Alberta, Saskatchewan, and Manitoba—during the culmination of the 19th century. They also settled in Midwest area states such as Michigan, Wisconsin, Minnesota, North and South Dakota, and Montana. They often arrived for reasons of religious freedom sought by the General Baptist, Evangelical Covenant, and Evangelical Free. Originally these sects were the Norwegian-Danish Evangelical Free Church and the Swedish Evangelical Free Church which merged in 1950. They too by race are Caucasian and by religion Christian.

The Dutch arrived in the New World approximate to the English and French during the early 1600s. They are credited with founding the city of New York originally named by them as New Amsterdam. Following conclusion of the Napoleonic Wars, the Dutch immigrated to the New World in larger numbers although not quite equal to that of the Germans or Irish. In large numbers Scandinavians settled in locations such as Holland, Michigan, and South Holland, Illinois. Religion assumed a significant role in their circumstances. Most were Protestant Christians originally referred to as the Dutch Reformed Church that eventually became the Christian Reformed Church. They too by race are Caucasian and by religion Christian.

Arriving in the 1890s immigration from Eastern Europe included Russians. At the time there was a change in laws that allowed for more immigration to the United States and Canada. Previously most Europeans had immigrated from western Europe. Just as other Europeans, Russian immigrants came for reasons of freedom, and they were Christian Caucasians. Their numbers were slowed by the Great Depression. Following World War II saw a minimal increase in Russian immigrants that has recently decreased to very little.

Last but not least among European immigrants are Italians. From about 1890 to 1930 the United States saw a large number of immigrants arriving from Italy. Prior to a change in laws the United States and Canada saw few Italian immigrants coming to their shores. In the United States, large numbers of Italians settled in east coast cities such as New York and Philadelphia and in states such as New Jersey and eastern Pennsylvania. Italians are Caucasian and Christian (Wiseman, 2014). Subsequently, immigrants from Europe who were Christians and Caucasian were seeking citizenship in a nation that for the most part was Christian and Caucasian. In their manifestations of racism from whence colorism emerged were commissions of some of the most heinous crimes in US history characterized by lynching.

Among the most violent of racist murders in American history is the lynching murder of a black American child named Emmett Till. Till was a 14-year-old boy born in 1941. His home was located in a middle-class black community in Chicago. Till had made a trip South to visit family in Money, Mississippi, during 1955. At the time of his visit, Till stopped at a grocery store where he encountered a white clerk named Carolyn Bryant. She was a cashier who waited on Till who was to have made a sexual comment to her about which she complained. When her spouse found out he decided on murder. He and his half-brother decided to abduct Till and kill him on sight. Once they abducted him, they beat the child to the point where his face was no longer recognizable as human. Multiple shots had been fired into his head.

Eventually Till's murderers were arrested and tried for murder. They were found innocent by an all-white, all-male jury. Years later Carolyn Bryant, who made the accusation, admitted that she had lied (Biography, 2019). Such a tragic event was repeated before and after Till as a brutal tradition of white racism.

In the aftermath of World War II, immigrants arriving to the United States left from areas of the globe other than Europe. Many are neither Christians nor Caucasian. Their arrival is commensurate with a decrease in European immigration. These newly arrived immigrants benefit from legal changes that broaden opportunities for religious and racial groups otherwise excluded. They too like European immigrants seek religious freedom and a better quality of life. However, they are for the most part exotic in race and religion. Unfortunately, their commission of racist acts would prove no less violent than that of European immigrants before them. In fact, many are dark-skinned which contrasts with Caucasian light skin. Their experiences unlike that of Caucasian Europeans was not one of "welcome" but tolerance at best and hostility at worst from the American public (Wiseman, 2014).

Modern-day America remains a destination of immigrants seeking freedom and access to a better quality of life. In locations such as Los Angeles in 1990 saw an increase of nearly one-million residents and in the metropolitan New York 400,000, and Chicago nearly 360,000. These increases were due largely to the births of recent immigrants. The majority of the nation's fastest-growing cities where they live are located in the West and Southwest. There too city growth is a function of immigration. Unlike earlier European immigration of light-skinned immigrants from Europe dark-skinned immigrants from third-world nations posed unique challenges that the country has yet confronted. They are more than half of the residents of New York City who are immigrants or children of immigrants. Among the most formidable obstacles they face pertains to some manner of race.

Population experts' projection is that the proportion of immigrant Americans who by miscegenation are biracial will consistently rise. In some areas that rise may be dramatic. Therefore, by 2030 it is projected that white Americans will compose a much smaller sector of the nation as a whole. That sector will be smaller in both proportion as well as absolute numbers. The Latinx population will see a projected 100%increase from 24 million in 1990 to 60 million by 2030. Black Americans currently just over 13%of the population, will increase but at a much slower pace. The Asian population will see similar increases in that it too will also increase by 100%.

The increase of non-white populations will be dramatic in select states. By 2030 it is projected that the state of Florida will see an increase of 100%. At that time white Americans now seven times as numerous as both black and Latinx-Americans will decrease to merely three or four times as large. Further West in California of 30 million residents, 56%are white, 26% Latinx, 10% Asian, and 7% are black. By 2020, where California's population is expected to increase by 20 million, half of them will be newly arrived immigrants. By then no more than 35% of its residents are projected to be white. Another 40% are projected to be Latinx, 17% are projected to be Asian, and 8% are projected to be black (Hochschild, 1998). These projections manifest in what some authors refer to as the "browning of America" (Frey, 2015). Although the author Frey who coined the term does not directly define the browning reference, his work pertains to the dramatic increase in the non-white population, i.e., Mongoloid and Negroid juxtaposed with a dramatic decline in white Americans, i.e., Caucasoid. Given the increase of non-whites and their active miscegenation, biracial births will similarly increase making racial identifications less discernable. The fact that racism per se will become non-existent and race less discernable will morph into colorism as a manifestation of racism in the 21st century spurred by inter-racial marriages.

Most marriages currently are intra-racial and will remain so into the foreseeable future. However, rates of inter-racial marriages vary significantly by group. Statistically, 93% of white and black Americans marry intra-racially. Additionally, only 70% of Latinx- and 70% of Asian-Americans marry intra-racially as do 33% of Native-Americans (Moran, 2001, p. 103). As a matter of statistical fact "Latinos" as Cubans, Mexicans, Central Americans, and South Americans evidence higher rates of inter-racial marriage than Puerto Ricans and Dominicans (Gilbertson,

Fitzpatrick, & Yang, 1996). As pertains to Asian inter-racial marriage is a complexity brought by the definition of Asian. Considering Asians such as Filipinos and Vietnamese inter-racial marriage is higher in part due to the Vietnam War and the military bases located in the Philippines such as Subic Bay. Despite being notorious for endogamy, the highest rate of inter-racial marriages belongs to the Japanese and Chinese-American. They marry white partners almost exclusively (Kitano & Daniels, 1995). Said marriages are consistently white male to Asian female. The lowest rate of Asian inter-racial marriage pertains to Southeast Asians. As pertains to colorism, in this Asian case "whitening" is more likely for offspring of Asian-white and Latinx-white couplings than for those of black—white couplings. Black heritage results in dark skin and by virtue of the "one-drop theory" dominant genes. It is also a master status due to societal stigma. Subsequently, given to the fact that only 22% of the black fathers' and white mothers' offspring are classified as white, the children of the same couplings among Asians are twice as likely to be classified as white. This ultimately by skin color enables colorism (Waters, 1999). The same scenario for Latinx-Americans is even more dramatic as those of Cuban, Mexican, and South American descent have high rates of inter-racial marriage compared to Puerto Ricans and Dominicans (Gilbertson et al., 1996). This may be due to colorism according to Moran (2001) in that Puerto Ricans and Dominicans may be closer to an African heritage which causes them to have darker skin. Distinct from their non-white counterparts who by having lighter skin are afforded access to a status known as "honorary whites" (Bonilla-Silva, 1997).

The original term of "honorary whites" is derived from South Africa's apartheid regime. Those so designated were offered an opportunity to assume almost all of the rights and privileges normally attributed to whites, i.e., Caucasians if they were the member of a favored non-white group. Designees included the Japanese in the 1960s. They were given favor to assist a trade pact negotiated between South Africa and Japan. It involved Tokyo's Yawata Iron & Steel Co. which agreed to buy 5,000,000 tons of South African pig iron. Such purchase was worth more than $250,000,000 over a span of ten years. Given the potential for such a huge profit, the South African Prime Minister determined profit was more important and thus decided not to subject the Japanese people to the same restrictions as other non-white peoples. In the aftermath, Pretoria's Group Areas Board made an official announcement that all Japanese people were to be considered white for reasons of residence. What's more Johannesburg's city officials "in view of the trade agreements" declared all municipal swimming pools open to all Japanese visitors. This made the Japanese almost equal to white South Africans except for the right to vote or serve in the military. In a country that today has a tradition of colorism being designated as "honorary whites" the Japanese were popularly welcomed.

In South Africa there lived a small Chinese community of about 7,000 residents at the time of the Japanese "honorary whites." They were disappointed that an Asian population that had once invaded China (Chang, 2011) would be elevated above them as white. In a statement of colorism one Chinese observer noted: "If anything, we are whiter in appearance than our Japanese friends." He was a Chinese businessman that now questioned that if Japanese are considered white would his interactions break the law's Immorality Act?'"

To circumvent discrimination Chinese people wanting to claim honorary white frequently passed for Japanese. In this way they could enter swimming pools as proclaimed by the chairman of the city council's Health and Amenities Committee. Said official reported that "[i]t would be extremely difficult for our gatekeepers to distinguish between Chinese and Japanese." Thus in 1984, the South African Chinese community became officially honorary whites. This meant that they were to be treated the same as South African whites as pertains to the Group Areas Act. Following the Japanese and Chinese came other non-white Asians to claim the status of honorary whites. They included East Asians, South Koreans, and the people of Taiwan. Ironically not a few black Western entertainers were reported to have gained an honorary white status for entertainment visits (Honorary Whites, N.D.). In the extreme of honorary white that included a few blacks, was a new brown version of white racism carried out by non-whites no less brutal and violent. It is called colorism as expressed in the primary, secondary and tertiary manifestations.

Colorism Racism

Primary colorism, as implied by Banton (1992), refers to the efforts of a lighter-skinned group to exclude a darker-skinned group from sharing in the material and symbolic rewards of status and power. Primary colorism differs from various other forms of colorism by its idealization of light skin exclusively contingent upon observable race related traits (Wilson, 1992). Said traits such as light skin imply the inherent superiority of brown race groups who are then rationalized as a natural order associated with whites of the human biological universe (Minor & McGauley, 1988).

The most zealous proponents of primary colorism profess that lighter-skinned brown groups are superior to darker-skinned black groups as a matter of social and scientific fact (Welsing, 1970). They postulate that they much as Caucasian have been endowed with capacities necessary to make evident their superiority. So-called superiority is a thinly veiled submission to white otherwise Caucasian domination. This domination culturally justified their colorism devoted to rationalizing the right of light-skinned brown groups to subjugate all criteria associated with Africa (Daly, Jennings, & Leashore, 1995). By way of white domination and white ideals brown people of color left no terrain of the non-white third world untouched. After centuries of white domination, the mission to rescue brown heritage from the feared denigration associated with black via dark skin has necessitated a universal, almost mystic belief in the power of skin color to elevate or taint (Hyde, 1995). Subsequently colorism was sustained as an operative force in justification of white supremacy and by association brown superiority.

Primary colorism pertains to macro interactions on a light-skinned versus dark-skinned group level. Secondary colorism pertains to micro interactions on a light-skinned versus dark-skinned personal level. Secondary colorism is a social product of brown individuals in the aftermath of slavery and colonization (Stampp, 1956; Canizares, 1990). It differs from primary colorism in that perpetuation is sustained by a light-skinned operative individual who casts insults of inferiority at a dark-skinned subject despite lack of justification. Their thoughtless insults enable white supremacy and their own demise. Thus, similar to primary colorism directed by light-skinned brown populations at dark-skinned populations, secondary colorism is directed by light-skinned individuals from light-skinned populations at darker-skinned individuals from dark-skinned populations which imposes upon their personal interactions. Subsequently, personal contacts between blacks and whites and whites and browns are more numerous. Personal contacts between blacks and browns are all but non-existent. This minimal contact may occur despite a lack of evidence suggesting any historical confrontations between the two dramatically suggested by marital patterns, i.e., eurogamy (Hall, 2003).

As pertains to brown colorism is eurogamy by Asian prospective brides. Eurogamy is the tendency to exclusive Caucasian partnerships as a form of hypergamy. As a brown group notorious for endogamy Asian women pursue fantasies of a white husband as their ideal mate. In fact, not a few white males fetishize Asian women for purposes of sexual exploitation. Therefore, in a given year any number of Asian hopefuls post their photos with mail order magazines. Among the most prominent and successful is *Sunshine Girls*. In acting out secondary colorism via eurogamy brown women are exposed to transgressions which the mainstream marriage and family academy has ignored as it does not fit the white supremacy narrative.

In search of the facts, Hall (2001) requested random samples of the *Sunshine Girls* magazine for years 1991–2000 (one issue for each year). The number of women who participated were an approximate total of 620 girls. They ranged in ages from 18 to 30 years. The racial and ethnic categories included Japanese, Chinese, Korean, Indonesian, Malaysian, and "other" to accommodate the application of an occasional non-brown Russian. Most of the selected women adhered to racial taboos in their requirements. However, of those most intense about race ignoring the implications of racism approximately 96% requested Caucasian and/or white men, only 2% requested Asian men and another 2% requested Latinx men. The brown individuals who selected Caucasian men most often were by far the Chinese at 30%, the Japanese at 27%, and the Koreans at 14%. If male purchasers of the magazine were black, they were advised to inform the women in correspondence ahead of time and treat their being black as a handicap. This dramatic demonstration of colorism concurs with such individuals having been dominated by white power structures whereby they adhere to human ranking via skin color (Hall, 2001). Other brown individuals at the micro level such as Indonesian and Malaysian requested Caucasian men as well (12%). Ironically some may be much darker than the aforementioned Northern Asians. This subtle but pronounced evidence of colorism is reflected in the works of Washington (1990) who first constructed the concept of brown racism. He contends:

> (1) that brown racism exists not as isolated episodes of prejudice but as an integral part of a white-oriented global system of racial stratification which emerged during the post-colonial phase of Western imperialism; (2) that brown racism differs from the ethnocentric color prejudice-defined as antipathy towards persons whose color and physical features differ from those of one's own group-found among traditional societies with a history of isolation from the outside world; (3) that, in contrast, brown racism is distinguished by antipathy toward blacks and attraction toward whites and by ideological beliefs about the innate inferiority of Africans; (4) that brown racism has been manifested in two historical forms-a minor colonial form which operated in geographically localized systems of racial stratification and a major neocolonial form operating in a global system of racial stratification. The latter emerged with the demise of colonialism, as overt ideological expressions of white racism underlying Western imperialism were obliged to assume a more covert form through processes of cultural hegemony; (5) that brown racism has the consequences of affirming the principle of white racial superiority, supporting structures of white domination and weakening the solidarity of third world peoples of color in their struggle against Western domination; (6) and that, finally, because they are interdependent, the problem of white racism cannot be solved without finding a solution to the concomitant problem of brown racism.
>
> *(Washington, 1990)*

Unfortunately, brown racism via colorism has not been resolved but persists in reference to attitudes toward black Americans that ended in an Atlanta, Georgia Emmit Till-like murder.

In 2006, two journalists at the Atlanta Journal-Constitution named Beth Warren and Jeffery Scott reported on the brutal murder of a black American woman named Sparkle Reid-Rai (Warren & Scott, 2006). Her original name before marriage was Sparkle Reid. Her Asian husband had confided to her that his parents had died by the time they were to be married. The husband's motivation for telling an untruth was attributed to the fact that colorism may have caused parental refusal in that Sparkle Reid was black. The parents wanting to prevent the marriage had gone so far as to offer Sparkle Reid $10,000 to break up with their son. When Sparkle Reid refused the money the elder patriarch Chiman Rai, acted to have his daughter-in-law at the time murdered.

Sparkle Reid-Rai had not known that her Asian fiancé's parents were alive and well on the day that the couple was to be married in Atlanta's Fulton County. When word of the marriage reached the 67-year-old patriarch he was deeply distressed. The Atlanta police contend that he prepared a plot to have her murdered. In carrying out the plan the elder Rai sought and obtained the services of a contract killer. After being paid, the killers arrived at the Rai's home in Union City, Georgia under the pretense of delivering a package. When the 22-year-old black bride opened her door, a 300-pound ex-convict who had been hired by the elder Rai attacked her with a knife. When the attack was over Sparkle Reid-Rai lay dead. She suffered from a brutal assault being stabbed at least 13 times in the back, neck, chest and ribs. To ensure that she was dead her attacker then strangled her and slit her throat. The Asian husband discovered the body after returning home from work according to police detectives. Fortunately, the couple's 7-month-old daughter who was situated in the room next to where the murder took place had not been harmed. Initially the case was assumed unsolved due to lack of evidence. Eventually four years later a witness who had been arrested on another charge came forward in exchange for their freedom. It was due to their testimony that the Asian patriarch was found guilty. A local detective opined:

> I think almost from the beginning his family opposed their relationship, said Lt. Lee Brown, an investigator with the Union City police department. They're Indian, and it was real taboo for him to marry outside the family, and it was even more taboo for him to marry a black girl.
>
> *(Warren & Scott, 2006)*

In conclusion of the Rai murder, it should be emphasized that in no way is it representative of the entire Asian community. Indeed, Asian persons intermarry successfully with black and other Americans much as is expected. However, due to colorism and the domination of white power structures when Asian brown populations in general intermarry, the women at least seek out white mates to rescue their feared inferior status. This fear also has a history in black America that began during the antebellum among the free black people of North Carolina.

During the 1700s there existed in North Carolina black Americans who referred to themselves as "free people of color." Most were biracial in their ancestral heritage. Subsequently, they were light-skinned and very adamant about passing on the genes for light skin to succeeding generations. In their marital traditions antebellum free people of color were no less given to brown racism and colorism than their modern-day Asian brown descendants. According to Milteer (2020), free people of color devised their own perspectives of race and racial identity that often conflicted with society at large. A few segregated themselves totally from black slaves or those who were emancipated as they may not have been born free. Free people of color lived in segregated communities called "colonies" and via colorism were insistent upon endogamous marital patterns in maintaining light skin. So intent upon preserving light skin some practiced a form of incest in cousin to cousin marriages or other familial arrangements. They rejected slaves as spouses and rarely received visitors from outside the community. Some free people of color identified with whites and had children with whites. In fact, according to Milteer (2020), the extent of colorism was such that some among free people of color were known to conceal their blackness and join the Confederate Army in defense of slavery. They encouraged their children to associate with white children exclusively in hopes of a white marriage. Such sentiments for black colorism live on in modern-day Louisiana matrimony.

Amber Rose is a light-skinned black American whose family networks refer to themselves as Creole. Creoles are located in such Louisiana cities as New Orleans and Baton Rouge. Not a few among them have suffered familial rejection after marital unions involving a dark-skinned mate such as that of Amber Rose's choice. Her situation reached public discourse attributed to her being a light-skinned Creole black entertainer. After her family learned of her finance's dark skin color both were rejected by them. Overall, their traditional marital matters are a dramatic display of secondary colorism. While members of the same racial group they identify as differentiated. In essence such displays of colorism harken back to the light skin exclusivity of North Carolina's free people of color as a dramatic illustration of secondary colorism.

Secondary colorism consists of micro interactions between two different racial/ethnic groups as in Asian and black. Tertiary colorism is also micro interaction but distinctive given to the interactions of perpetrators belonging to the same racial/ethnic group. In contrast to Indian-Asian/black colorism is black American/black American colorism. The race and ethnic heritage of personnel may be common but also by some exception irrelevant. In fact, Indian-Asian/black colorism can occur if the Asian prospect is dark-skinned and not perceived as Asian. Furthermore, if the black prospect is light-skinned enough to pass for white no tertiary colorism occurs. While Amber Rose is light-skinned her features and color prevent her from passing for white possible only in the perceptions of the most uninformed of observers.

The existence of tertiary colorism among non-white people of color is now contained in official litigation documents of the United States. One of the first cases of tertiary colorism in the modern era was that of the dark-skinned Felix—plaintiff-versus the lighter-skinned Marquez-defendant. That case was litigated in 1981 by the US District Court of the District of Columbia. Both plaintiff and defendant were of the same Puerto Rican group. Both were employees of the Office of the Commonwealth of Puerto Rico in Washington, D.C. (OCPRW). According to litigation records, the plaintiff alleges that the defendant did not promote her on the basis of what would be described as colorism. At trial, the plaintiff introduced the personnel cards of 28 of her former fellow employees that she had worked with. She then testified that among them, she suggested only two were as dark-skinned, or darker-skinned in color than she. Her presumption was that all were light-skinned. Based on the rules of law in such a legal proceeding, the court determined that the plaintiff did not legally suffer from the effects of colorism (Felix v Manquez, 1980). However, it is plausible that failing to prevail in a court of law as pertains to charges of tertiary colorism does not suffice. The mere charges brought is evidence of the existing problem.

Colonization and slavery as the mainstay of racism have subsided as traditionally carried out among the people. A black American has occupied the White House as

President of the world's most powerful and wealthiest nation. He was succeeded by no less than a black woman as Vice President. Black athletes and black entertainers have amassed financial fortunes beyond the imagination of anyone black or white. Indeed, Oprah Winfrey and Michael Jordan are billionaires. Unfortunately, their wealth and their power have not afforded them the opportunity to escape their denigration. Both as black Americans are dark-skinned and while they enjoy the privileges of wealth and power absent its acknowledgment, they remain relegated to a status of the inferior and the despised. Violence and overt hostility directed at their person only emerge on the rarest of occasions. Unlike in years past word of such events bring immediate expressions of universal outrage. In aftermath of criticism and a return to calm those fortunate few characterized by dark skin via colorism will once again settle into their subjugated status. The longevity of what they daily encounter is colorism as racism in the 21st century. Unfortunately, absent resolution by the totality of mankind being one raceless species will render unnecessary pain and suffering upon humanity for generations to come.

References

Banton, M. (1992). The nature and causes of racism and discrimination. *International Sociology, 7*(1), 69–84.

Biography. (2019). *Emmett Till biography.* Retrieved April 11, 2019, from www.biography.com/people/emmett-till-507515

Bonilla-Silva, E. (1997). Rethinking racism: Toward a structural interpretation. *American Sociological Review, 62*(3), 465–480.

Canizares, R. (1990). Cuban racism and the myth of the racial paradise. *Ethnic Studies Report, 8*(2), 27–32.

Chang, I. (2011). *The rape of Nanking.* New York: Basic Books.

Daly, A., Jennings, J., Beckett, J., & Leashore, B. (1995). Effective coping strategies of African Americans. *Social Work, 40*(2), pp 40–48.

Felix V. Manquez. (1980, September 11). WL 242, 24 Empl. Prac. Dec. P 31, 279 (D.D.C., No. 78–2314).

Frey, W. (2015). *The browning of America.* Retrieved November 17, 2021, from www.milkenreview.org/articles/charticle-3

Gilbertson, G. A., Fitzpatrick, J. P., & Yang, L. (1996). Hispanic intermarriage in New York City: New evidence from 1991. *International Immigration Review, 30*(2), 445–459.

Hall, R. (2003). *Skin color as a post-colonial issue among Asian-Americans.* Lewiston, NY: Mellen Press.

Hall, R. (2001). *Filipina eurogamy: Skin color as vehicle of psychological colonization.* Quezon City, Philippines: Giraffe Books.

Hochschild, J. (1998). *American racial and ethnic politics in the 21st century: A cautious look ahead.* Retrieved November 17, 2021, from www.brookings.edu/articles/american-racial-and-ethnic-politics-in-the-21st-century-a-cautious-look-ahead/

Honorary Whites. (n.d.). Retrieved November 17, 2021, from http://dictionary.sensagent.com/Honorary%20whites/en-en/

Hyde, C. (1995). The meanings of whiteness. *Qualitative Sociology, 18*(1), 87–95.

Kitano, H. H. L., & Daniels, R. (1995). *Asian Americans: Emerging minorities* (2nd ed.). Englewood Cliffs, NJ: Prentice Hall.

Milteer, W. (2020). *North Carolina's free people of color 1715–1885*. Baton Rouge: Louisiana State University Press.

Minor, N., & McGauley, L. (1988). A different approach: Dialogue in education. *Journal of Teaching in Social Work, 2*(1), 127–140.

Moran, R. F. (2001). *Interracial intimacy: The regulation of race and romance*. Chicago: The University of Chicago Press.

Stampp, K. (1956). *The peculiar institution*. New York: Vintage Books.

Warren, B., & Scott, J. (2006). Kin grapple with alleged contract killing. *Atlanta-Journal Constitution*. Retrieved April 19, 2009, from www.bnvillage.co.uk/1376008-post1.html

Washington, R. (1990). Brown discrimination and the formation of a world system of racial stratification. *International Journal of Politics, Culture and Society, 4*(2), 209–227.

Waters, M. C. (1999). *Black identities: West Indian immigrant dreams and American reality*. Cambridge, MA: Harvard University Press.

Welsing, F. (1970). *The Cress theory of color confrontation and racism*. Washington, DC: CR Publishers.

Wilson, M. (1992). What difference could a revolution make? Group work in the new Nicaragua. *Social Work with Groups, 15*(2–3), 301–314.

Wiseman, R. (2014). *Short history of European immigration to North America*. Retrieved November 17, 2021, from https://bloomp.net/articles/european-immigration-to-north-america.htm

13
CONCLUSION

According to white American sociologist Andrew Hacker (1992), "No white American, including those who insist that opportunities exist for persons of every race, would change places with even the most successful black American." Black American comedian Chris Rock concurs adding that despite the fact he's "rich!" Therefore, any number of Americans, black and white, dark- and light-skinned, would suggest that race is critical to the American social experience (Bonilla-Silva, 2001). Absent race what prevails globally as the most powerful sovereignty in the Western world and beyond would be dismissed from admiration and forced to completely redefine itself. To maintain themselves at the zenith of civilization Americans as Western have consumed so much of the race ideology that they are apt to be lost without it. Absent the race construct, they are clueless in the conduct of their lives, the direction of their institutions, and their overall quality-of-life inspiration. Thus, race has been elevated to a sacred level of operation that is little known and to the surprise of many includes the participation of oppressed people of color per their racist participation (Kitano, 1985). Afterall, people of color are no less racist than their most racist counterparts albeit via nuanced manifestations. As victims oppressed people of color are no less consumed by the ideals of white supremacy that casts fictions of inferiority upon those such as themselves. They labor to escape into the white world and superiority status of their oppressors never hinting at the reality of who and what they really are in the grand scheme of a contrived human hierarchy.

From the contrived concept of race is derived an impediment to the ultimate of human civil potential. Said impediment directs the most urgent and divisive interactions which consume the good and the holiest of aspirations that mankind might intend. Unfortunately, this being a formidable pessimism that rises from the toxic disdains of race, racism is sustained by the newfound tenants of colorism. Among the tenants of colorism is intra-group racism. The Eurocentric perspective as standard validation of knowledge has dismissed colorism from the significance of scholarly speculation and legitimate discourse (Herrnstein & Murray, 1996). The conscientious and the curious agonize over the manner in which colorism has been ignored while perpetuated worldwide. On more than one occasion, they have challenged the contemporary icons of social work, psychology, sociology, and other social science disciplines. Social science academics who study the keenest aspects of human behavior remain oblivious to the implications of skin color in the 21st-century new millennium. In fact, most social science faculties at universities throughout the United States, Canada, Europe, and elsewhere West have gone through their entire educational experience without a word mentioned about colorism or its potential to impact human behavior in the most critical of social circumstances. It should therefore come as little surprise that students, and faculties of today have not understood the consequences and social stirrings of colorism. They then overlook the role of colorism in the formulation of models and theoretical constructs that might accrue an immediate path to its resolution. For many reasons, the topic of colorism in practically every sector of the mainstream white Western academy and thus the society at large has remained an unspeakable taboo for serious scholarship and polite conversation (Santos, 2006). The outcome links well-intended curiosity to an intellectual stagnation that nourishes prospects of regression. That nourishment is digested by an intellectual power structure, that given to the virtue of self-preservation, is committed to the scientific status quo. Under such circumstances any attempt to investigate colorism or rescue facts from its obscurity must confront its origins.

The origins of colorism are not commensurate with the simultaneous birth of human existence or civilization. Prior to the emergence of today's national and continental arrangements mankind existed merely as a conglomeration of various ethnic groups distinguished more often by language, religion, and culture. In fact, culture was arguably the most significant factor of differentiations between one individual and another (Agier, 1995). Race and skin color were both secondary characteristics. Skin color as pertains to colorism was little more than a trait similar to height, weight, or hair texture. Race until recent history did not exist contingent upon Europe and the emergence of Western civilization. Once previous tribes and various other populations settled into distinct arrangements of identity Europe was the outcome. The relative isolation of populations encouraged language, traditions, and cultural identities from which separate European nations came about. Race was still little acknowledged given to fewer consequences or practical application. Therefore, the existence of Africa and its dark-skinned peoples was not unknown but limited to folk tales and references by travelers and traders in search of desired goods and services.

Eventually what would become nations and races became the focus of intellectual discourse. European travelers coming into contact with Africans took immediate notice of their dark skin and at some point, began to assign meaning. In the interests of wealth and an increasing desire for resources Europeans allowed profit to dictate both their impressions and their treatment of Africans and other non-white peoples. The end results were the Atlantic slave trade and upon discovery of the New World colonization. In their ability to exploit Africans and New World populations required Europeans to reduce the human status of such peoples to something less than. In fact, Africans would come to be regarded as less than human and New World indigenous people as heathens (Cooley, 1902).

Religious reference to people of color provided a rationale for the exploitation of non-white populations that rescued Europeans from any notions of guilt. Africans as slaves could then be bought and sold much as any other livestock. Native-Americans when not found useful for slavery were officially exterminated if they would not submit to the dictates of Christianity to save their heathen souls. By this time slavery had been symbolized by African and heathen by Native-American. The skin color of both by European standards was dark. While there existed some antebellum reference to skin color, endorsed by science race was the official vehicle that organized human categories (Kitano, 1985). Thereby, race was the reference in conversation, but race was acted out in reference to skin color. As a consequence, any determination or reference to race category was determined by trait in color of skin.

The treatment of Africans and indigenous Native-Americans in what would become the United States was brutal, violent, inhumane, and tenacious. No amount of deed or accomplishment could rescue either one from the beliefs in race that defined them as inferior via biological heritage. Slave uprisings were a constant fear on the part of the plantation class such as that led by Nat Turner. Native-American scalps brought a premium from the US government as proof that the taking of a scalp was evidence of its owner's death. Despite years of such racist brutality, Africans both free and enslaved as well as Native-Americans were existing under a system of unintended indoctrination. The science, the traditions, and the religion that defined them as an inferior component of mankind was slowly being internalized. With each succeeding generation the belief in non-white inferiority had been consumed absent African- and Native-American objection (Beiser, 1988). The succeeding birth of African- and Native-American offspring complicated matters to an extent unprecedented in human history. Biracial Native-Americans so inclined passed for white. Biracial African-Americans so inclined emerged as a separate non-white category referred to as "House Negroes." House Negroes by not a few were dedicated to the interests and ultimate welfare of the plantation that was more of a priority than their own interests. They were trying to survive.

While a few among House Negroes resented their birth circumstances, others in a will to survive embraced it. More often than not they were the sons and daughters of the planation patriarchs who sexually exploited the mothers of such offspring. This otherwise criminal activity had become an acceptable tradition in white access to subjugated black women that no less than the third President of the United States was a participant. For years following his death the family members of Thomas Jefferson denied his sexual exploitation until it was substantiated by modern DNA evidence (Russell, Wilson, & Hall, 1994).

The offspring of master slave unions were particularly noted for their light-skinned attractiveness as colorism in their physical appearance. Being the children of slave masters and the forced concubines of American Presidents light-skinned black females were referred to as "Fancy Girls" and black males as "Run 'Round" men. Run 'Round men were reputed to own the affections of women in both the black and white communities. Their light-skinned black female counterparts were particularly subject to sexual exploitation by white males introducing the concept of legitimate and illegitimate children into American jurisprudence. In this way white male offspring by black women could be legally denied access to their father's wealth. To be legitimate required parents to be legally married.

Light-skinned black males were often the victims of lynching whereby a few had been known to have had intimate contact with white women. Unlike white male contact with black women these affairs were consensual. On the occasion said affairs were exposed such women might be put at risk which led to accusations of rape to save themselves. Their accusations prevail well into the modern era and often a prerequisite lynching. Thus, while contact by white males with slave children brought silence, intimacy between Run 'Round men and white women might lead to death. Consequently, while some historians criticize House Negroes who dismissed their Field Negro counterparts taking advantage of their light skin to survive House Negro life was not at all an absolute bliss (Edwards, 1973).

In addition to greater attractiveness assumed by their proximity to white heritage, House Negroes as the sons and daughters of white fathers might exceed what was expected of an assumed inferior race. While often distinct by light skin House Negroes were considered no less black and no less inferior. A few were educated and allowed to go into businesses where they excelled. To explain this ability of an inferior race prospect from science came the mulatto hypothesis (Reuter, 1969). Having white blood was assumed to allow such blacks referred to as mulattoes to do things not possible for unadulterated Field Negro blacks. Thus, light-skinned biracial blacks were both tolerated and feared as they had the potential to compete on every level with the white masses. If given the opportunity, they could excel in education as they might reach the Sorbonne in Paris. If given the opportunity, they might amass a fortune in business putting a desperate white Irishman in the position to ask them for work. Indeed, as pertains to an indentured working class Irish overseer a house slave could be assessed as superior to them intellectually and otherwise which would dismiss the white supremacy narrative. Amid disbelief of black intellectual superiority dark-skinned black Americans reached the height of irony in that the highest human IQ on record to date was eventually scored by a nine-year-old black American girl who was not a mulatto but described as being of "unmixed African decent" (Theman & Witty, 1943).

The trials and tribulations confronting black Americans during the early periods of the nation's history have prevailed into the modern era (Rose, 1964). Slavery was dismissed by Lincoln's Emancipation Proclamation and the last colonial territory was dissolved well into the 20th century. However, the ravages of these human atrocities remain existent. They are not overt but covert in sustaining the oppression and exploitation of black Americans and other people of color marked by the observations of their dark skin. Educational programs in the aftermath of

Civil Rights and political activism have given opportunities to black Americans previously non-existent. However, numerous social science investigations attest to a direct correlation between skin color as independent variable and education as dependent variable (Hertel & Hughes, 1988). In the outcome is representation of the mulatto hypothesis where it is the light-skinned among black Americans who have most benefited from the Civil Rights educational programs. While such research is documented, its documentation is by far the exception versus the rule. What's more many HBCU institutions in years prior to Civil Rights required prospective students to submit a picture with their application which could be used to reject or accept them considering colorism in their application. Still, when educational programs are assessed today those who conduct the investigations are more inclined to frame their conclusions in the context of race.

The educational gains made by black Americans resulted in commensurate occupational gains. In practically every field of occupational endeavor black Americans are today evident in their participation. Similar to the educational advantages encountered by light-skinned black Americans, the same advantages exist in occupation dramatically displayed in the entertainment industry (Lyman, 1990). Casting calls and news operatives who appear in front of a camera are all but exclusive to dark-skinned people of color regardless of their racial or ethnic heritage. Some icons of the rapper music genre such as "Whitenecious" and "Black Chyna" promote bleaching creams and celebrate the attractiveness of their light skin. Their influence upon an entire generation is beyond comprehension. Dark-skinned especially black American women have encountered the pain and suffering such entertainers cause brought by bleaching cream products that have influenced some to commit suicide (Bell, 2014). For this the entertainment occupational industry has remained silent and the white social science academy such as social work seem no less committed to prioritizing white issues. This they do at the expense of black Americans and other people of color negatively impacting their quality of life. Numerous events of litigation have been filed by people of color today charging job discrimination that provide documentation of the problem ignored by society at large.

Advances in occupation have facilitated a rise in black American incomes. Once rejected on the basis of colorism in skin color the increased numbers of black American doctors, lawyers, CEOs, bank executives and other high-income occupations have allowed black Americans to amass fortunes in wealth as never before. Those who are light-skinned are considered less threatening and thus more tolerated for the incomes they earn from prestigious occupations. This unprecedented wealth has contributed to the emergence of a stable black American middle class. In years past the black American middle class similarly accumulated a measure of wealth. They owned various assortments of property and frequently traveled abroad to exotic destinations. However, regardless of wealth they lived exclusively in the black community. Today in the aftermath of segregation, middle-class black Americans have options that their predecessors did not have. Many frequent gated white communities and are all but completely removed from the black population.

They are less visible by the sight of their light skin which somehow justified their middle-class incomes.

The inability of black Americans to escape the stresses brought by colorism have imposed upon their decision-making process which negatively influences their physical well-being. Given to the trivialization of colorism per skin color by social scientists dark-skinned women in particular worldwide apply bleaching creams to lighten their dark skin (Al-Saleh, Elkhatib, Al-Rouqi, Al-Enazi, & Neptune, 2012). Daily application of such creams can be life threatening due to their toxic ingredients. Many contain arsenic, mercury, and hydroquinone. Arsenic and mercury are natural poisons, and hydroquinone is a carcinogen. Black American women who bleach their skin while pregnant succumb to stillbirths having passed poisons by way of the placenta to their unborn children. Those who apply creams that contain hydroquinone may develop skin cancer by compromising their natural melanin protections. In addition to the social science academy medical institutions such as the Skin Cancer Foundation have trivialized this colorism as unworthy of a research funding priority.

The physical well-being jeopardized by colorism may have psychological consequences as well. Those persons confronted by the implications of skin color especially if it is dark seek to alter those aspects of themselves which prevent their full participation in society and preferred quality of life. In addition to bleaching their skin, they may demonize and distance themselves from any and all matters associated with Africa and its blackness. They may support political candidates who oppose black progress or black authority sitting on the highest courts of the land. Their music preferences, dress styles and friendship choices reflect little if at all of the nation's diversity. Indeed, the Bleaching Syndrome they display is a psychological strategy devised to overcome colorism. In the end those who succumb to the Bleaching Syndrome are reduced to victims of self-hate that will ultimately tax their physical well-being to no end (Clark & Clark, 1980).

In a world so dominated by colorism, brown racism has emerged as a pathology in non-white communities. Unlike slavery and colonization brown racism per colorism is not overt but more often covert. For this reason, it is much more insidious which helps sustain its longevity. As an extension of white racism and white supremacy brown racism will prevail as the foundation of colorism that unless resolved currently will impose upon the civility of humanity for years and perhaps decades to come. In the aftermath of Loving v Virginia that legalized inter-racial marriage, the increased levels of miscegenation will limit the possibilities for racial identification merely by observation (Duignan, 2016). The previously distinct racial categories such as Caucasoid, Mongoloid and Negroid will lack distinction to the extent of being unrecognizable. The masses will be comprised of individual citizens whose skin is dark, whose hair is wavy-straight, whose eyes are blue and settled into exotic eye-folds. America, and indeed the world will accrue to a final "melting pot" of biracial human beings whose physical characteristics will be distinct only in being indistinct. Unfortunately, transgressions in colorism will prevail as racism in the 21st century and beyond.

Most people of color who occupy third world nations failed to anticipate the potential of Western domination for colorism as racism in the 21st century. They did not anticipate that slavery and Western colonization would carry on indefinitely to a global colonial system of domination. Western economic power managed cultural dependency between itself and previous colonial subjects including those that had escaped the domination of colonialism. Significant literature has been published about the economics of colonial domination, while little has been published as pertains to cultural domination. Economic explanations are too myopic. They overlook the voluntary, non-coercive social psychological processes underlying cultural domination. Subsequently, they overlook the impact that Western cultural hegemony will have in sustaining colorism as racism in the 21st century and beyond. For what was previously brought by overt domination could be achieved through cultural domination of third world people of color. They were convinced that cultural domination was a civilized and modernizing thing to do. A major vehicle for this occurrence was the advent of cultural communication technologies.

Under the control of white Western authority, cultural communication technology facilitated the dispersion of Western culture as a form of domination (Kitano, 1985). Given to films, radio, television, etc. made available throughout the third world community extended such domination. The impact of this cultural domination was much more potent than was slavery or colonization. It commenced to transforming the ideal cultural identities of non-white people of color via the ideals conveyed by media technologies. Subsequently, people of color in the third world aspire to white characters of various media dedicated to them by imitation. Unlike the era of slavery and colonization, when media technology was less available, cultural domination at the time was less possible. This made for the possibility of sustaining distinct local cultural values free of domination and less conducive to colorism. Unlike years past, matters today are different in that there exists a union between Western domination via media communication technology and Western cultural forces. These unions act to undermine the validity of cultural independence and native authority for third world people of color. The technology through which cultural domination is conveyed is under total control of Western operatives. The end result is not only domination but the homogenization of cultures. For the process to work will require the existence of a homogeneous market which cultural domination provides.

Attributed to this market of homogeneity, is the creation of people of color who by domination prefer what the market has to offer. This hegemonic cultural phenomenon is effective because it diminishes the worth of native ideals that make domination possible. In the grand scheme of colorism is the effect of this cultural hegemony and homogenization for the idealization of light skin and the denigration of dark skin on a global scale (Poussaint, 1975). It is not racism per se but no less potent in the emergence of racist outcomes. Among said outcomes are white Western ideals willfully internalized by dark-skinned people of color who act out color valuations as a consequence of assumed white racial superiority. This assumption is apparent in the global rankings of skin color in the modern world. Unlike the geographically confined under overt colonial domination, the new global media technology provides for a system unrestricted by locale and popularized by native as well as international icons (Trainor, Andzulis, Rapp, & Agnihotri, 2014). This should not suggest that local elites are purposely drawn to idealizing light and/ or white skin but that aspiring to light skin is evidence of modernization separate and apart from the uncivilized heathen. Thus, the internalization of alien ideals via global stratification is perceived not as a product of domination but simply modern. The truth of this conclusion comes by way of white Western media technology in films, magazines, television, and news publications that project its ideals by subliminal communication (Baumann, 2008). Therefore, the alien notions of white superiority in ideal light skin largely escape the notice of dominated third-world societies. Subsequently, the same market schemes used to sell Western products convey to people of color both at home and abroad the preference light over dark skin. People of color residing in third world countries under these influences of domination and cultural hegemony, eventually succumb to colorism. When circumstances warrant, they then express positive valuations as pertains to light skin and negative valuations as pertains to dark skin. Separate from natural forms of ethnocentrism indicative of geographically isolated populations, colorism by way of technology pertains to a global system of white values. Whereas the original form of colorism where it exists extends from actual contacts between people of color, the modern-day version exists independent of personal contact. This newer version is globally advanced by the reaches of communication technology which advocates the belief in black inferiority (Washington, 1990). Therefore, Africans and others via dark skin absent contact or conflict with same is an invention of Western technological ingenuity. In the aftermath, its termination will necessitate a Western technological solution.

References

Agier, M. (1995). Racism, culture and black identity in Brazil. *Bulletin of Latin American Research, 14*(3), 245–264.

Al-Saleh, I., Elkhatib, R., Al-Rouqi, R., Al-Enazi, S., & Neptune, S. (2012). The dangers of skin-lightening creams. *Toxicological and Environmental Chemistry, 94*(1), 195–219.

Baumann, S. (2008). The moral underpinnings of beauty: A meaning-based explanation for light and dark complexions in advertising. *Poetics, 36*(1), 2–23.

Beiser, H. (1988). "I ain't nobody": A study of Black male identity formation. *Psychoanalytic Study of the Child, 43*, 307–318.

Bell, T. (2014). For Brown Girls, Karyn Washington, Light skin vs. Dark skin, Low self-esteem. *The ReadyWriter*. Retrieved September 21, 2016, from https://conversationsofasistah.wordpress.com/2014/04/11/she-committed-suicide-because-of-her-skin-color/

Bonilla-Silva, E. (2001). *White supremacy and racism in the post-civil rights era*. Boulder, CO: Lynne Rienner Publishers.

Clark, K., & Clark, M. (1980, November). What do Blacks think of themselves? *Ebony, 36*(V), 176–182.

Cooley, C. (1902). *Human nature and the social order*. New York: Scribner.

Duignan, B. (2016). *Loving v. Virginia, Encyclopedia Britannica.* Retrieved February 23, 2020, from www.britannica.com/event/Loving-v-Virginia

Edwards, O. (1973, June). Skin color as a variable in racial attitudes of Black urbanites. *Journal of Black Studies, 3*(4), 473–483.

Hacker, A. (1992). *Two nations.* New York: Macmillan.

Herrnstein, R., & Murray, C. (1996). *The bell curve.* New York: Simon & Schuster.

Hertel, B., & Hughes, M. (1988). The significance of color remains. *Social Forces, 68,* 1105–1120.

Kitano, H. (1985). *Race relations.* Englewood Cliffs, NJ: Prentice Hall.

Lyman, S. (1990). Race, sex, and servitude: Images of blacks in American cinema. *International Journal of Politics, Culture and Society, 4*(1), 49–77.

Poussaint, A. (1975). The problems of light skinned Blacks. *Ebony, 85.*

Reuter, E. (1969). *The mulatto in the United States.* New York: Haskell House.

Rose, A. (1964). *The Negro in America.* New York Harper & Row.

Russell, K., Wilson, M., & Hall, R. E. (1994). *The color complex: The politics of skin color among African Americans.* New York: Anchor.

Santos, S. (2006). Who is Black in Brazil?: A timely or a false question in Brazilian race relations in the era of Affirmative Action? (O. C. Anya, Trans.). *Latin American Perspectives, 33*(4), 30–48.

Theman, V., & Witty, P. (1943). Case studies and genetic records of two gifted Negroes. *Journal of Psychology, 15,* 165–181. doi:10.1080/00223980.1943.9917144

Trainor, K., Andzulis, J., Rapp, A., & Agnihotri, R. (2014). Social media technology usage and customer relationship performance: A capabilities-based examination of social CRM. *Journal of Business Research, 67*(6), 1201–1208.

Washington, R. (1990). Brown racism and the formation of a world system of racial stratification. *International Journal of Politics, Culture, and Society, 4*(2), 209–227.

INDEX

21st century 133–137; colorism racism and 138–143; honorary whites and 137–138; immigrants to New World and 133–136

Abrams, S. 66
academic bias 11–13
ACLU *see* American Civil Liberties Union (ACLU)
adaptation 4–5
Affirmative Action policy 88–90, 93
African-Americans 4, 7–8
Akee, R. 87
American Civil Liberties Union (ACLU) 92
American Community Survey data 87
American Dilemma (Myrdal) 45
American Dream 24, 109
Americanization 108
antebellum period 7, 8, 11, 18, 28, 37, 50, 141; assimilation products during 110; plots and rebellions during 29–30
Arce, C. 115
Argentina 97
arsenic 99–100
assimilation 108; mode of entry of minority group and 110; products of 110–112; by race 109–110; residential redlining and 108–109; stress of 115–116; wealth and 109
autonomous minorities 78

Bailey, S. 93
Baird-Pattinson system 97
Bakke case (1978) 90

Banton, M. 5, 122, 138
behaviorism 28–29
Bell Curve, The (Herrnstein and Murray) 59, 67, 69–70, 73, 76
bias theories 77
biological deficiency theories 76
biology of colorism 97–99
biopsychosocial environmental experience 3, 4, 5
biracial people 91, 141, 147, 150; African-French population 110; Americans 41, 44; births 8, 12; black women 44; blacks 48, 50, 52–55, 58, 66, 73, 84; blood 47; Fancy Girls 42, 44; idealization of 48; light-skinned 42, 45, 47, 53–55, 58, 60, 65, 75, 78, 80, 148; miscegenation and 136; Run Round men 45–48
black Anglo Saxons 112
Black Anglo-Saxons, The (Hare) 112
black bourgeoisie 112
bleaching cream, and stillbirths; market 100–102; toxicity 99–100
Bleaching Syndrome 107, 150; Maslow's hierarchy of needs and 114; meaning and significance of 113–116; *see also* assimilation
Blumenbach, J. 121
Bodnar, L. 96
Bolivia 93
Brigham, C. 59
Brooks, P. 44
Brown, J. 30
Brown, S. A. 52

Brown, W. W. 52
browning of America 136
brown racism 118, 150; background of 118–123; colorism and 126–128; non-white racism and 123–124; significance of 124–126
Bryant, C. 135
Burgess, E. 108
Burkina Faso 101
Byrd, S. 70

California 136
Cameroon 101, 102
caste theory 78
Caucasoids, characteristics of 120
Center for Disease Control (CDC) 102
Cervantes, R. C. 115
Césaire, A. 19
Charleston Heart Study 79
Chase-Riboud, B. 42
Cheng, K. 98
Chicago, immigrants to 136
Child, L. M. 52
Chyna, B. 101
Civil Rights Act (1964) 89
Clark, R. 72
Coates, T. N. 66
Cobett, W. 42
Colombia 93
colonial mentality, notion of 20
colonial origins, of colorism 17; aftermath of colonization and 23–25; colonization and 19–23; colorism as alternative to racism and 25–26; identity formation and 23; print media and 18; sexual contact with female slaves and 17–18; slavery and 18–19
colorism, significance of 8–10; *see also specific aspects/types*
communalism, in peer review 13
Congo 101
Congressional Records (1935) 89
Connell, J. P. 71
Cooley, C. 23
Costenos 126
Crania Aegyptiaca (Morton) 122
Crania Americana (Morton) 121
creation myth, central African 53
Creoles 33, 112, 142; black 110–111; community 111; plaçage 44–45; significance of 34
Cuba: hierarchy in 21; skin color issue in 126
Cuban-Americans 7

cultural deficiency theories 76–77
cultural implications, of slavery 29

dark skin, in post-colonial era 22–23
Darwin, C. 118
Datcher-Loury, L. 72
Declining Significance of Race, The (Wilson) 123
deficiency theories 76–77
Dio Chrysostom 53
discontinuity theories 77
disinterestedness, in peer review 13
Dlova, N. 101
Dominican Republic 93
Dornbusch, S. 72
double consciousness 77
Douglass, F. 32–33
dual perspective 77
DuBois, W. E. B. 56, 58, 77, 126
Dutch immigrants, to New World 134

ecological perspective (EP): importance of 3–5; of Western civilization 119
education 65; and *Bell Curve, The* 67, 69–70; black male and women educational comparisons and 71–72; black women accomplishments and 70–71; family dynamic and 72–73; Hampton Institute and 65, 66; SAT test and 70–71; white privilege and 67–69; white supremacy narrative and 69–70
Egypt 97
El Salvador 93
EP *see* ecological perspective (EP)
Erickson, E. 23
Essence 9, 127
ethnocentric(ity): bias 12; and white supremacy, comparison of 122
eumelanin 98, 127
Eunice Kennedy Shriver National Institute of Child Health and Human Development 96
Eurocentric bias 12, 13, 24, 25
eurogamy 139
exchange theory 111

Fancy Girls 35, 37, 39, 41; biracial 41, 42; feminine ideal of 42; Jefferson issue and 42–43; plaçage and 44–45; Quadroon Balls and 44
Fanon, F. 19–20
Faulkner, W. 52
Field Negroes 7, 8, 26, 30; brutality experienced by 32–33; dark-skinned

30–31; and House Negroes compared 34–36; marriage of 31–32; selling through auction of 32; slave psychology and 36–37; women of 31; *see also* House Negroes
Florida, non-white population increase in 136
For Brown Girls organization 115
Ford, D. 72
Frazier, E. F. 112
free people of color 141–142
Freud, S. 29
Frisbie, W. 115

German immigrants, to New World 134
Gibbs, J. 71
Gill, S. 72
Glidden, G. 122
glutathione 99, 100
Goffman, E. 29
Goldenberg, R. 102
Goldsmith, O. 51
Graham, L. O. 112
Grape, H. 91
Guatemala 93, 103

Hacker, A. 145
Hall, R. 42, 139
Hall, R. E. 126
Hamed, S. 101
Hampton Institute 65, 66
Hare, N. 112
Harper, F. E. W. 52
Hauser, R. M. 80
Hemings, S. 42, 43
Herrnstein, R. J. 59, 67, 69
Hersch, J. 92, 93
History of the Earth (Goldsmith) 51
Hoetnik, H. 52, 53
Hong Kong 96
honorary whites, in South Africa 137–138
House Negroes 7–8, 26, 47, 147, 148; categories of 33–34; demeaning of 35; and Field Negroes compared 34–36; seasoning process of 33, 34; slave duties of 34; slave psychology and 36–37; *see also* Field Negroes
Hughes, M. 67, 79
humanity, categories of 121
Hume, D. 51
hydroquinone 99, 100, 150
hypergamy 139

idealization: of biracial black heritage 48; of light skin 75, 113
income 86; Affirmative Action policy and 88–90; origin, meaning and significance of 86–87; skin color and 87–88, 91–93
India: ancient 9–10; during British times 10; early neonatal mortality in 97; skin bleaching in 95–96; stillbirths in 102
intermediate racism 6–7
International Stillbirth Alliance 102
inter-racial marriages 39–40, 136–137
involuntary minorities 78
"Iola Leroy; or Shadows Uplifted" (Harper) 52
Italian immigrants, to New World 135
Ivory Coast 101

Jablonski, N. G. 97
Jackson, M. 70
Japan 11, 96
Jefferson, T. 42–43, 147
Jensen, A. 76
Jeter, M. 39
Johnson, K. 70
Jones, A. 56
Jones, M. 87
Jordan 51, 52
Journal of Psychology 59
Jung, C. 13

King, M. L., Jr. 5
Kitano, H. 20, 108
Klein, A. 82
Koehler, J. J. 13
Korea 96
Korematsu v. United States (1944) 40

Latino National Political Survey (LNPS) 80
Latinx people of color 17–18, 77, 81, 82, 83, 87, 136
"Life of Frederick Douglass, The" (Douglass) 32–33
"Light in August" (Faulkner) 52
light-skinned mulattoes 50–51; black 52; light-skinned 50–51; tragic 52
Linneaus, C. 121
LNPS *see* Latino National Political Survey (LNPS)
Looking Glass Self 23
Los Angeles, immigrants to 136
Loving, R. 39
Loving v. Virginia (1958) 39–40, 150

mankind, classification of 121
Maslow, A. 114, 119
MC1R *see* melanocortin 1 receptor (MC1R)
McAdoo, H. 71
McIntosh, P. 67, 68, 69
McKissick, F. 112
McRoy, R. 91
Mead, G. 23
melanin: as filter for protection 99; as operative of skin color 127; quality of 98; among races 126–127; significance of 97, 126–128; tyrosinase activity and 100
melanocortin 1 receptor (MC1R) 98
Meltzer, B. 29
mercury 99
Merton, R. 13
Mestizos 126
Milteer, W. 141
minority, concept of 22
miscegenation 18, 45–47, 124, 128, 136, 150
mobility thesis 81–82
Mongoloids, characteristics of 120
Moran, R. F. 137
Morison, W. 126
Morrow v. the IRS (1990) 126
Morton, S. 121–122
"Mulâtre, Le"(Daute) 52
mulatto hypothesis 48, 148, 149; light skinned mulattoes and 53–55; origin of 52; somatic norm image and 52–53; Talented Tenth and 55–59; victimization of dark-skinned blacks and 53
Murgia, E. 115
Murray, C. A. 59, 67, 69
Myrdal, G. 45

NAEP *see* National Assessment of Educational Progress (NAEP)
Naim v. Naim (1965) 40
National Assessment of Educational Progress (NAEP) 83
National Labor Relations Act *see* Affirmative Action policy
Native-Americans 17, 47, 50, 87, 133
Negro and Mulatto Families Questionnaire (Bureau of International Research) 58
Negroid, characteristics of 121
Negro Problem, The (DuBois) 56
neuromelanin 127
New Africans 33–34
New World, immigrants to 133–136
Ngoc, N. 97

Nicaragua 126
Nigeria 100, 102
Norton, D. 77
Nott, J. 122

occupation 75–76; public opinion on 82–84; research investigations on 78–82; theoretical explanations of 76–78
ochronosis 100
Oedipal complex 29
Old Africans 33, 34
one-drop theory 45, 46, 73, 137
On the Natural Varieties of Mankind (Blumenbach) 121
organized skepticism, in peer review 13
Our Kind of People (Graham) 112

Pakistan 102
Panel Study of Income Dynamics 81
Paraguayans 93
Park, R. E. 108
passing process 45–48; definition of 46; as physiological phenomenon 47; Run Round male quadroons and Octoroons and 47–48
passivity: in adaptation context 5; resistance through 29, 30
"Peace and Freedom" 67
Penner, A. 93
Peru 97
phenotypic discrimination and occupation 80–81
pheomelanin 98, 127
Philadelphia Negro, The (DuBois) 58
Philippines 21
plaçage 44–45
Porter, S. 87
primary colorism 138
primary racism 5–6
psychological colonization 24
psychoanlaysis 29

Quadroon Balls 44

Race, Evolution, and Behavior (Rushton) 122
race and behavior, link between 121–122
racism 5, 9, 45, 150–151; Affirmative Action and 89; brown 116, 124–126, 139–140, 150; colonization and slavery and 142–143; colorism as, in 21st century 133–143; colorism as alternative to 25–26; ecological theory of 119; education and 68–70; intermediate 6–7; lynching and 135; non-white 123–124;

occupation and 77, 79; primary 5–6; tertiary 7–8; *see also* brown racism; *specific aspects/types*
redlining 108, 112
Reid-Rai, S. 140–141
repudiation 13
Reynolds, A. J. 72
Ritter, P. 72
Rock, C. 145
role-playing 28–29
Roscigno, V. 81
Rose, A. 142
Run Round men 37, 39, 41, 45, 148; biracial 46–47; idealization of biracial black heritage and 48; one-drop theory and 45; passing for white by 45–48
Rushton, P. 122
Russell, K. 42
Russian immigrants, to New World 135

Saleem, S. 102
saltwater Negroes *see* New Africans
Saperstein, A. 93
SAT test 70–71
Scandinavian immigrants, to New World 134
Scott, J. 140
secondary colorism 138–139, 142
Séjour, V. 52
Sextus Empiricus 53
significant other 29
Skelton, M. 42–43
skin bleaching 95
Skinner v. Oklahoma (1942) 40–41
SLC24A5 gene 98
Snowden, F. 53
socialized prejudices 13
social structural deficiency theories 76
somatic norm image 22, 52–53
South Africa 97; bleaching cream market in 101; honorary whites in 137–138
Steinberg, L. 72
Stember, C. 126
Stevenson, H. 77
Stillbirth Collaborative Research Network Initial Causes of Fetal Death protocol 96
stillbirths 95; biology of colorism and 97–99; bleaching cream market and 100–102; early neonatal mortality and 97; maternal obesity and 96–97; and miscarriages compared 96; toxic bleaching creams and 99–100; women of color and 102–103

Stowe, H. B. 52
Study of American Intelligence, A (Brigham) 59
Sue, S. 11–12
Sumner, C. 44
sunlight 99
Sunshine Girls 139
Systema Natura (Linneaus) 121

Talented Tenth 55–59, 111
Terman, L. 59
tertiary colorism 142
tertiary racism 7–8
Thomas, W. I. 108
Tikmani, S. 102
Till, E. 135
Togo 101
tragic mulatto 52
Tsoka-Gwegweni, J. 101
Tunisia 102
Turner, N. 147
Turner, N. 29
tyrosinase activity 100

Uncle Tom's Campus (Jones) 56
"Unequal Race for Good Jobs" (McCourt School of Public Policy Center on Education and the Workforce, Georgetown University) 82
universalism, in peer review 13
US Census report (1990) 87
UV rays 99

Vargas-Willis, G. 115
Vaughan, D. 70
Vietnam 97
vitamin D 99
voluntary immigrant minorities 78, 110

Wagner, R. F. 89
Wagner Act *see* Affirmative Action policy
Walker, A. 8–9, 66, 127
Warren, B. 140
Warren, J. R. 80
Washington, B. T. 79
Washington, K. 115
Washington, R. 124–125, 140
"weness" 23
white privilege 67–69
"White Privilege" (McIntosh) 67, 68
white supremacy ix–x, 11, 28, 107, 125; in *Bell Curve, The* 69; colorism by education and 69–70, 73; and ethnocentricity compared 122; mulattoes

submitting to 52; support for Caucasian race and 122–123
Wilson, G. 81
Wilson, M. 42
Wilson, W. J. 123
Women's International League for Peace and Freedom 67

women: of color, and stillbirths 102–103; and mobility thesis 81 World Health Organization 101

X, Malcolm 7

Znaniecki, F. 108

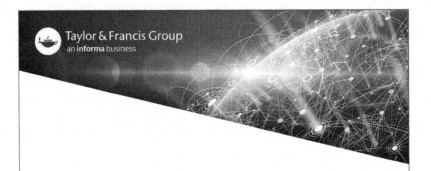

Printed in the USA
CPSIA information can be obtained
at www.ICGtesting.com
LVHW021736041124
795688LV00040B/1265